# Courage in the Congo

## *A Doctor's Fight to Save the Pygmies*

Kent Galloway

Printed in the USA

First Edition

Cover design by Jill O'Neall

Library of Congress Control Number: 2021905971

Publisher's Cataloging-in-Publication Data

Name: Galloway, Kent
Title: Courage in the Congo
Subtitle: A Doctor's Fight to Save the Pygmies
Description: Trade paperback
Subject: Non-fiction / Biography / Christian Ministry / Missions


ISBN   978-0-578-87712-9 (Paperback)
ISBN   978-0-578-87713-6 (E-book)

# Dedication

I am honored to dedicate this book to the family and friends of
Dr. Jerry Galloway, CICM.

# Contents

# Foreword

My uncle, Dr. Jerry Galloway, spent his entire adult life helping the poor. He had no interest in wealth but instead used his medical degree to work for the people's good. He devoted 27 years to the Pygmy people in the African rainforest, living among them, working as a Catholic missionary at Mission Pendjua in the Republic of Congo (formerly Zaire).

He taught them about sanitation; ran the hospital and pharmacy; started "barefoot doctor programs" so that remote areas, available only by foot, bicycle, or jeep, could receive medical care. He taught them to clear the forest and grow their food. He saved many lives and gave the people of Africa a better way of life. He endured many hardships due to the economic and political instability, but by God's grace, he stayed focused on his work.

He opened boarding schools, one for boys and one for girls, and made it possible to receive an education. He wrote letters home to his parents every week for 27 years about the "happenings at Mission Pendjua." My grandmother spent countless hours deciphering his handwriting, typing, copying, and sending letters to family, friends, and benefactors.

When my grandmother was no longer able to do it, my aunt Sister Mary Blaise, Jerry's sister, took over the task. Sister Mary Blaise turned all the letters over to me, and she was intent on finding someone to write Jerry's story. When my cousin Kent Galloway volunteered, we were thrilled. I scanned all of Jerry's letters, pictures, and newsletters and sent the CD to Kent. My uncle was not only the "Apostle to the Pygmies," he was a Saint!

Thank you, Kent Galloway, for telling Uncle Jerry's story in this book. God bless you.

Cindy (Galloway) Haverstick

# Preface

In 2008, after returning from a mission trip to Uganda, my aunt gave me some letters that Dr. Jerry Galloway wrote. Once I read them, I knew I needed to learn the rest of the story.

In 2009, I heard about a student in Iowa, Olivia Grubbs, who won second place in a national speech contest. She spoke about Dr. Jerry's life among the Pygmies. After emailing Olivia's parents, I received a call from Joyce Grubbs (Olivia's grandmother). She told me she worked with Dr. Jerry and said she knew I was the one to write a book about his life. Joyce not only planted the seed but provided encouragement and advice during the past ten years.

In late 2009, I learned from Jerry's niece, Cindy, that she had copies of all the letters for the 27 years that Dr. Jerry wrote them. She sent me a CD, and I printed out all 1,500 pages. During 2010, I read all the letters, and then, in 2011, I reread them.

In late 2011, I discussed my concerns about writing with Joyce Grubbs, Author from the Grassroots. After our call, I had peace about writing the book. In early 2012, I started to type the manuscript. After much reflection, I decided the story must come directly from the letters in the way Dr. Jerry wrote about the events. I did not want to embellish or change any anecdote. At one point, I was disappointed with how hard and slow the writing process seemed. Joyce reassured me that "the book will happen, and it will be in God's good timing, as well as yours."

Once I read the letters, I knew I had to share them. The account of Jerry's transformation, his great faith, and dedication encouraged me. His ability to overcome the many challenges he faced in a remote part of the Congo inspired me. I believe it is an honor to be entrusted to share Dr. Jerry's story.

# Acknowledgments

I am very grateful to Robbi, my wife, for the encouragement to finish the book and allow me countless hours to work on it.

A very heartfelt thank you to Joyce Godwin Grubbs (Author From the Grassroots) for encouraging me to write the book.

I appreciate Cindy Haverstick's efforts to provide me the letters that Jerry wrote that are the basis of the book.

I offer my thanks to Kelsie Vargas for assisting in the initial editing of the manuscript.

Thank you to Gary G. Steele (author of The Gypsy Family Circus historical fiction series) for your advice and encouragement when I experienced "writer's block."

Thank you very much to Jill O'Neall for her creativity in designing the cover and page layouts.

I am honored to have connected with those who knew Jerry from the Peace Corps, fellow missionaries, members of CICM, doctors who worked with him, and young Pygmy men who Jerry befriended, and for the photos and anecdotes you shared.

# Introduction

The story is based solely on the letters that Dr. Jerry wrote. It is likely one of the longest histories of the Pygmy people, as told by someone who lived with them. The story coincides with world events such as the outbreak of AIDS, the Rwandan genocide, the overthrow of President Mobutu, and the Congo wars.

Dr. Jerry promised his family that he would write a letter home each week. Over 1,200 letters document his life with the Pygmies. The letters share the "good, bad and ugly" as Jerry wanted the readers to know the successes and failures.

"It was a great pleasure to share his abundant life and to grow spiritually and technically. Dr. Jerry fought against racial and social injustice. He took many risks to travel across roads, lakes, and rivers to provide medicines and teaching. His heritage is one of reconciling differences and helping people in need."
- Dr. Brian Bakoko – Development Alternative, Inc (Congo)

"Dr. Jerry's work in Pendjua, one of the hardest-to-reach areas, both geographically and culturally, provides fascinating, personal, and inspirational insights into the challenges and rewards of working in DR Congo. This story is an excellent read for understanding past and future paths for health care in DR Congo."
- Dr. Franklin Baer, SANRU Basic Rural Health Project (Congo 1981-1991)

"I met Jerry when he was a Peace Corps volunteer, and I taught at a local mission college. Later, I learned that Jerry joined our congregation of CICM and became a missionary. I am happy that finally, a book will be published about Jerry. His missionary dedication deserves the attention of as many readers as possible."
- Fr. Romain Clement, Provincial Archivist CICM (Belgium)

# Prologue

At a young age, Jerry ventured to the creeks that meandered through the woods in central Illinois. He loved to fish in the local farm ponds. Mendota was a great place to grow up. The downtown had the typical outlets of many small towns, like diners, a dime store, grocery store, and small shops. There were no foretelling events that pointed to the path that would take him 7,000 miles away to the Congo rainforest.

The 1960s ushered in an era of civil rights and turbulence in America, just as Jerry started medical school. His only ambition was to be a medical doctor, go into private practice, and live a comfortable life. He joined the U.S. Public Health Service. While in Savannah, Georgia, he encountered the civil rights movement and his first experience with segregation. Growing up in a small town, he had never known of these things.

During this time, he met some priests, who introduced him to a young Afro-American paraplegic boy named Ronald. This contact began a change in the direction of Jerry's life. Ronald belonged to a family of twelve who lived on a plantation in almost slave-like conditions. One year earlier, Ronald broke his back in a fall from the roof of a tobacco barn. At that time, one priest took Ronald to the university hospital. He paid the bill as the family did not have insurance and earned slave wages. The priest visited the family until one day when the plantation owner ran him off the land.

The NAACP came to the family's aid and moved them to Savannah, and they requested that Jerry take care of Ronald. Ronald's condition became severe the night Jerry received a call. Distraught by what he saw, Jerry went to a public telephone and frantically called some of his doctor friends. Jerry did not have staff privileges at the city hospital. As each doctor gave an excuse why they would not accept Ronald as a patient, Jerry's eyes filled with tears. As he pleaded with God to help him, he promised to serve the poor and not go into private practice.

Jerry marched from the phone booth, picked up Ronald, put him in his car, and sped to the hospital. He carried Ronald into the emergency room to the surprise of the staff. It wasn't until Jerry promised to pay the bill that a doctor came to see him.

#

In 1968, the three priests he befriended had to leave the diocese. Jerry speculated that the church leaders did not like the priest's involvement in civil rights. Seeing the injustice triggered Jerry's crisis of faith. He left the Catholic church and became a self-proclaimed socialist and an atheist. Jerry decided he did not need God or the church to do humanitarian work.

Jerry returned to Marquette and completed his internal medicine residency. The late 1960s were a rebellious time for Jerry, and he joined the Students for a Democratic Society (SDS), an anti-war and anti-capitalist student organization. This choice epitomized his disillusionment with America, the government, and God.

#

In 1974, still a socialist and an atheist, Jerry grew restless to work in Africa. He joined the Peace Corps, and they sent him to Zaire. Jerry insisted he not be assigned to a missionary hospital. However, they sent him to a hospital run by Canadian Sisters in Mwene-Ditu. Jerry did not like how the Sister responsible for patients treated Africans. After six months, he left for a nearby hospital run by Africans. There were two Missionhurst priests and a brother at a nearby mission. Even though Jerry was anti-missionary, they became friends. In 1977, Jerry completed his time in Zaire.

#

Upon returning to the U.S., Jerry became the Medical Director at a health care center in Iowa, and his clinic nurse was Joyce. She began to have strange conversations with Jerry that he initiated. Jerry brought up obscure Bible passages or stories to challenge her. No matter how obscure the verse or challenge he put forth, Joyce always knew the answer.

Eventually, the health center staff noticed a change in Jerry. One day, during a staff meeting, he announced that he would leave for a week of vacation. The following week, during an all-staff session, the Clinic Director walked in with two priests in tow. One introduced himself, then the other. They were from Missionhurst. They advised that they would "take good care of their doctor."

When Jerry returned, he acted differently. Joyce knew he would leave. Later, Jerry informed his staff that he would leave to become a Catholic missionary, a brother through Missionhurst[1]. Jerry told them that he would go to the seminary, take vows, and hoped to return to Zaire. The news stunned the staff.

Jerry realized God had waited for him to come back and fulfill the role he had for his life. When Jerry met with Missionhurst, he thought that he shouldn't have to go to the seminary. Jerry rationalized that as an Internal Medicine Specialist going to do medical work, he shouldn't need to take time out for seminary. They convinced Jerry though his medical skills were essential, he would help people find what he had: God. Jerry later confirmed that he could have given up medicine but not the teaching of God's word and sharing of God's love to others.

---

[1] Missionhurst – CICM (the Congregation of the Immaculate Heart of Mary) has almost one thousand priests and brothers who serve the poorest of the poor around the world.

# Path to Pendjua
*October 1980 – April 1981*

As we drove through the outskirts of Kinshasa, thousands of people trod along both sides of the road. Outdoor markets emerged every five or six blocks. Each market consisted of 100 or more tables lit up by homemade oil lamps. All kinds of odors overwhelmed my senses, from the smell of meat sizzling on a barbeque, the garbage piled up along the road, and the exhaust fumes that spewed out from old trucks without mufflers. Surrounded by crowds of people and absorbing all the odors, I knew I had arrived back home in my beloved Africa.

#

On October 12, 1980, I wrote my first letter home upon arriving back in Zaire. Many questions flooded my mind: How am I going to learn Lingala, the dominant language here? Who will teach me Lotwa, the unique language of the Batwa Pygmies? How did I end up here?

I spent the first few weeks of my new life with Zairian Brothers, who attend a Jesuit college. The brothers are warm and open, and they touched the depths of my heart. Their friendliness made the transition from America to Zaire an easier one. Their prayerfulness and oneness humbled me.

1

Everywhere I went, sweating bodies jammed the buses. It was impossible to get a seat. The Zairian passengers shot looks of surprise at me since white people typically traveled by car.

On one outing, I went to Mama Yemo Hospital, named after President Mobutu's mother. Some of the brothers' friends had been in an airplane crash. Three of the thirty-seven students on board survived, though two of them had severe burns. The hospital situation appeared worse than when I came here with the Peace Corps several years earlier. Patients received one meal a day, and it consisted of just rice and beans. I gave them some money to buy canned fish.

My next visit took me to a parish in the slums. Two young priests lived in a small house, similar to the ones in which locals lived. There were no beds, no refrigerator, no stove, no water, and no electricity. They ate Zairian food, which consisted of manioc, rice, beans, fish, caterpillars, ants, and monkey meat.

The little children love to teach the "mindele" (whites) their language of Lingala. Like children everywhere, I noticed that no matter how miserable their existence seemed to be, they always had ready smiles on their faces.

By 1980, the economy had deteriorated even further. Gasoline cost $7.00 per gallon, and beef sold for $25.00 per pound. A teacher's salary amounted to $45.00 a month. Almost no one in the slums ate meat, and malnutrition had intensified. Eighty-five percent of the people lived in abject poverty. I wondered how much longer they would endure this injustice. Most state clinics and hospitals operated without equipment and medications. Most people could not afford to buy medicine. Aspirin sells for 50 cents per tablet and penicillin for $1.00 a pill.

There were signs of hope as I saw evidence of the development of Christian communities. They provided economic cooperatives, agricultural co-ops, and education. People realized that the current system made a small group very rich and left the rest in abject poverty. The road would not be an easy one. I longed to head to Pendjua.

*Kabuika*

Sunday morning found me in church when I received word that a child in Kimbanseke was in critical condition. I hurried as fast as I could on the half-mile walk to the Kimbanseke clinic. As I entered the pediatric ward, a mother sat with her eight-year-old boy cradled in her arms. I could tell by the way his eyes stared off into space and how he struggled to breathe that he was semi-comatose. When I looked at him, all I saw were skin and bones. I knew that starvation caused his condition. Helplessness overwhelmed me as Kabuika died just five minutes after I arrived. Perhaps he could have been saved by blood transfusions and oxygen. However, those are not available here.

I trudged back to the church. As I thought about little Kabuika, my heart broke. Perhaps a year ago, the young boy may have been healthy and happy as he played with his friends. During the past year, his parents saw their meager income eaten up by one-hundred percent inflation. Soon they had no meat, fish, or eggs to eat. They only subsided on manioc, a starchy vegetable that filled one's stomach but contained no bodybuilding protein. Kabuika would not have known about protein, carbohydrates, and fats. He may have noticed his pants started to slide down his narrowing waist. Then he may have realized he did not have to eat as much.

Kabuika would not understand economics and politics, capitalism, and communism. These were not a part of his visible world. He would not know that ten percent of the people had control of eighty percent of the wealth. As weeks passed, Kabuika noticed he got tired more quickly when he played. He went to bed hungry and woke up hungry. Then, one day, he did not have the strength to get himself up. He wondered why this happened and why his life was not fun anymore. His mother understood the gravity of the situation, but she did not have money to go to a doctor.

Then one day, he caught a cold, and that turned into pneumonia. His weakened body could not fight anymore. His mother, in desperation, brought him to the clinic, but it was too late. I wondered if Kabuika saw my pale face looming over him. If he did, could he know the grief and anger that welled up inside me?

Why should Kabuika, and thousands more like him, suffer from such misery and agonizing deaths? I felt ashamed to think I recently complained about two canker sores in my mouth.

My thoughts continued. Why does God allow this to happen? I knew God does not have to give us the "why" of it all. When it came down to it, wasn't it the fault of humankind that Kabuika died?

Do we not have the means to prevent starvation in this world? Is there not some crazy, distorted value system where nations arm themselves to the teeth while children starve? Is it right that ten percent of the people of Zaire control eighty percent of the wealth? Isn't there something wrong when we worry about being too fat and fret over watching our calories? All the while, Kabuika could not even get a piece of fish once a month. Is it right that a high percentage of U.S. aid to underdeveloped countries goes for military equipment instead of food? I wondered how Jesus would answer these questions.

#

On February 14, 1981, after two more months passed, I was set to depart for Pendjua. However, they told me the boat would not arrive until February 20. The 20th came, and no boat arrived. Word came that the craft would not arrive until the 28th and would not depart until March 7. All the waiting had tested my patience, and I knew this would be a virtue to have in Zaire.

On March 2, the barge arrived. The twenty-ton craft hauled produce from the farm cooperatives. Each passing day seemed to bring a new delay and my discouragement increased. Seven very long days later, I left Kinshasa, not by boat, but on a small private plane. The small four-passenger plane took us to a cattle ranch near Mushie. The cattle rancher who operated it used it to transport meat to Kinshasa, and he allowed missionaries to fly on it for free. Next, we took a boat to Mushie.

From Mushie, the boat ride would take two hours to Bandundu. Once there, we had to meet with the regional medical director, as he had the required papers to sign. Of course, the director had left, so once again, we waited. After three long days, the barge arrived. Now I understood the meaning of "African time." Watches and calendars did not mean much in Zaire.

Early the following day, the second leg of our journey began. The barge had a small cabin with one bed, a stove, a table, and chairs. We traveled under a full moon that reflected on the rivers and swamps. Many fishermen in dugout canoes fished with gill nets. After we docked in Kutu, we waited for almost another week for them to unload the barge. Finally, we continued to Inongo, another twelve-hour boat ride away. The trip continued to the headwaters of Lake Mai-Ndombe. We followed the long, curving, narrow river filled with cypress trees.

The barge arrived in Kiri, a small town of 15,000. The locale did not have one store or car except for the jeep at the mission. We planned to stay and rest until Monday and then drive to Pendjua. I did not know my medical skills were about to get their first workout. A priest burst into the room and said they had a medical emergency. I rushed after him to find a woman with a ruptured uterus. She needed immediate surgery, and I dashed to the hospital. I discovered they had no equipment for blood transfusions, no intravenous fluids, and no sterile equipment. Without hesitation, we loaded her into the jeep and raced to Pendjua, where I could operate.

Thirty-eight miles separated Kiri from Pendjua. The road passed through dense rainforests and swamps and over seventeen log bridges. The trip usually took two hours, but on that morning, in a torrential downpour, the trip took an agonizing four hours. I prayed the entire way there, "God, please don't let us get stuck or fall through any rotted log bridges."

Upon our arrival, we rushed the patient to the operating room. Medical mission Sisters ran the hospital starting in 1958. Five courageous Sisters, all nurses, worked there. We performed the surgery on a "wing and a prayer." The patient lost a lot of blood, and she went into shock. Her baby had already died. The rupture caused severe damage to the woman's uterus. The nurses and I struggled for three hours, and we saved her with the help of the Lord.

How and when I had arrived in Pendjua did not go according to plan. The trip, which started on February 14 and should have taken seven to fourteen days, took six weeks to complete. I have begun to grasp that Pendjua is so remote, and I have started to feel like I am at "the end of the world."

My new home is the mission house that consists of plain cement blocks. It is the width of one large room, with windows on the north and south sides to allow the breeze to blow through. The house includes a dining area and a recreation room. It also has a kitchen with a wood-burning stove and a refrigerator that runs on kerosene. Drape partitions separate the four bedrooms. We each have an office area, a cot, and a mattress.

### Batwa and Ekonda

Let me introduce you to two groups who live in the region: the Batwa and the Ekonda. The Ekonda are of the Bantu race, which is what most Africans were at the time. The Batwa are Pygmoid, that is, Pygmy-like. The real Pygmies are called Bambuti, and they live in the Ituri rainforest east of Pendjua. The Batwa lifestyle and that of the Pygmies are almost identical.

In the past, the Batwa were nomadic and did not have a permanent home. They lived in the forest. They stayed in one place four to five months, the time it took to kill most of the game and harvest the fruit and roots in the area. However, since 1960, they have settled into more permanent villages, but their lifestyle did not change. They did not take up farming but remained hunters and fishermen. However, as game and fish began to diminish, health problems began to occur, mainly from malnutrition.

A significant problem the Batwa faces results from their centuries-old relationship with the Ekonda. Between the two, there exists a "master-slave" relationship. Every Ekonda family holds the position of a master over several Batwa families. This "master-slave" relationship does not occur by force. No actual ownership takes place in the sense an Ekonda cannot sell a Batwa. Long ago, the relationship had been mutually beneficial. The Ekonda farmed but did not hunt, and the Batwa hunted but did not plant. So, they bartered goods.

The Ekonda consider the Batwa to be significantly inferior. They are not even allowed to eat with, sit with, or marry an Ekonda. In the mission hospital, the two groups have separate wards. The Ekonda live in a development located in the center of a region. The Batwa live in small communities or clans surrounding the primary, or Ekonda, part of Pendjua. This setup creates a problem since many Batwa do not come to the hospital or the church. Batwa cannot appear in public with Ekonda. The mission school accepts students from both groups. However, Batwa children do not stay in school because the Ekonda bully them. About one in every thousand Batwa completes six years of school.

The Batwa have not learned the cash economy, so they exchange their game and fish for vegetables and cassava. The people use cassava, an edible, starchy root, to make bread. They never receive adequate compensation in their trades. The Batwa have little or no money, and therefore they rarely buy clothes. Most of them dress in rags and are too embarrassed to go to the mission church, school, or hospital. Most of them do not have enough money to pay for medical care. At the mission hospital, we charge them one-half of the standard fee. I noticed that they have many medical problems and a high infant mortality rate.

However, I can see that the young Batwa adults are in a transition period. They want to learn new skills so they can earn a cash income. Several groups of men hand saw trees into planks. Since most sawmills are inoperable, they sell the planks, even though they are not perfect. I believe we can start several projects such as rice, peanut, and bean fields. Everything will have to be hand cultivated, as they do not have the right equipment or the knowledge to use it. I need to be able to take health care to the villages. I hope to train "barefoot doctors" to work in remote communities. This concept of "barefoot doctors" started in China. Each area will select young adults to receive first aid training, and they will learn to treat common diseases like malaria and worms.

#

I have encountered an enormous number of tuberculosis patients. I only have three types of drugs to treat it. Unfortunately, fifteen percent of the cases are resistant to drugs. There are many other infectious diseases I cannot address for the lack of the right antibiotics. I can only do my best, and somehow, I will have to accept that some people will die. I realize that many of these deaths would be preventable if we were stocked with medications and had the right equipment.

In the first weeks, I learned that fifty-one villages exist in the Pendjua area, and thirteen have government-run dispensaries for medicines. Of these, five have medical personnel, so the other eight are not functioning. I met with the chief nurse, and he informed me he had not received any medications from the government in the last ten months. I found the lack of medicines to be absurd. This urgent need required a pharmacy depot to supply the dispensaries.

My mind began to race. First, I would have to write proposals to receive funds. However, even if we received funds, it would take another six months to get medicines here. I took some deep breaths, tried to remain patient, and accepted my limited power to make rapid changes.

During the initial weeks, I visited six Batwa villages on the edge of Pendjua. At first, the people were afraid. After a few smiles and handshakes and the greeting "Mbote Bandeko" ("hello, my brothers and sisters"), all fear evaporated. Everyone talked at once. They spoke of their favorite activities, which were hunting and fishing. They showed me a small pig-raising project and a few fields cut from the forest. They started to raise chickens, but a viral disease had wiped them out. Two pigs already died of sleeping sickness.

As I thought about their needs, I made plans to start two fish ponds and stock them with a pan fish called Tilapia. I imagined we could grow rice in the swamps and plant peanuts and beans for protein sources. At present, people produced starchy foods such as manioc and sweet potatoes that are low in protein. I knew I needed to bring agriculture and nutrition education to the people. Without an improvement in these areas, the thousands of dollars spent on medications would be a waste.

*Luba*

I selected a Batwa youth named Luba to help me learn Lingala. During the lessons, we talked about the life, beliefs, and hopes of the Batwa people. At sixteen years old, he still lived with his mother, brother, and sister. His father deserted their family two years prior. The desertion of fathers had become a common problem. Men often fled to other regions to escape oppression by the Ekonda.

Luba, one of few Batwa who had attended grade school, could read and speak French. He wanted to further his education, but his family did not have money to pay for seventh grade. Instead, he worked with his uncle in a field. I began to teach him how to give health education lessons on tuberculosis, intestinal worms, and nutrition. I used flip charts, and then Luba translated them from French into Lingala.

I asked him, "Since tuberculosis is so prevalent, how do you believe people catch it?" He explained, "When someone with tuberculosis coughs and spits on the ground, and another person steps in it, they will catch the cough."

At least he had a basic understanding of germs and had begun to understand how someone contracted tuberculosis. He listened as I explained how breathing in small, infected droplets coughed up by a tuberculosis patient spread the disease. Because a whole family lived in a small one-room hut, entire families were often infected. I envision Luba as one of the first barefoot doctors.

Since Luba went to school for six years, he did not learn hunting and fishing techniques. Luba had just built his own house and prepared to move out of his family's home. Most boys left their homes at age fourteen because houses typically had only one room. Their customs did not allow two men to live in the same place. Luba was polite but definitely not timid and quite adamant that he would never be a slave to the Ekonda. I witnessed his leadership capability and knew it would be interesting to follow his life's journey.

#

One day, I invited some Batwa men to talk about their way of life. They explained that they wished to be independent of their

Ekonda masters. "How do you think you can do that?" I asked. "We need to make enough money to buy food so we can be independent," they responded. "The Ekonda exchange corn, manioc, and peanuts for the game we kill."

"How do you plan to make money?" I asked. They replied, "The mission and the hospital need to hire us." I said, "But only eighteen people work at the hospital, and hundreds of men need work, so that is not the solution. If the reason you are dependent on them is agriculture, couldn't you learn to farm?"

To most, the answer may seem self-evident. However, the Batwa and their ancestors had only hunted and fished for centuries. The thought of cutting forest to clear a field, hoe it, and plant crops did not seem feasible. Eventually, a few men agreed to grow food. They would sell a portion of their game to the Ekonda. We decided to meet each Sunday to continue the discussions. They educated me on their way of life, and I taught them how to attain independence.

#

In mid-April, I went to the Batwa village of Bokote, and some people asked me to examine a nineteen-year-old boy. He had been sick for six months and afraid to go to the hospital. He had deteriorated to nothing but skin and bones due to tuberculosis. I talked him into coming to the hospital sanitarium. He had no one to bring him food, as his parents had died. He wore only a pair of raggedy shorts and a tattered shirt, so I gave him a t-shirt. I promised to provide him with some work in the mission's garden when he regained his strength.

Another seventeen-year-old Batwa boy with advanced leprosy arrived. His terrible condition surprised me, and I discovered he had already lost three toes and the tips of three fingers. His hands were crippled but still functional. I gave him a job weaving baskets and mats to be able to make a little money. Weaving would be excellent therapy for his hands.

A cure for leprosy existed, and if treated early, it left no crippling or loss of fingers or toes. The hospital in the boy's village did not have medications for leprosy. With treatment, I would be able to stop the disease from progressing. With physical therapy, he could make a living. Such suffering tore my heart to pieces.

#

In need of a break, I went to Ngondo Banga, a nearby Batwa village, and taught them how to play volleyball. After I explained the rules, using poor Lingala, they chose sides of seven. The first time the ball went over the net, thirty people rushed onto the court and batted away at the ball. When the ball went out of bounds, thirty or forty more ran after the ball and hit it back onto the court. After I eventually restored order, they played some actual games. Since the children were all about three feet tall, I lowered the net. The experience was so much fun that I planned to travel to other villages to teach them how to play.

#

I needed to continue to learn more about the Batwa, so I invited Luba, Bola, Mpia, Mbomba, and Bilimbeya for a meeting. I asked them if they knew the origin of their people. Each African group had a history and a story with parts that were true and pieces that were mythological about how they began. A legend about a chief named Ikulua-Loleke provided the source for the Batwa history and their Ekonda "masters."

Chief Ikulua lived on a prairie near the rainforest, and he had two sons. At an old age, he became ill, and his death appeared imminent. At that time, the older son entered the forest with a large hunting party, and the younger son remained at home. The younger son, who ordinarily did not have the right to become chief, talked the old leader into giving him the prairie land and the chiefdom. The older man agreed to this on the condition the older brother and his clan controlled the forest. They would also have control over the animals, fruits, and trees that existed there. The latter group is the Batwa or 'Forest People.' During the meeting, the boys did not get to the part that explained how the Ekonda became "masters" and the Batwa "slaves."

# Becoming a Real Man
*May 1981 – August 1981*

I observed that malnutrition cases had increased each week, especially among Ekonda children. The problem stemmed from a scarcity of wild game, and the people did not raise animals for food. I needed to convince them to plant high-protein vegetables like corn, beans, and peanuts. Then, I had to teach them how to change their eating habits and grow proper vegetables. The hospital agreed to plant one acre of peanuts, corn, and kidney beans as a demonstration. Malnutrition did not usually become a big problem among the Batwa as they ate everything that moved. Their diet included snakes, crickets, birds, monkeys, rats, and mice.

I also noticed that medical missionaries were very involved with the technical aspects of patient care. However, they did not take time for personal aspects of living and working with people. Rarely did the Sisters who provided health care visit the villages, and they infrequently socialized with the people. I encouraged the health care workers to have more contact with the Batwa. I planned to build a one-room mud hut in a Batwa village. Then, I could spend six days a month living and working with them. I needed to learn more about their way of life.

#

In mid-May, the hospital had many adults and children with critical illnesses. One child, a little eight-year-old Batwa boy,

12

Boombo, came from a distant village. I could not believe that the villagers carried him on a stretcher for seventy miles. He arrived in critical condition. The diagnosis included double pneumonia, heart failure, an infection of his heart valve, and his blood count dropped to twenty percent of an average boy. Somehow, he survived the first twenty-four hours after administering intravenous fluids, blood transfusions, antibiotics, and heart medicines.

For six days, I observed Boombo and watched him improve. He flashed a smile when I visited him three times each day. He fought so hard to survive. Then, after each succeeding day, I saw his condition worsen. His blood count dropped. Without hesitating, I gave him 3/10 of a liter of my blood. Despite my efforts, Boombo died quietly and gently. Sad tears ran down my flushed face. All I thought about is why did young children have to suffer like this?

#

After they buried Boombo, we held a prayer meeting. The young men wondered how Mary, the mother of Jesus, could be so joyful if she was as impoverished as they were. They thought that only rich people who had everything were happy. The Batwa had no possessions outside of their one-room mud huts. They did not have any instruments, pans, plates, or glasses. Most had no more than one shirt and a pair of pants, and those were often hand-me-downs from their masters. They did not have soap or a toothbrush. They had nothing since they did not have any money. The group talked about Jesus and His poverty and learned that He had happiness and joy. They sensed they had inner happiness and joy, despite their poverty.

I explained, "I have fewer belongings than ever before, but I'm happier than I've ever been." One man replied, "Yes, the Lord can make you happy even when you are poor if you allow Him to enter into your heart." Another man questioned, "What can we do to help ourselves? The only way we can make money is to get a job as a nurse or teacher."

"You're right," said another. "We only have a sixth-grade education, and we do not want to go to high school. It is sixty miles away." I learned that the men were afraid to leave their village. A member of the group spoke up, "What if we earned a living from farming?" Two other members agreed it would be a good idea. "We can cut a field," they responded. My hopes rose for these men. "I will buy you machetes and help select a site for the field," I offered.

### Cutting a Field

It did not take long to learn that cutting fields required backbreaking work. We planned to clear two acres by August. The young men wanted to plant peanuts and hoped to yield eight to twelve sacks of peanuts per acre. I suggested they could use the wood they cut to build pig pens. I promised to buy them a female pig to start a pig-raising business. My medical training did not prepare me for this.

Luba, Bola, and Mpia decided to try farming. I went to the village to help them select a field to cut. Each family had its allotted ancestral land. The senior member of each family gave permission where one could acquire a piece of property. Luba's birthplace was the village of Liamba. He asked his uncle for a property, and his uncle agreed to give him an acre of land.

My excitement increased as I went to help them on their first day to cut a field. As I approached the village, I heard several loud voices and came upon a very heated argument. A group of three young men squared off against another group of three. A group of twenty-five women tried to keep them separated. They fought over the fact that the young men did not want Luba, Bola, and Mpia to cut the field. After all, they did not live in their community.

"What if you go to the village chief to settle the situation?" I suggested. They had already done so, but the chief got mad and left. The groups squared off again. The men yelled and hurled insults at one another, and I worried that someone would get hurt. "Please, please settle down. " I urged. "Let's talk this through. Ngambe (God) gave us an enormous forest, and there is plenty for everyone. Luba, since you live in Ngondo Banga, don't you think it is better to cut a field there? Then you can watch and guard it."

I sighed as the young men backed off. They thought this idea could work and decided to return to Ngondo Banga. Their uncle agreed to give them an excellent, large plot to cut. The area of about an acre and had ten giant trees and hundreds of smaller trees growing on it. We cut for three hours and made a swath around the plot.

Two more members agreed to cut a field. The area they received had dense brush and trees. The young men usually did not chop down the trees for more than two hours a day and perhaps only four days a week. When they grew tired, they grabbed their fish lines and bows and arrows and headed into the forest. They stayed there for hours, days, or even weeks. They did not worry about the future because both God and the rainforest always provided for them. The Batwa believed the provision would continue. They did not realize that the wild game population and the fish had steadily diminished.

#

When I arrived back at the mission, Luba and his little brother stood out front, stripped to the waist. Tears ran down their faces as they held several chickens in their hands. I rushed over to them, worried. "What's wrong, boys?" In between sobs, Luba said, "Our grandmother died this morning. I pleaded with her all night to come to the hospital, but she would not. So, we need to buy a piece of cloth to wrap her in."

I had one piece of cloth I bought for a sheet, but I gave it to Luba and told him to keep the chickens. My heart went out to these boys. Their grandmother might have had a chance to be saved if she chose to go to the hospital. Many of the older generation Batwa had a fear of modern medicine and doctors. So, at sixteen, Luba had become a man. As the head of his mother's household, he now had to provide food, and he had to arrange his first funeral.

After the funeral, I visited Benga-Nkelete to encourage the prayer group members who just started to cut a field. I took an ax to help chop down trees. The Ekonda and Batwa were amazed a doctor did manual labor. I wanted to show them farm work was not inferior to other work, as they believed. As I worked and sweated alongside my Batwa brothers, I learned about their culture and customs. Slowly, I built up a level of trust with them. I have already received so much from this slow process of "give and take." I believe that it is essential for them to see a white man - a missionary - on an equal plane, willing to share in their sufferings and joy.

15

*A Real Man*

In late June, I participated in a fishing trip with the boys. The river we chose to fish in required a two-hour walk from Ngondo Banga, Luba's village. The group prepared two hundred bank poles and took two kerosene lanterns. The narrow trail to the river wound through dense underbrush and swamps. There were many low-hanging limbs. All sorts of roots and vines grew on the ground. We set off at a rapid pace. I learned to look at where I placed my feet. Vines, roots, thorns, and venomous ants could inflict severe wounds.

Since the first part of the dry season had begun, the river had a low water level. We set up camp about one-quarter mile from the river. The young men cut small trees and constructed two beds, and built a fire between them. They made the beds by sticking four forked sticks in the ground. Then they laid small trees in the forks to make the frame. When they finished the stick bed, the boys smiled and exclaimed, "That's your bed."

"That is so kind of you, but I'd rather sleep on the smooth ground," I responded. A wave of disappointment came across the boys' faces. "Oh, I am kidding," I said with a nervous laugh. "I am happy to sleep on the bed."

The group set out and placed one hundred bank poles along a four-kilometer stretch of the river. The river looked like a natural paradise for catfish as it had tree stumps, drop-offs, and curves. After dark, we grabbed the kerosene lamps and continued to check the bank poles. After we had caught sixty more fish, we returned to our tents to sleep.

I rolled up in a blanket on my lumpy stick bed, and the sticks indented my back. When the boys saw me sleeping on my back, they talked excitedly. The following day, I asked them, "Why were you so nervous last night?" "Because we never sleep on our backs," they responded. "Sleeping on your back is the position of a dying person, and if someone sleeps on his back, his spirit will leave him and go up into the sky." The boys feared I would die.

That morning, we checked the poles to find we caught another fifty-six catfish. At ten o'clock, we arrived back home with our catch. The villagers greeted us and kept chanting to me, "Yo azali mobali!" (You are a real man). I learned that until a Batwa boy traveled deep into the forest and spent the night there, he could not be considered a man.

#

In June, the school gave out report cards. All the students assembled, and the principal announced the top three students in each class. Luba's little brother, Mbomba, came back to my house just before dinner. His beaming smile could not hide his pride in being first in his class of twenty-six students, of which eighteen were Ekonda. I mounted his report card to some cardboard and covered it with plastic so Mbomba could hang it on my wall. Mbomba decided that if he placed it in his hut, it would get covered with smoke, and he would be unable to read it.

The Batwa built a small fire in their shelters every night to keep warm as they did not have any blankets. Everything they owned smelled of smoke, and the Ekonda made fun of them and called them "stinking Batwa." I allowed Mbomba to hang the card on my wall, and every time he came to visit me, he could look at it.

#

In July, during a Batwa prayer group meeting, I received yet another culture shock. One boy stated that the Batwa were terrible and inferior to all other humans. The negative self-image surprised me. I asked the others, "What do you think?" They all talked at once. "Well, black skin is evil, and it is a punishment from God," one of them replied.

"Yes," said another. "We are poor because we are evil, and whites are rich because they are good, and God blesses them."

Hearing these things saddened me. Another said, "We fear white people, and no white person thinks good of us or trusts us."

"Well, what about me? Do you think this way about me?" I asked them. "We do not know yet, as we do not know the inner thoughts of your heart," one responded. Luba spoke up, "I believe Dr. Jerry trusts us because he lets us keep his tools in our village and eats our food."

The entire discussion agonized me. I wondered why the Batwa had such great fears and such negative self-images after

17

twenty years of missionaries here at the hospital, school, and church. I believed we missionaries must follow His example by living like the people.

#

In early July, a man accidentally discharged a shotgun in another village. The pellets hit three people, and one, a three-year-old boy, received a fatal wound. They brought the boy to the mission hospital, but he died within an hour. The deceased boy's family tied up the man who fired the shotgun and planned to kill him. The village chief sent for the military, but before they arrived, the man escaped. He fled to Kiri and turned himself over to the police for protection. The military showed up in Pendjua and raised havoc. Many soldiers were thieves and stole the people's tools and food.

Imono, a member of the prayer group, came to my door. He said a soldier came into his hut, took his ax, a duck, and a basketful of palm nuts. Furious, Imono and I marched over to the building where the soldier stayed. We asked him what right he had to break into someone's house and steal their things. I cited a book of Zairian laws. It stated no soldier could enter a home unless he were in pursuit of a criminal. The soldier raised his eyebrows in amazement that I knew the laws. Then, he gave back the ax but kept the duck.

During the prayer meeting, the group talked about their life situation. They stated, "The Ekonda are jealous because you help us." Several weeks ago, I told the group that I would like to build a hut and live part-time in a Batwa village. The group shared their fears at the thought of me moving into their community. They thought the Ekonda would kill them with either evil spirits or with poison. They said the Ekonda would not kill me but would undoubtedly kill them, and they feared for their lives. I assured them I would not do anything to endanger them. I realized I needed to learn more about their beliefs about evil spirits.

#

When I returned home, a fifteen-year-old boy named Ikengo sat on the church steps. I asked why he sat there looking so troubled. When he held up his right hand, I could see the destroyed third finger and the three holes in the palm with pus pouring out. Shocked, I asked, "Why didn't you come sooner?" He replied, "I do not have any money, and I am afraid to go to the hospital."

I learned that both of the boy's parents were dead, and he had to fend for himself. I felt sympathy for him, sat him on my bicycle, and took him to the clinic for treatment. The suffering the people endured before they came for help amazed me. Situations like these made the barefoot doctor program even more necessary.

Seven Batwa villages selected barefoot doctors who I planned to train in September. I received another lesson in the Batwa culture through this process. Intermarriage connected the two villages of Ngondo Banga and Liamba, so they were to select one person to serve both communities. Ngondo Banga wanted Luba to be their barefoot doctor, but the people of Liamba refused. The situation baffled me since Luba's father came from Liamba, and he also had three uncles who lived there. One of his uncles held the position of the village chief.

### Marriage System

To understand the situation, I had to understand the marriage system and family structure. I learned that when a young man wished to marry, he and his family paid a dowry to the bride's family. The full payment rarely occurred; however, the young couple could lead a life as husband and wife, except at night. The girl had to stay with her parents for the night. The couple may have children. The children belonged to the girl's family until the boy paid the entire dowry.

When the man paid half the dowry, the woman and her children could live in the husband-to-be village. However, they still belonged to the wife's family until the final payment. In Luba's situation, his father paid half of the endowment. Therefore, Luba's mother, brother, and sisters lived in Liamba, their father's village.

In 1977, Luba's father deserted the family and moved to Inongo, a three-day voyage from Pendjua. At that time, Luba's mother took the children and moved back to Ngondo Banga, her village. This situation caused an absolute disgrace for the father's community. The survival of the clans and villages depended on having many children.

Luba, being of marrying age, and having a sixth-grade education, made him a real asset to the village. Luba's youngest uncle pressured him to move to Liamba. When Luba said he would think about it, his uncle became angry. The uncle scolded Luba and said, "You are not fit to be a barefoot doctor because you do not obey your elders." A heated argument ensued, and the uncle insulted Luba and his mother. Luba retorted, "I will never live in Liamba." He said he would stay in his mother's village, get married, and his children would belong to Ngondo Banga.

Everyone considered Luba's threat to be the worst thing that could happen to a paternal community. In retaliation, the uncle threatened to have Luba arrested, for which there were no grounds. I counseled Luba and encouraged him not to desert his younger brother and mother. "Your father's family has no claim on you because he only paid half of the endowment," I advised.

\#

After Sunday's prayer meeting, the group visited the marketplace. The Ekonda chief confronted them and warned, "Be careful getting involved in politics. The doctor and Miguel (a co-worker at the mission) are trying to obtain independence for you. That isn't right." The group returned, all excited and frightened, and told me what happened. We discussed the dangers and risks of seeking independence and liberation.

I told them, "If you think it is better that I should not come to your village or work with you, I understand. I'll stop my activities if I must." Luba spoke up. "Jesus told us, what good is it for a man to save his life here only to lose it for eternity? If I lose my life for being Christian and wanting freedom, let it be that way." The rest of the group did not respond with as much drama. They agreed to work for independence through non-violent means.

I believed the Ekonda would not do anything as they were peaceful people. However, I thought they controlled the Batwa through "psychic violence." They did this in part through stories passed from generation to generation. As a result, the Batwa developed deep fears that kept them enslaved. I knew that liberation from these fears would allow them to be independent.

#

On Sunday, the prayer group held a "limpati" or feast. They asked many questions about white people, as they viewed them as superhumans. I always tried to dispel these myths. I wanted them to see white persons were no better than they were, and white people had weaknesses and faults. They thought white people were more intelligent because they had so much technology. I asked them, "Do I know the forest better than you?"

"No," they replied. I continued, "Do I know which trees are good for firewood and which ones are good and strong for building houses?" They answered, "No."

"Can I make traps of vines and catch animals?" Again, they replied, "No."

"See, you know more than I do," I responded. "We never thought about it that way," they said. "We are superior to you when we are in the forest, our world."

After our discussion, I prayed about the idea that I should go on a retreat alone in the forest for one week. I asked Luba, Mpia, and Bola if they would take me to a quiet place by a brook or spring. There I would stay and pray for one week. The young men were astonished and afraid, as they had never spent a night alone in the forest. "The Bengondu hunt and kill anyone who stays alone in the forest at night," Luba warned me. "What are the Bengondu?" I asked. "Evil spirits?"

"No!" they exclaimed. "Animals?" I asked. Again, they shouted, "No!"

"Well, what are they?" I inquired. "Bato batam-boli na nzamba (Men who walk in the forest at night)!" they shouted.

I asked, "Have you ever seen them?" Mpia replied, "No, but others have. You can't stay alone in the forest at night."

My heart sympathized with them. On Saturday, I packed up food and blankets. I filled my bag with dried beans, rice, coffee, palm oil, sugar, manioc, and five cans of sardines. On Sunday, the group arrived and began to talk all at once. Luba said, "Mitema na biso bayoki mawa mpe nsome (Our hearts are full of fear and sorrow). Zabola (the devil) will take you from us."

I asked, "Well, my friends, which is stronger, the devil or Jesus?" The group replied, "We think Jesus is, but we're not sure because didn't the devil kill Jesus?" I replied, "Yes, but didn't Jesus rise from the dead and become victorious in the end?" They responded, "Yes, we know the resurrection of the dead will occur, but we don't want you to die and leave us."

The group proposed to come to the camp, stay the night, and leave me alone during the day. In the end, they agreed that Luba would spend each night there and return to the village each morning. When my retreat ended, the young men were thrilled that I survived. The people from Ngondo Banga came to meet me and were relieved the "Bengondu" did not take me.

#

Upon my return, a mother of eight children needed emergency surgery. She ruptured her uterus during the labor of her ninth pregnancy. The lady lived sixty miles away, and twenty-four men transported her to the hospital on foot. I could not believe they made the two and a half-day journey. Though she appeared to be near death, her blood pressure steadily rose after administering intravenous fluids and medications. We decided we could operate. The woman had gas gangrene in her abdomen, and the odors were terrific. Somehow, she lived through the operation but died three hours later. Once again, the incredible suffering saddened me.

# Traditional Beliefs
*September 1981 – December 1981*


In mid-September, we held the first barefoot doctor class. The class consisted of five young men who were eager to help their brothers and sisters. Two men could barely read. Luba explained things in Lotwa to those who did not understand Lingala. The first lessons addressed the causes of illness, traditional beliefs, and scientific concepts. The conventional views were that serious diseases resulted from breaking a taboo, breaking a rule of their ancestors, or sorcery.

I learned about several beliefs. If a pregnant woman ate porcupine meat, she would have an abortion. No one entered the forest on Thursdays, as on that day, the ancestors looked for food. If a person went into the rainforest, they would die. If someone went into the forest while it rained, they would contract skin abscesses.

They called the primary agent in sorcery a "ndoki," the word for an evil spirit. The Batwa believed there were four ways the ndoki could pass onto a person. An enemy could invoke the ndoki to provoke an illness. An older family member had the power to initiate the ndoki. A person's "double" could leave him while he slept. The "double" would invoke the ndoki and cause illness to another family member. Or, an unhappy ancestor could invoke the ndoki.

However, they believed this latter cause was preventable. The family must throw a big feast for the dead family member within the first year after their death. The Pygmies thought the ancestor would be unhappy and cause illness if the family did not provide a feast. The family usually spent everything they had to satisfy the dead person's spirit.

When someone had a severe illness or died, the family met with the local witch doctor. A family included everyone to the fifth cousin. The witch doctor asked many questions and performed certain rituals to find out who sent the ndoki. Afterward, the witch doctor would prescribe a treatment that included some fetish to drive the ndoki away.

#

After learning about some new beliefs, I went to see a seven-year-old boy in Ngondo Banga who had a large abscess on his thigh. He also had a high fever, so I told his father to bring him to the hospital to have it lanced and receive antibiotics. The father refused since he feared even the most minor operation. I gave Luba antibiotics to take to the boy, along with ointment, to help bring the abscess to a peak. A few days later, I grabbed some sterile instruments and went to the village. The father agreed to let me lance it as the villagers watched. I removed a half pint of green pus, and the little boy let out a wild scream. Afterward, he sat on my lap and smiled from ear to ear.

Then, the people asked me to circumcise the boys, as the man who used to do it died. When the boys were seven to twelve years old, they were circumcised. They held the boys down without the use of anesthesia, and a machete completed the circumcision. Afterward, they smeared red hot pepper on the wound and wrapped it in banana leaves to stop the bleeding. Circumcisions were carried out in the dry season when fish were plentiful to eat. Therefore, the body had iron to replace the lost blood. I told them I did not have the heart to do circumcisions without the use of anesthesia.

### Ngondo Banga

In early November, I went to Ngondo Banga. Luba and I examined stool samples and found ninety percent were positive for hookworms, roundworms, and whipworms. People surrounded the table, and each one looked through the microscope to see the worm eggs. They all asked for worm medicine, but I refused to give them any. Before they received treatment, each family needed to dig an outhouse to use. The people grumbled that they had to wait. I knew that without improved sanitation, they would continue to get re-infected by worms.

I met with the village elders to discuss the problems they faced. They told me that they did not have money for education, clothes, or books. Very few could afford to come to the clinic. They lamented that game and fish were becoming scarce, and the people did not eat as well as before. I asked them, "How do you plan to get more food and money?"

"We need to cut more fields to plant peanuts and rice and raise animals," they responded. "However, we do not have machetes, axes, seeds, or animals. We don't have money to buy any of those things." I said, "I will supply each extended family with five machetes and an ax, plus seed, to begin. I'll also try to get you some pigs and chickens to raise."

To start, I gave them five spades and encouraged them to dig outhouses. I told them to cut the weeds around their homes to reduce the mosquito population. They were happy when I announced that the clinic would accept firewood and bamboo mats in place of money for their visits and medications.

#

Each Batwa village consisted of a clan, which meant they had a common ancestry. Within the group, there were up to ten extended families. Each clan had an "ebanga," a structure similar to a picnic shelter, where the men ate and met. Men and women never ate together. The little girls ate with the women, and boys over three years old ate with the men. One extended family may consist of up to ten or fifteen households. If one family killed an antelope or a monkey, they shared the meat with the other families. However, they did not share any fish they caught, possibly because the fishes were too small.

Ngondo Banga consisted of five extended families. Luba and Mbomba belonged to one family, and Mpia and Bola, to another family. They invited the whole village whenever a dance or celebration occurred.

The Batwa are wealthy in the sense that they find joy in the little things of life and share them. There are times when I am questioned and challenged, times when they misunderstand me, and times I misunderstand them. The Batwa and I are barely beginning to understand one another. The Batwa long for a life of independence and one with less suffering and disease. They want their children to make it to adulthood, as 35-40 percent die before age five. Medicine alone is not enough, and there must be economic and social change.

#

In December, I rode my bicycle to Bongili. I started to train Yende, the oldest of the five barefoot doctors. He had a talent for technical work, though he was timid and had the least education. While I worked in the village, a skinny and frail sixteen-year-old boy came. He had bloody diarrhea for the past three weeks. He did not come to the clinic because he did not have any clothes, only a rag wrapped around his waist. I told him if he went to the hospital, I would give him a pair of shorts, a shirt, and food for one week.

The next day, the sick boy arrived. Our diagnosis showed he had amoebic dysentery and severe ulcerations of the bowel. Amoebae were a severe problem because the springs and creeks were contaminated with them since they did not have outhouses. Of those who had latrines, the children did not use them.

I returned to Ngondo Banga to examine stool samples. Each sample contained two or three types of worms. I still refused to give them worm treatment, as they had not dug any outhouses. The people were slow to change, and they did not associate germs or worms with diseases. They believed all conditions came from breaking taboos or from evil spirits. The people believed kwashiorkor (a Lotwa word for a type of malnutrition where a child's body swelled up) resulted from eating sand. They did not realize the children ate sand because they did not have enough protein to consume.

When I first revealed to a group of women that kwashiorkor resulted from a lack of specific foods and protein in the diet, they laughed. I even had a difficult time getting the barefoot doctors to accept the reason.

### Prayer Groups

Luba, Bola, Mpia, and Mbomba stopped by to see me on their way to school one day. Luba announced that if Imono and Banzolo came to the prayer meeting, he and his brothers and friends would not show up. They had another inter-village squabble. The previous night, Imono told Luba he and his friends would beat up Luba. Before too many fists flew, a group of adults broke up the fight. Luba said nothing could make him come to pray with Imono and Banzolo again. Later, I ran into Imono. "What happened?" I asked. Imono replied, "Nothing to cause the break-up of our prayer group." His reply upset me, and I became more upset to think the prayer group might end.

I met with the adult prayer group. Afterward, the members asked me if they could discuss a "likambo" (problem). "We are cutting a field to plant rice and peanuts and thought we each would get a machete," one stated. "We do not want to share one among each family. We also want shirts," another said. Flustered, I replied, "A part of being a Christian means learning to share. Did you only join to receive material things?"

Both prayer groups were on the rocks. I prayed on my way home and recognized the events were a test. *Lord, you have put me here, and you were the one to inspire these two prayer groups into formation. I put my trust in You. Please help us find a way to resolve these problems.*

I canceled the prayer meeting because the young men did not amend their differences. I felt empty, as though part of me was missing, so I prayed. Then, I heard a knock at my door, and there stood Imono, Banzolo, Luba, and Mbomba. They came to talk about their dispute.

Luba spoke for the group. He said, "Frere (Father), Imono, and Banzolo became jealous of me, and so they wanted to beat me up. I got angry and even allowed myself to hate them so much I didn't want to pray with them anymore. They have asked me to forgive them, and with the Lord's help, I have, and they have forgiven me. Please do not stop the prayer group."

I almost did a cartwheel on the inside. *Alleluia Lord! You never let us down. You just tested us to make us stronger.*

#

On Christmas Day, we celebrated the Prince of Peace's birth in this isolated corner of the world. There was no Santa Claus, no commercialism, and no gift-giving. However, we had a prayer-filled and song-filled celebration. On Christmas morning, I provided tea and cake for the prayer group. This snack would be the best that they would eat today. The hunters had come back empty-handed, so they ate manioc and boiled leaves. On Christmas night, the Sisters invited me to dinner. It bothered me that we dined so well, while the people did not. I became painfully aware of the vast chasm between the "haves" and the "have nots."

# Youth of Light

*1982*

I returned to Ngondo Banga to find every family dug an outhouse. I agreed to treat every person for worms, free of charge. Digging latrines would be a small step forward in their health improvement. While there, I learned that four young men harvested their peanut field and had almost one hundred kilograms worth 400 Zaires ($36.00). Then, I found out that the adults formed four groups and began to cut fields to plant peanuts and rice due to the boy's results. I thought about how my greatest pleasure occurred when I toiled with them, and it helped me get to know them better.

Once I returned to the mission, Mr. Mputela, the local congressman, came to visit. He was an Ekonda, but he had a favorable attitude toward the Batwa. He supported my work. However, he came to warn me that many Ekonda were upset because I helped the Batwa, taught their children, and even allowed them into my house. He said the worst offense was that I ate food cooked by them. I had previously heard these complaints.

## Fishing Trip

Even though I had much work to do, the five oldest prayer group members and I went on a fishing trip. On the last night, they asked me how much money I made. "I make four hundred Zaires a month ($40.00)," I said. "Why did you spend all those years in school to make so little?" they wondered. Luba replied, "Jesus sent you here, and if you work for Him, money isn't important."

The others asked, "Why aren't you mean like the other white men we have met? Why are you willing to get your hands dirty and work with us?" I answered, "I guess that is the way the Lord wants me to be, and He has given me the grace to do these things."

Before we left, the boys retrieved the seventy catfish they placed in a gunnysack in the river. They returned with much disappointment. All the fish were dead. They had put the sack in a small brook that stopped running during the night, and the lack of oxygen caused them to die. The boys planned to sell them to buy the things they needed. They could sell three catfish for 5 Zaires ($.50), which was a lot of money. They did not understand when I tried to explain how the lack of oxygen killed the fish.

"The ndoki (evil spirit) killed them," one boy said. Another claimed, "I dreamt a man died at the hospital, and his spirit came and killed the fish." Bola suggested, "Maybe God doesn't want us to have these fish." "I agree," Luba stated. "We will give the fish to the patients at the hospital. The fish are not yet spoiled."

They were still sad and did not want to eat breakfast. I couldn't let the trip end on a sad note, so I offered to buy the fish to feed the hospital patients. This offer brought shrieks of joy. Then they ate breakfast, and we made the three-hour march back home.

### *Bilenge Ya Mwinda*

During my free time, I read several books about the "Bilenge Ya Mwinda" (Youth of Light). The Bilenge Ya Mwinda was a Christian youth movement established by Bishop Motondo in 1970.

Once a month, the groups will come together for a conference and prayer meeting. Once a year, they will go into the forest for a five-day retreat. The program takes three years to complete. In the first year, they become brothers in Christ through a sixteen-step process.

The first step, "Komona Clair" (see clearly), requires them to give up everything false. These things include lying, slander, extra-marital sex, and other behavior. In the second year, they receive the option of giving themselves to Christ. During the third year, they will go out and proclaim the gospel to others.

After much reflection and prayer, I decided to reach out to other Batwa youth, so I started a three-person study group. Luba and Bola were the other two selected, as they were the most mature ones in the prayer group. We began with a book for the Yaya (Big Brother). After six days of study in the past two weeks, Bola asked me if they had to give up sex.

"Sex is a way of life for us," he explained. "Do you have the courage to become a true Christian and be an example for the younger boys?" I asked. Luba said, "I will try because I want to be a big brother and help my younger brothers. I will need a lot of help from the Holy Spirit to change my ways." Bola looked uncertain. "I want another week or two to pray about this, but I will continue to study the way of life for a Yaya."

When a Batwa boy reaches fourteen or fifteen, he often finds a concubine to satisfy his sexual desires. Rarely does this result in a personal relationship or any emotional attachment. Most of the time, neither party intends to get married. In our next prayer meeting, Imono asked, "Did God make us male and female to procreate?" "Yes, He did," I replied. "Well, then, why is having sex with my concubine a sin?"

Bola answered, "God created marriage, so when a man and woman become one, they can have children." Imono wondered, "Is sex only for married people?" I led them to what the Bible says. Afterward, they said, "It looks like we have to give up sex if we want to be true Christians."

One member did not want to accept this, and he said, "If we don't sleep with our concubine, how do we know we are fit for marriage?" I asked, "Are you looking for a wife?" The boy said, "No." "Well, then why do you need to know this?" I asked. Others jumped in and said, "We aren't looking for wives; we are looking to satisfy our mposa na mzoto (bodily passions)."

I asked, "Do you believe marriage is just sex?" This question led to a discussion on the emotional and love relationship in marriage. Then we discussed parental responsibilities. The boys talked about their mothers' difficult situation, as none had a father living at home. Bola did not even know his father. A worried Banzolo said, "If I don't have sex with my concubine, she will refuse me and look for another boy."

Luba replied, "So what? If she refuses you because you won't sleep with her, she doesn't love you. Besides, do you go with her because you love her?" During the remaining time, they prayed for grace to change their ways and give up bonsoni (sex). They asked me to lead another discussion on these topics. Their desire showed real progress on their journey to follow Jesus.

#

The pounding on my door sounded like someone wanted to break it down. I went out to find Luba and Bola standing there. Bola bled profusely from a severe machete wound to his knee. I rushed him to the operating room and found that he cut two arteries, the ligaments and knee joint bones. By the time I sewed the wounds and hospitalized him, he had lost a lot of blood. I prayed he would heal.

Then, one of my patients, who had chronic tropical ulcers on his lower leg for several years, arrived. When he came to the hospital, his shinbone had eroded, and his blood count measured at ten percent. I told him that he either had to have an amputation or return to the village, as no medication could help him. He agreed to the amputation, and though I had many apprehensions, the operation proceeded without any complications. I had just performed the first amputation ever done here. It was the very first one because people preferred to die than submit to an amputation.

My week did not end before I performed three more significant operations. A lady with a ruptured extra-uterine pregnancy arrived first. With the Lord's help guiding my hands, I stopped the bleeding. Next, I operated on a patient with a ruptured appendix and an enormous three-week-old abscess. The third patient, a Batwa man, arrived at 10:00 one night from a distant village. He had a strangulated hernia. During the operation, I found three feet of the dead gangrenous small intestine. I had never done a bowel resection and reconnection.

I took out my surgical atlas with step-by-step pictures of general surgeries. For fifteen minutes, I studied the illustrations. Then, as a nurse held the book by my side, I removed the dead bowel and reattached the two good ends. We had to use local anesthesia to operate, and we did not finish until 3:00 a.m. Several days later, the man could eat.

After an exhausting week of surgery, I prepared for the day of prayer and orientation for the new group of Bilenge ya Mwinda (Children of Light). I shared with the group about my transformation and decision to follow Christ in 1977. Luba shared his testimony on how the four "B's destroyed his life and how he changed with the Holy Spirit's help. The four "B"s were bitumba (fighting), basanga (alcohol), bangi (marijuana), and bonsoni (illicit sex).

#

Later, I met with the adult prayer group. They asked many questions and expressed concerns about marriage. The bride price system had become very distorted and impeded those who wanted to marry. In the past, the bride price consisted of donated food or meat. It was more of a symbolic gesture by the husband-to-be that he valued his wife. With the introduction of currency, parents exploited the system to make money. The price among the Batwa represented two or three years of income. As a result, fewer and fewer couples got married.

#

I returned from a well-baby clinic in Liamba. By then, I had a temperature of one hundred four degrees and stomach pain. By night time, I had severe diarrhea, and the next day, my diarrhea included blood. Upon examination, I learned I had another extreme case of amoebae. To combat dehydration, I took fluids. When Luba and the prayer group arrived at my house, they turned pale upon seeing the IV bottle. They thought I would die. I assured them I would be fine, but they must hold the prayer meeting without me.

At the next prayer meeting, we talked about doing good deeds. The discussion brought a new revelation to me about the Batwa's culture. Bola said that if you tried to help an older person, he or she would refuse because they feared you wanted to trick them.

Another boy added if you offer someone food, they will not eat it because they believe you are trying to poison them. A third boy stated if you prayed for a sick, non-Christian, the people would chase you away. The Batwa believed you would be trying to invoke the ndoki (evil spirits). I observed that many Batwa spent their entire lives fearing that others want to harm them. The group decided to help fellow Christians to show others they intend to help them and not commit harm.

### Lofokoloko

We left for Lofokoloko. This village would be the most challenging destination we had to reach on our trip. The jeep could only go as far as Tweya, and then we went on foot for four hours through dense forest. We stayed in Lofokoloko for two nights to recuperate for the return trip. The Ekonda there had more prejudice toward the Batwa than in other places we had been. When we arrived, the people gathered to shake hands. A group of young men shook my hand and then Mfutus. When Luba extended his hand, they withdrew theirs. I turned toward Luba, whose face had filled with anger, and a few tears tumbled down his cheek.

I put my hand on his shoulder. "Kango motema (have courage, hang in there)," I kindly said. I then gave him a cigarette, took out some matches, and lit it for him. The Ekonda were astonished. I did this as a small sign to show them I regarded the Batwa as my equal.

Luba and I went off to the nearest Batwa village. I told the people that everyone is equal in God's eyes, and they were children of the God who created all. The people yelled and shouted with joy. Then they proceeded to tell me the woes and problems they had with the Ekonda. Luba prayed for the Ekonda. He prayed God would change their hearts, and he forgave those who slighted him.

Now Luba had confidence in me, and he began to tell me about the Batwa's beliefs. Up to this point, we still had a barrier between us. Even though I learned more about them and tried to understand the local languages, they saw me as an outsider. The Batwa were a very closed people. However, Luba got past his embarrassment and fear of talking about his culture. I realized that few white people ever got to know the Batwa because they shied away from making genuine friends. I still had to overcome a significant handicap, my inability to speak and understand Lotwa, the Batwa's challenging language. Luba spoke French and Lingala, so he and I communicated well.

#

Several weeks later, I traveled to Liamba to hold a well-baby clinic. Only thirty-five out of a possible one hundred and thirty women showed up. Batwa women were slow to accept modern medicine or any modern ways. The men were a little more receptive to change, which may have been because more boys than girls went to school. Until last year, only three Batwa girls attended primary school. In the past year, two schools opened in Batwa villages, and about twenty-five percent of students in the first classes were girls. Outside of Pendjua, almost no Batwa children attended school.

The schools were a small beginning to help the Batwa in their struggle for a better life. While the population increased, the game and fish decreased. I knew that the Batwa must change to survive and become independent from the Ekonda.

In late July, the hospital filled with patients, and a higher number of children had malnutrition. The problem occurred when the rainy season, which usually ended in June, continued. When the water levels are high, the Batwa catch fewer fish. Usually, June through August were dry periods when fish were available, and malnutrition did not become a problem.

The extended rainy season made it more critical to encourage the Batwa to plant rice, peanuts, and beans since they are good protein sources. The daily diet, when there were no fish, consisted of manioc leaves and roots. The manioc filled them up, but it did not contain enough protein.

## Journey to Kinshasa

With the advice of the missionary Sisters, I agreed to take Luba on my trip to Kinshasa. It would be a long drive from Pendjua to Mbandaka. From Mbandaka, we would take a boat to Kinshasa.

We began our journey on August 16. We drove 156 miles in eight hours. After we arrived in Mbandaka, we learned the craft we planned to take became stuck on a sandbar. We waited for five days, then we gave up and took a plane to Kinshasa. Luba suffered from culture shock, as he had never seen buses, trains, cars, skyscrapers, elevators, and large crowds. His first bus ride resulted in quite a frightening experience. The busload of people pushed, shoved, and shouted. I looked into Luba's bewildered eyes and sensed his fear.

We visited a large open-air market. A soldier stopped Luba and asked for his ID card. In Zaire, everyone over 18 had to have an ID card. Luba only had a student card. The Batwa, who lived in the interior lands, were not issued ID cards. Despite our explanation, the soldier became nasty and insisted we go with him to the police headquarters. When I agreed to go, the soldier asked for a bribe. I refused, so we started toward the police station. Suddenly, several more soldiers joined him, and they tried to take us down an alley. I again refused. "We must stay on the main route," I exclaimed.

The soldiers argued, "We are taking Luba. You are a foreigner, so it is not your affair." Luba looked at me with wide eyes. I felt uneasy, so I agreed to pay the soldiers. They asked for 500 Zaires but settled for 50 ($5.00). After they let Luba go, he broke down and cried. Kinshasa crawled with soldiers who terrorized and robbed people. Luba and I agreed that Kinshasa would be a terrible place to live. He could now tell his friends that Kinshasa is not the paradise they imagined it to be.

#

After our return from Kinshasa, I met with the chief of Ngondo Banga and some of Luba's older uncles. I asked for permission to build a hut in their village on Luba's clan's land, to which they agreed without any hesitation. However, the villagers did not understand why I wanted to become poor like them. One of Luba's uncles decided to take charge of construction and cut poles. I met with the three other missionaries to get their support. They were not surprised that I desired to move into the Batwa village.

#

Luba's little brother, Mbomba, accidentally knocked over and broke Luba's new kerosene lamp. He got angry and beat Mbomba with a branch. Luba stopped by on his way to school and told me about the incident. I said, "Luba, there is no possession worth enough to cause you to beat your brother." Luba remained unconvinced. A while later, Mbomba came by. Tears filled his eyes. "I don't love my brother," he cried. "I will die before I ever talk to him again."

I saw scratches and welts on his head and legs from the beating. How could Luba do such a thing? I left a note in my office for Luba since he always stopped on his way home from school. Luba did not come back for his regular study session, but he sent a letter. His message said he could not come to study until he found Mbomba and asked for forgiveness.

#

On November 26, Luba's fiancée, Ndongo, gave premature birth to twins. They died twelve hours later. I felt very sorry for her and Luba. Ndongo had a healthy pregnancy with no problems until Thursday night when she went into premature labor. Luba took Ndongo to the maternity ward, and she delivered twins at 10:00 p.m. However, Sister Paula knew they were too small to survive, so she did not notify me. Luba came the following day and told me about the delivery. He prayed all night. He and I went to the maternity ward to find out the twins died just before we arrived. Luba broke down and cried. We prayed and planned the burial.

*Marriage Custom*

To help understand Luba and Ndongo's arrangement, I will explain the marriage custom here. Batwa boys between the ages of seventeen and twenty usually have "fiancées" who live with them. A marriage takes place in three stages. When a boy and girl decide to marry, the two families hold several reunions to discuss the bride's price. The boy's family must make a payment to the girl's family. They call stage one "mbongo na mama" (the mother's fee). The girl's mother receives money because she gave birth to the girl. Upon receipt, the girl is allowed to stay overnight at the boy's house. Most girls became pregnant during this stage.

Then, in stage two, "mbongo na tata" (the father's payment) occurs. The father receives compensation because he worked to raise the girl. "Mbongo na libola" (marriage payment) takes place in step three. After this payment, the boy and girl become officially married. Marriage in the church can occur after stage one, but most wait until the father makes the payment. This whole process takes up to five years to complete.

#

During December, I went to visit the dispensaries in several villages. The last dispensary was in Booke, a community located deep in the equatorial rainforest. To reach there, we walked two hours to Boyele. Then, we hiked two miles along a winding creek, and the scenery was stunningly beautiful. Once we reached the river, we boarded dug-out canoes. After we arrived at the landing site for Booke, we still had to walk almost two hours through manioc fields and banana groves to get there. The villagers gave us a rousing welcome. Before the dancing began, towering storm clouds gathered. The chief and elders tried to drive the rain away to no avail. A torrential downpour postponed the festivities until the following day.

Late the next day, we walked through Ekonda and Batwa villages. We went to see a famous nganga nkisi (traditional healer, or witch doctor) in Booke. She was a Batwa woman, as all healers were. Her site had two rows of huts, one for the Batwa and one for the Ekonda. She made her diagnosis in her "sun laboratory," a ten-foot dirt mound she stood on. She would stand on the hill, staring into the sun, and then go into a trance to come up with a diagnosis. For medicine, she used various roots and herbs. The villagers also said she helped people who had psychological illnesses.

That night, it rained, and the torrential downpour continued until morning. The trail to the river became nothing but mud. We had three paddlers for the canoe, as the return trip would be upstream. We came back to where we had parked the jeep and headed home. When we were ten miles from Pendjua, villagers told us that we could not cross the Bilamba River. We went on to the river and found the water to be waist-deep, so we stayed at a nearby dispensary for the night. The following day, a driver with a large truck met us and loaded our gear. When we got to the river, the water had risen even higher, and we could not cross. On the other side of the river sat another truck on its way to Pendjua. We struggled to carry our items across the deep river. Exhausted, we threw our gear in the vehicle and proceeded home.

# Measles Epidemic
## *1983*

Wherever I went, I could see the country's values and morals deteriorate due to governmental corruption. People were willing to do anything to make money. Teachers sold grades, and nurses stole medications, police officers took bribes, and so on. Even with its corruption, the government had the support of outsiders such as Belgium, France, and the U.S. These countries traded for cobalt, diamonds, copper, and other precious metals from Zaire.

After being gone eleven days on a retreat, I returned for four days. My team and I then loaded two trunks of medications, inspected the jeep, and fueled up. Two days later, after battling a tropical rainstorm, we arrived in Itendo and reopened the dispensary. Our next stop brought us to Bunga. We were surprised to see they were building a large clinic with mud bricks. The villagers constructed a two-room house for Miguel and me to stay in whenever we came there.

Miguel and I headed for Booke. Because the river did not have enough water, we could not take canoes. So, we took a route through the forest on foot. The hike took over two hours on a very rough trail. When we arrived, Miguel became tired and weak. He had an insulin reaction. I gave him sugar and forced him to eat. We stayed an extra day to let him rest. Upon our return, I looked forward to time at home to get refreshed.

#

I left for the U.S. and stayed during the summer with my family for some much-needed rejuvenation. Then, I returned to the Congo in August. I arrived in Kinshasa, and while there, I bought pots, pans, clothes, shoes, nylon for traps, and metal plates. I also purchased books for school, combs, medical books, children's Bibles, spare parts for sewing machines, vaccines for chickens, and more. There were policemen everywhere, and they asked everyone for ID cards.

I wondered how Kinshasa's people survived, as most made less than 300 Zaires ($12.00) a month. An egg cost 5 Zaires ($.20), a banana cost 1 Zaire, meat sold for 50 Zaires per pound, a pair of shoes cost 22 Zaires, and a simple school notebook cost 10 Zaires. I could not imagine how a family of four or six survived on those wages. Zaire did not have a middle class. Due to such low pay for school teachers, nurses, and white-collar workers, they fell into the same category as the poor. Even state doctors received only 1,000 Zaires a month ($40.00).

Three days before my flight to Kiri, I stayed at a small motel. I read the book "Ekonda and Their Batwa," written in 1969, and learned about both races' beliefs and traditions. The Ekonda gave the Botoa the name of Batwa. From then on, I decided to refer to them by their correct name, Botoa.

Another guest at the motel, a Trappist monk, became ill, and I went to see him. He had diabetes and had vomited all day, accompanied by stomach cramps. He did not take his insulin because he feared a reaction. I sent him to the hospital to check his blood sugar and urine. When he arrived, they did not have a doctor on call. The hospital called for a doctor, but he refused to come and ordered a shot for the vomiting.

Later, the monk continued to vomit and sweat profusely. He took some insulin, but we had no idea if his sugar levels were too high or low. So, we gathered and prayed. The following day the monk felt better. He did not have any pain, and he could eat. Tell me the power of prayer is not greater than medication. I know the Lord gave us the gift of modern medicine to alleviate suffering, but we must not neglect prayer. After witnessing that miracle, I planned to organize a group of Bilenge to gather and pray for healing.

Bola and Luba took my bike to Kiri and waited at the airport. I arrived at a tearful and joyous reunion. We stayed at the mission and talked most of the night. The next day I went to Pendjua, and on Saturday, I walked through the villages and greeted my friends. Luba's wife started her sixth month of pregnancy. We prayed she would carry this baby to full term. Luba and Ndongo planned to marry in the church in October.

#

Several days later, I met with the seven men who built my mud hut to discuss payment. "What do you think it is worth?" I asked them. They replied, "You are our boss. You fix the price." Another older man said, "You are smarter and wiser than us, so pay us what you want." I said, "You are the elder, and therefore, wiser. I value your opinion." The men were astounded that I valued their opinion. Once we agreed on a price, the men did not want money. They wanted payment in clothes, buckets, pans, nylon cord for traps, and other items.

### *Family Feud*

On Friday night, a massive fight took place in Ngondo Banga. It began when one of Luba's uncles killed an antelope and brought it to the mission to sell to earn money to buy clothing for his three wives. Luba, Bola, and I butchered the antelope, making the uncle save some meat for his family. I cooked the heart, liver, lungs, spleen, and kidneys for supper and shared it with Luba, Bola, and Mbomba. The fight began when the uncle gave some meat to his third wife, who lived at one end of the village, and he put the rest of the antelope in Luba's old house. The uncle's first wife accused Luba of stealing the meat when she found it in his former home.

I advised the uncle to take the antelope meat to his first wife. I did not know the uncle had fabricated a story and told his neighbor his dog ate the meat. The dog's owner came to make amends, and Luba's uncle demanded an exorbitant price. The man said he had no way to pay for the meat. However, so there would not be further trouble, he offered to kill his dog and then broke the dog's neck.

The affair did not end there, as the uncle's stepbrother sided with the dog's owner. A fight broke out, and five more men joined in with clubs and machetes. Luba and two others tried to separate the men. At 1:00 in the morning, the affair calmed down. However, the clan of the dog's owner arrived, armed with machetes. The family patriarch declared a "tofokufa," which meant they fought to the death or until no one could stand. Luba and Mbomba locked themselves in their hut in fear. Eventually, Luba's uncles had enough fighting for the night and declared a truce, and the other clan left.

Luba suffered an injury during the fight, and his right wrist became swollen and painful the next day. Out of anger, he refused to talk to or eat with his uncle. I declared, "There will be no feast in my new house until peace reigns in the village." With that, I canceled the house warming party they planned for my new mud hut. Soon, calm returned in Ngondo Banga. However, the clans involved still did not speak to each other.

### Measles Outbreak

Children who suffer from measles and its consequences filled the hospital. One or two children died each week. The people often give the child an enema laced with red pepper and other herbs. They believe the treatment rids the body of measles, but it makes the problem much worse. Some children die from these caustic enemas. The grandmothers have a great deal of influence on the younger women, as far as home remedies are concerned. They keep the young women from bringing sick children to the hospital. Luba's cousin had a two-year-old son who died the week after his grandmother gave him an enema to chase away three evil spirits. They carried him to the hospital, but we could not save him.

Hundreds of children in the region get sick and die from a disease we have almost eradicated in the U.S. Without proper treatment, a case of measles can cause blindness, deafness, brain damage, or even death. The epidemic passes from village to village, and new outbreaks appear daily. Many of the sick children do not come to the hospital. The people think they need to treat it with indigenous medicine and do not trust modern medicine.

In some villages, there have been funerals every day for the past two months. Measles is serious because the children already have infestations of worms and parasites. They suffer from malaria, and most are malnourished, so their frail bodies are too weak to fight measles. The death rate has been 15 out of every 100 cases. Most families have been affected. I struggle with all my might to try to save the children. The barefoot doctors desperately try to save as many lives as possible by vaccinating all babies in the villages.

As the epidemic rages, we do not have enough room in the hospital, and beds fill the hallways. With so many sick children and not enough beds, three to four children often share a bed. We have had to turn away many patients with other needs.

The mayors from two villages came and insisted I send nurses with medications to their communities. "If I had a nurse, I would send medications, but I do not have any extra nurses," I explained. "How many youths have you sent to the nursing school?" They replied, "We have not sent any." I responded, "The only way things can improve is to send students to nursing school."

The mission received some measles vaccines from Kinshasa. A public health nurse and I went to Tweya to vaccinate children. We took 200 doses of the vaccine. When we arrived, we were overwhelmed by over 500 people, some of who walked 25 miles to get their child vaccinated. We tried to get the people to line up, but our efforts were futile. I stationed myself at the entrance to the clinic. I allowed one Ekonda to enter and then one Botoa, alternating until all the vaccines were gone. More than 150 children did not receive vaccinations. They did not want me to leave, even though I promised to return with more vaccines.

Upon my return, I learned that on November 29, Luba's wife gave birth to a healthy five-pound girl. Everyone celebrated the successful delivery. I praised God for protecting their little girl.

#

The following week, I went on a trip to review the dispensaries with the nursing director, Mfutu. Two weeks prior, the

44

nurse in Booke had a dispute with the mayor. The mayor accused the nurse of lodging elephant poachers. The police arrested the nurse, tied him in chains, and paraded him through the villages to the county seat. Of course, the charges turned out to be false. I still paid 200 Zaires to free the nurse from jail, and when I did, the nurse refused to return to Booke. Without another nurse to send, I closed the dispensary.

Mfutu and I planned to go to Itendo first, but we changed our plans and arrived in Mbungo at 8:30 a.m. The nurse just came, though his starting time began one hour earlier. The nurse looked shocked to see us. I did a quick inspection and found the dispensary to be a mess. The needles and syringes were not sterile. We asked him for his monthly report and found he had not even started it. Upon further review, we learned the medication counts were wrong. I became upset and reduced the medicine supplies by fifty percent.

The following day, we went to Itendo. From there, we decided to go to Monio. We traveled a tough stretch as the road passed through a dense forest and swamp. Twice we got stuck in the swampy part of the roadway. When we arrived, though exhausted, I thought about bathing in the creek and going to bed early. However, ten minutes after we came, the nurse thought he had a strangulated hernia. I examined him, and sure enough, he had a hernia and required emergency surgery. The doctor and nurse supervisor had already unloaded the jeep. They were upset when I told them to load up, as we had to return to Pendjua.

I did not like to drive through the dark rainforest and murky swamp at night due to the sheer danger. There could be anything on the road at night, and the visibility would be terrible. Though filled with great apprehension, I had no choice. I drove with great caution, and we arrived at the hospital. When the clinic staff heard the noise and saw the jeep's headlights, they came running to help. We operated on the nurse just in time. His intestine became trapped in the hernia sac and had already turned blue due to a lack of circulation. The nurse recovered, for which I was thankful.

*Christmas in the Congo*

I canceled all elective surgery as there were no beds for surgery patients. Children with measles continued to fill the adult wards. I hoped the epidemic would end before Christmas.

Christmas in the Congo differs from what we experience in the States. On December 19, it did not seem possible Christmas would be here in less than a week. It hardly seemed like Christmas in the hot equatorial rainforest. Decorations did not exist, stores did not sell gifts, and there was no Christmas music to hear.

On Christmas Eve, the Bilenge came to practice the Nativity play and the songs for the service. I hung my Coleman lamp outside the hut to give light to read the Bible and songbooks. After the readings, each Bilenge shared what the birth of Jesus meant and how it affected them. The 200 people who came were utterly silent.

# Beya and the Bengondu
## *1984*

Upon seeing the man, I knew that his condition was critical. His infected leg had gangrene. Sister Paula and I debated on whether or not to operate. The poor man begged us to do it. Reluctantly, we proceeded with the amputation. As we finished the surgery and started to suture the wound, his heart went into arrest. Despite our frantic efforts, I could not detect a heartbeat or any sign of respiration. We informed the relative, who stayed in the operating room, that the man died.

We required a family member to be present when we operated. People had many distorted ideas about what happened in the operating room. With a family member present, he or she acted as a witness for the family. I had just walked up to the relative and informed him the patient died when I heard a sound behind me. Suddenly, the patient began to inhale and exhale. He gasped for breath at first, but slowly, he started to breathe, and his heart began to beat again. I and everyone in the room could not believe it; the man had come back to life. I excitedly told his relative, and he began to cry and said, "God has pitied us."

After that traumatic event, I went to Ngondo Banga since I wanted more time to study and speak Lotoa. On Saturday night, I visited Liamba to participate in a feast and ceremony to mark the end of Bola's wife's wale (wah-lay). It had almost been a year since she gave birth to her little girl. During this period, she lived with her mother. Bola was thrilled the wale ended. We celebrated with a dance, and Bola presented his wife and child with gifts. Later, Luba and I visited Luba's father, who returned from a hunt. He killed two giant forest rats and a large snake. He gave us part of one rat and part of the snake, which we wrapped in leaves and hung over the fire to cook overnight. I returned home to prepare for what may lie ahead in the new week.

This week, I witnessed the most incredible case I have seen, and I have seen many. A 13-year-old Botoa boy arrived at the hospital with a strangulated and perforated hernia. He lived 100 miles away, and villagers carried him to the hospital on a stretcher. Three weeks prior, he had a strangulated hernia, and his intestines became necrotic and perforated through his scrotum. Unbelievably, the boy had bowel movements through his scrotum. We gave him IV fluids, antibiotics, and other medications to prepare him for surgery. Medical school had not prepared me for a circumstance like this. I put my surgery atlas on a table and followed it step-by-step. Sister Elise assisted with the operation, and we removed one foot of the small intestine and then did a reconnection. It was an absolute miracle that the boy did well the following day.

### Traditional Burial

This week, I witnessed a traditional burial of a 36-year-old woman. The villagers gathered in front of the family's home. Four pallbearers carried the light wooden casket on a bamboo rack upon their shoulders. A female relative acted as the funeral director. She "communicated" with the deceased's "spirit." The first event would determine who "killed" the woman.

The Botoa believed the cause of illness and death resulted from either a dead ancestor or a living person who wanted to harm another. The pallbearers received instruction from the "spirit" to parade through the villages. They marched around the houses, into the forest, and around all the people gathered for the funeral. I learned that they did this to look for the killer. After forty-five minutes, the "spirit" informed the directress that the "killer" was the deceased woman's former husband. The husband deserted her ten years earlier, and he now lived in Ikongo.

The second event began, and the pallbearers asked the "spirit" where she wanted her burial place. The "spirit" directed the pallbearers to run through the village and behind the houses to find a burial site. After thirty minutes, the directress proclaimed the dead lady wanted her burial in Ikongo. The sun had begun to set, and it would take over two hours to walk there.

The eldest clan members went and talked to the deceased. They explained that due to the late hour, they could not go to Ikongo, and she had to choose a place in Ngondo Banga. After another twenty minutes of negotiating, a location still hadn't been determined. The villagers sang to the deceased and pleaded with her to choose a closer place. After five more minutes, they found a burial place. They dug a hole and buried her, much to everyone's relief. Afterward, Mbomba asked me, "Do you think that the directress or the spirit of the deceased directed the pallbearers?" I said, "I think the funeral director directed the whole affair." I don't think he believed me.

#

One April afternoon after the funeral, I went to Ngondo Banga to meet with the adult prayer group. We had just sat down to eat when a group of people arrived from a distant village. They carried a man who had been mauled and bitten by a wild boar. Luba and I examined him, and we realized that he needed emergency surgery. The boar tore a ghastly hole in the man's abdomen. His intestines hung out. He also had deep gashes on his chest, arms, and legs, and his right fibula had shattered into small pieces. We rushed him to the hospital, and Sister Elise and I operated until late into the night. The next day the man did well, except for the nightmares.

A few days later, I encountered a custom I had not known. One of Luba's uncles lived and worked in Inongo. One of his two wives died last week. Since she came from Pendjua, he had to inform her family and make a payment to them. I learned that if a man's wife died, he had to transport the body to her village for burial. Even if he brought the body, he still went through a two or three-week period of punishment. He had to pay the family several hundred Zaires and give them a goat. Luba's family had tried to raise 600 Zaires among their clan.

They had buried the woman in Inongo, a three-day trip from Pendjua. Therefore, Luba's uncle arrived in Pendjua alone. The wife's family proceeded to beat him with tree limbs until he couldn't walk. They tied him up and placed him in a three-foot-by-three-foot hut. They only gave him water to drink and manioc leaves to eat. They told me that some families even forced the poor husband to drink his urine.

At our next prayer meeting, the older group of Bilenge discussed this custom. The men were very much against this. Some believed that they would be better off not getting married. At the very least, if they did marry, they hoped that they would die before their wife did.

### Luba and Ndongo

There were two common traits among the Botoa. First, jealousy dominated their lives. Second, they got angry very quickly and often ended up in a fight. They did not fight with weapons. The one who put the other on the ground first became the winner. The women argued and fought even more often than the men.

On Monday, a woman from a neighboring clan told Luba's wife, Ndongo, that Luba slept with another woman. She happened to be an enemy of Ndongo. Rather than wait to talk to Luba, Ndongo went to the other woman's house and struck her. Well, the affair did not end there. A cousin of Ndongo's, who did not like Luba and happened to be an assistant to a police officer, decided to take Ndongo to the police station. Her cousin wanted to have Ndongo fined so that Luba would have to pay a fine, all out of jealousy. This event took place about noon, and when Luba went home to eat lunch, he met the group on the trail.

They exchanged words, and before long, fists flew. The police arrested Luba for disorderly conduct. Luba exclaimed, "I never had an affair with the other woman." He stated he struck the assistant to the police because the man mistreated Ndongo. The man who tried to arrest Luba's wife had no jurisdiction to apprehend someone since only police officers had that authority. Assistants to the police could only report incidents to the police, who may arrest the involved parties.

They held a hearing before the magistrate, and I asked my nursing supervisor to attend. Through his knowledge of the laws, he could determine if Luba received justice. An unfortunate situation occurred right at the start. As everyone entered the mud hut that they used for a courtroom, they searched them. They found the pocket knife that Luba kept in his pocket. The Ekonda judge declared that he had a dangerous weapon and fined Luba 200 Zaires. Then, they discussed the disorderly conduct charge for over two hours. In the end, the judge fined everyone 150 Zaires, so I loaned Luba the money to pay the fines.

Two days later, when tempers cooled, I talked with Ndongo and Luba. Ndongo accepted Luba's statement. Ndongo explained that she became so angry when she heard the news that she did not think to wait to talk to Luba. The Botoa believed in any such rumors since fidelity between spouses rarely existed. Luba and Ndongo wanted to end the wale within a week. Then they could once again live together as man and wife.

This event with Luba and Ndongo, along with a similar fight between teenage boys, prompted me to talk to the chief and elders of Ngondo Banga. We discussed the need to restart the tradition of judging these small affairs in the village rather than at the county court. The Botoa threw away the little money they had by always accusing one another in court. In the past, the elders settled all minor battles, and there were no hefty fines. The money from any penalties remained in the Botoa village. The chief and elders agreed with me to begin to hold village meetings.

#

Later that week, the prayer group discussed more Botoa traditions. We discussed the custom of paying a bride price, knowing that many young men could not afford it. This custom increased the number of couples that cohabitated. The group talked about another tradition called "likota," where two villages unite as sister villages. If a sister village member visits the other community, he can take all the food he wants, and the other person cannot object. He can even sleep with another man's wife, and the man cannot oppose him. If the man objects, they believe he or his wife will die. The prayer group agreed that they should not continue this tradition.

### Beya is Lost

On the way to Ikongo, I stopped in Ngondo Banga to pick up Mbomba. When I entered the village, the only persons present were Mbomba and a few younger children. Mbomba explained that Beya, a 23-year-old deaf-mute, became lost in the forest, and everyone went to look for him. Beya belonged to the clan in Ngondo Banga. Beya received loving care from the clan members and the Bilenge.

Caterpillar season had begun, so the Botoa women and younger children wandered into the forest to gather caterpillars. I learned that Beya had joined the women and children. When the storm began, everyone panicked and ran for the village, and they forgot about Beya. Later, they realized he did not return with them.

Luba, his uncles, and other men went into the forest with kerosene lamps, but by 11:00 p.m., they were exhausted. The rain extinguished their lanterns, so they had no choice but to return home. The following day, everyone entered the forest to look for Beya.

I decided to go to Ikongo with Mbomba and the nursing supervisor because the clinic no longer had any medications. The trip turned into a difficult one as water covered the road, and three trees blocked the roadway. The dispensary nurse appreciated that we braved the weather to bring him much-needed supplies.

After we returned to Pendjua that evening, I went to Ngondo Banga. I knew from the exhausted, sad expressions on their faces that Beya remained lost. We prayed for the Lord to protect him, though we feared the worst. Beya did not know the forest, and he could not find food like the other Botoa. Beya only wore shorts, and when nightfall comes, the rainforest can become a cold and wet place.

Throughout the night, I had a fever and bone-rattling, shaking chills. These were the common signs of a malaria attack, so I took some malaria medicine. The sweating spells and chills continued. I couldn't stop thinking about my little friend, Beya. He remained lost in the vast, cold, haunting rainforest. I prayed and prayed they would find him alive. When I arrived in Pendjua on Friday afternoon, I stopped and asked the first Botoa I saw if they had found Beya.

"Yes!" he responded. "We found him this morning and took him to the hospital."

Relieved, I rushed to the mission, grabbed a handful of cookies, and went to see my little friend. Beya had fallen sound asleep in a hospital bed. I gently shook him, and he opened his eyes. When he saw me, a big smile lit up his face. I prayed a prayer of thanks that Beya had survived. He downed the cookie with some water and went fast asleep.

Later, Luba and Bola came to the mission, very happy but exhausted. They had spent forty-eight hours in a frantic search for Beya. They told me they came across him wandering in the rainforest. They gave him bananas and water, and Luba carried him on his back until he fell from exhaustion. Another man brought Beya to the hospital. Later, we were surprised when Beya showed up in Ngondo Banga. He refused to stay in the hospital, and he wanted to sleep in his hut. After we ate supper, we went to the community hut where the whole clan gathered. Beya recounted his ordeal by making gestures with his hands and arms.

### The Bengondu

Beya related how he ran through the forest as he cried and looked for his friends the first night and day. Beya used gestures and interpretation by the people to convey the story. He ate live caterpillars and some mushrooms to curb his hunger. He relayed that four Bengondu seized him on Thursday afternoon, tied his hands, and took him to a grass shelter. They gave him food to eat and then discussed how they would kill him in the morning. He made gestures and seized his neck to indicate how they grabbed him and threatened him. Beya claimed that later in the night, he escaped and ran through the forest when they slept. Then his brothers found him on Friday morning. The Botoa believed the story, and they were very angry with the Ekonda.

The Botoa had a firm belief in the Bengondu. They first told me about this belief when I took my five-day retreat into the forest in August 1981. The Botoa believed that certain Ekonda men wandered through the woods in search of Botoa people. If they encountered a Botoa all alone, they killed him, and in ancient times, they ate him. They called these Ekonda men the Bengondu. If a Botoa happened to die in the forest, they blamed this on the Bengondu. Whether the belief is true or false, I doubted that the Bengondu existed.

#

Several days later, the Botoa women went again to gather caterpillars that fell from trees. They gathered them each day during the caterpillar season. Ndongo left her baby with her sister and went to search for caterpillars. She did not return until 5:00 p.m., so the baby did not have any milk for the entire day. Luba became furious. I feared that he would beat his wife. I remained thankful for Luba's commitment to no longer follow the custom of beating his wife.

Botoa men often beat their wives when they were angry, and the wives expected this treatment. When I witnessed Luba, Bola, and other Christian men who quit the evil customs, I knew Jesus worked in their midst. Instead, Luba punished his wife by refusing to eat any caterpillars she gathered. For a Botoa woman, this hurt worse than a beating.

Later, I asked Ndongo, "Why didn't you carry the baby on your back, like you do when you work in the manioc field?" She replied, "If I had the baby with me, I would not find as many caterpillars, and the other women would laugh at me." Sister Paula explained to the women that their babies needed their mother's milk several times a day. She told them the babies would not be healthy if they had nothing to eat for seven to ten hours.

The next day, Ndongo's baby came down with a terrible cold and cough. Luba blamed Ndongo for the baby's illness, and by

Monday, little Mputu had pneumonia. I gave her penicillin and ordered Ndongo to stay home for several days to care for her baby. I had to accept that the process of health education would be slow and would require much patience and understanding.

#

A few days later, I met with the adult prayer group to discuss the issue of anger. Anger remained a genuine problem among the people. They got into horrendous arguments and battles, often over minor affairs. That night, Bola's uncle, a new member of the group, became involved in a big fight with his two sisters. One sister was Bola's mother. Last month, the two sisters asked a man to cut a field for them to plant manioc, as neither had a husband. The piece of land they cleared belonged to the clan. The uncle cut the giant trees seven years ago, planted the field, and, after the harvest, he left it idle.

Once someone cleared and planted a field, it must be left idle for six or seven years before replanting since they did not have fertilizer available. However, their customary law stated that the person who cut the large trees to clear a field remained the owner. Anyone who cleared and planted it later must have the owner's permission. Bola's uncle claimed his two sisters did not ask him. Of course, he did not say anything until they cut the field, burned, and readied it for planting. Then he claimed the area as his own and refused to allow them to plant it.

The parties asked the village elders to judge the affair, and they decided both sides were right. They divided the field, gave one part to the sisters, and the other part to the uncle, their brother. Bola's uncle wasn't satisfied. An argument broke out, and he beat his two sisters. As Bola made a move to beat up his uncle, several other adults intervened in the melee. I prayed for peace to return.

#

There was a woman who had two small children, and they lived in a nearby village. Her parents lived in the clan next to Ngondo Banga. The woman had suffered third-degree burns on her leg two weeks prior, and her mother treated her with local remedies and forest potions. Her condition did not get any better, and she had developed a severe infection. The family moved her to Ngondo Banga, but her mother told the family not to inform Luba or me.

On the day she died, Luba and I found out about her infection. We were distraught. Later, I talked to the deceased woman's father. He said the mother believed a dead ancestor caused the burn and infection; therefore, the white man's medicine could not help her. Though the men of the clan were Christian, the women refused to become Christians. Perhaps someday, they would have a change of heart and accept the liberating message of Christ.

A short time later, as Luba and I went to work in our field, a young man cried out to us from his hut. We entered the tiny house and saw the two massive abscesses on both of his thighs. The young man had been sick for two weeks, and his grandmother treated him with herbs and such, but he continued to get worse. "We have to take you to the hospital," I urged. He replied, "I will not go unless my grandmother agrees, and she has refused." I went, and I talked to the young man's older brothers and insisted that he needed treatment soon or he would die. The following day, his brothers carried him to the hospital, and I incised and drained the abscesses.

#

Two weeks later, Sister Ellie and I completed two abdominal operations. First, we operated on a Botoa woman who had two huge ovarian cysts. Then, we did surgery on a young woman with obstruction of her intestine. During the second surgery, I found new adhesions, and on further exploration, a wound on the surface of her uterus. I realized that the woman had used a sharp bamboo stick to provoke an abortion. She perforated her uterus, which bled and caused adhesions and then an intestinal obstruction. Witnessing a case like this brought on great sadness.

#

I went to my office, where I received a notice of a critical meeting for all doctors in the state of Bandundu. The conference would be at the end of October. A trip to the capital city always had challenges. If I went by water, it would be a week-long journey. With any luck, I could go by airplane. I left Kiri on Air Zaire and arrived in Kinshasa. The next day I caught a flight to Bandundu.

I had a most pleasant surprise when I saw a friend whom I admired so much. His name is Dr. Dan Fountain, an American Baptist medical missionary in Vanga.[2] I had visited him in 1975 as a member of the Peace Corps. Dr. Dan's dedication to Christ and to the work he did made a lasting impression. We spent a lot of time together during our week in Bandundu. Dr. Dan expressed his amazement when he learned how I became a brother and a missionary. We prayed together often that week and shared about the lives we lived for the Lord.

---

[2] The book "Health for All – The Vanga Story" by Daniel E. Fountain shares about Dr. Dan and his work in the Vanga hospital in the Congo for 35 years.

# Racial Discrimination
### *1985*

We began the year with a large New Year's celebration. The majority of the attendees were pagans, so they viewed the festival as more significant than Christmas. The people tried to buy new clothes for the event. The hunters stayed in the forest and attempted to accumulate game for the feast. No one waited up until midnight since they did not have clocks. On New Year's Day, the Bilenge came to the mission, and they killed and cooked a goat for their feast.

Forty-six boys came to the mission, and everyone had more than enough to eat. After the meal, Luba, Bola, and I headed to Ngondo Banga on our bicycles. We rode through an Ekonda village. The head of the clan claiming to be the Botoa's masters in Ngondo Banga yelled out to Luba. He told him to buy him a bottle of liquor. Luba yelled back that he did not have any money to buy him alcohol.

A little further on, Luba stopped at an Ekonda lady's home. He paid her 20 Zaires that his father owed for a bottle of alcohol. Bola and I continued to Liamba, where Luba's father and uncles lived. We chatted as we waited for Luba to arrive. It took him longer than usual to return, and when he did, he was infuriated. He told us that the Ekonda man and his grown son followed him and tried to beat him up. The Botoa men grabbed their machetes and clubs and prepared to fight the Ekonda. I desperately tried to persuade them not to go, but I could not stop them.

Then, I said, "How about just Luba and I return to talk to the man?" They reluctantly agreed, so Luba and I went and asked the man why he wanted to cause trouble. He replied, "This Batwa is my Batwa. I'm his master." My face turned hot and red as I said, "You are not the master or owner of any Botoa. Apologize, or I will not treat another member of your clan."

After that exchange of words, we returned to Liamba. Before we got to the end of the Ekonda community, almost forty Botoa men had armed themselves with clubs and machetes. They entered the village and went to the Ekonda chief's house and complained to him that the man struck Luba. I waited to see if he would try to prevent a fight, but of course, he stuck up for the Ekonda.

I pleaded with the men, "If you fight, it will spoil the New Year celebration. In the end, you will be the ones who suffer. If they call the police, they will let the Ekonda go free and put all of you in jail. Please go home to eat, dance, and celebrate the New Year. If you want the Ekonda to suffer, make a New Year's resolution to not cut any more fields for them." They returned to their villages.

#

When I returned to the mission, my state nursing supervisor came to ask me about what happened on New Year's Day. "There is a story going around that you had a revolver and organized a group of Batwa men armed with clubs and machetes to attack the Ekonda," he informed me.

Later, after we left the Ekonda village, we went to see the assistant mayor. The nurse supervisor heard the accusation and told the mayoral assistant he doubted the story could be true. He knew I did not have a gun. I informed the assistant mayor what happened and explained that I prevented a fight. Some Botoa leaders had told me that three Ekonda leaders accused me of stirring up the Botoa against the Ekonda.

The mayor arrived, and his assistant informed him of the accusation. He responded to the Ekonda, "You are jealous because Brother Jerry helps the Batwa and teaches them how to be independent." They had nothing further to say and left. For the next

59

week, as I passed through the Ekonda village, no one spoke to me. All I received were cold, hostile stares.

#

As I ate at Bola's house one quiet evening, Luba's uncle and his wife burst in, holding their nine-month-old child. The infant was having a convulsion. To our despair, he died within two minutes after they arrived. Within minutes after his death, the women gathered next door, and they cried and wailed most of the night. Luba and I prayed with his uncle to console him. He had lost four children in the past seven years, and this latest death devastated him.

#

On Saturday, Luba and Bola came to school and proceeded to tell me about another altercation with the Ekonda. On Friday night, as Luba and Bola crossed the marketplace, they met an Ekonda high school professor who was drunk. He proceeded to kick Luba and Bola. They told him to stop, and he just laughed and continued to kick them. Then Luba and Bola hit him. The professor slugged Bola, and Bola hit him on the back of the head with a flashlight. When he stopped beating them, Luba and Bola fled to a nearby store. The Botoa guard stationed there threatened to put an arrow through the professor's chest, and the professor ran.

I became furious when they told me about the incident, and I planned to write to the priest in charge of diocesan schools. These problems were due to the Ekonda being jealous. In the future, when the boys return home after dark, I will escort them to the end of the Ekonda section.

### Mbomba is Beaten

After the prayer meeting, Luba knocked on my door and told me that the police sought his younger brother, Mbomba. We rushed to the place where the policemen stayed. When we arrived, we found Mbomba with some friends. He had a bloody nose, a hemorrhage in his left eye, and bruises on his back. He said the police beat him. I marched to the station and demanded, "Why did you beat the boy? If he violated a law, why wasn't he arrested?"

The policeman replied, "The police did not beat him, but a man who lives at the chief of police house did." I marched over to the house and found the man. Luba lunged forward to fight, and I could barely restrain him. Mr. Mfutu, who lived nearby, heard the commotion and came over to investigate. By then, more than fifty people gathered. Mr. Mfutu asked the man why he beat the boy. The man refused to talk. The county vice-chairman arrived and yelled, "Everyone must leave. This area is the state's property, and you all must go home."

I pleaded, "Please leave and don't cause any trouble. I will file an official complaint to have the man arrested." I took Mbomba to Mfutu's house to examine him. The vice-chairman also came over. "How could the police stand by while an Ekonda man beat a schoolboy?" I asked him. "If the man were a Botoa, and the boy an Ekonda, the police would have beat and arrested the Botoa man in an instant."

"I will handle the case and the man. The police will receive punishment," he promised. Then I took Mbomba to the hospital and treated him before sending him home with Luba.

#

Though I doubted that justice would prevail, Mfutu and I left to go to Lofokoloko to open a new health center. We traversed many swamps, creeks, and rivers along the way and crossed twenty-seven log bridges. No one had used this road for years, and the villagers needed to redo the bridges and cut the brush. We arrived at the health center and gave the nurse the necessary equipment and medicines.

We returned home, hot, tired, and covered with road dust. Father Charles came to tell me what happened during my absence. The vice-chairman did not do what he said he would do. Instead, he called a meeting of the village elders, the village chiefs, Sister Elise and Father Charles. The vice-chairman accused me of inciting the Botoa to revolt against the Ekonda and the government. He made racist statements, saying, "a Batwa will always be a Batwa, inferior to the Ekonda." He threatened to arrest Father Charles and all the Botoa who worked at the mission.

A government official heard them. He told him he could not make such statements. The official said, "The government is happy Brother Jerry helps the Batwa. The Ekonda should also help the Batwa improve their standard of living." The meeting ended.

In the end, they did not arrest the man who beat Mbomba. Later, the police grabbed Mbomba as he walked to school. They took him to the station, stripped him naked, and made him crawl on the dirt floor. They jeered at him and called him an animal. When Luba heard they seized Mbomba, he ran to the station. The police released Mbomba for fear of repercussions.

Mfutu then took Mbomba to City Hall and filed an official complaint against the man who beat Mbomba. The next day a hearing took place. There were four Ekonda judges, and one was the vice-chairman. I asked Mfutu to represent Mbomba. Usually, an adult defended himself since there were no lawyers here.

The vice-chairman refused to allow Mfutu to represent Mbomba because he came from the Mosengili tribe. The judge did not want an outsider to help a Botoa. An altercation occurred, followed by accusations of racism and tribalism. In the end, Mbomba had to represent himself, but Mfutu stayed nearby to counsel him. Luba and I did not attend the hearing, as we feared we would get angry and make matters worse. The trial lasted five hours, and in the end, Mbomba received a fine of 175 Zaires. The Ekonda man paid a fine of 200 Zaires. Mr. Mfutu became furious and demanded a written copy of the hearing.

"I will go to a Superior Court in Kiri to demand a retrial and damages of 1000 Zaires," he exclaimed. I paid the fine, so Mbomba did not have to stay in jail. I then called a hospital staff meeting to explain what happened. Ninety percent of the staff were Ekonda, and they were good workers. Most agreed the Botoa were right, and the vice-chairman did an injustice to Mbomba. The vice-chairman refused to give us a copy of the hearing. He tried to persuade Mbomba's parents to drop the whole affair. He threatened that they would suffer if they went through with the decision to contest the judgment. I received a copy after I threatened to charge him with obstruction of justice.

A few days later, the assistant governor came for treatment. Before he went to the hospital, he stopped at City Hall. The vice-chairman told him that I organized the Botoa against the Ekonda. When the assistant governor came to the clinic, I explained my side of the story. He was a Baluba from the Kasai region, and he did not have any prejudice toward the Botoa. He showed sympathy toward my efforts to help the Botoa. I am glad to have some support from a higher level of government.

## The Congressman

In mid-March, the congressman from Kiri arrived. Over a month ago, I wrote to him and accused the vice-commissioner of racial discrimination against the Botoa. When he heard the accusations, the congressman became upset. He came to the mission to talk to the two priests and me. He read an article of the Constitution, which stated everyone is equal, and discrimination is forbidden. He said that their laws were excellent, though he admitted that many officials did not follow the rules and created injustices.

As I saw it, the relationship between the Ekonda and the Botoa resulted from the strong exploiting the weak. Their discriminatory practices were over 100 years old and would not change rapidly. The congressman congratulated the priest and me for our work among the Botoa. However, he warned us not to become involved in politics. He said only Zairians were to be involved in politics. The Ekonda were very jealous, and they had spread untrue rumors about me. The congressman disregarded the stories. He invited us to attend a meeting with the village elders and the people next week.

About 100 people attended the meeting, half Ekonda, and half Botoa. The congressman, Mr. Mputela, explained that they must apply the law equally to all citizens. Then he talked about the relations between the Ekonda and the Botoa. "You must all change to get along with one another. Medical work and development must go hand in hand. If Dr. Jerry works to improve the Batwa's lives, you Ekonda should be happy instead of jealous. If Dr. Jerry wants to live part-time or full-time among the Batwa, it is his business and not yours." I appreciated the support though I knew that words alone would not change the situation.

#

I left the meeting and went to the hospital when I received word that Bola's mother fell and broke her femur. I put her leg in a splint and then set it after administering spinal anesthesia. I set her leg and repositioned the broken fragments based on feel. Since I did not have an x-ray machine to take images, I had no other option. I looked forward to some rest, but that did not happen.

Villagers carried a lady to the hospital from a village in the Equator region, located 150 kilometers away. She had been in labor for four days. The woman suffered from shock, and her baby had already died. I gathered my strength, and we did an emergency cesarean section. The woman also had a sizeable pelvic cyst, which we decided we could not remove. We struggled to close the incision due to the infection of her uterus. By the end, my physical and emotional strengths had dissipated.

However, my night was still not over. When I left the operating room, I saw Mbomba waiting for me. "Two soldiers are looking for Luba and me to arrest us!" he cried. "Stay in my office," I told him. "I'll go to the city hall to see the mayor."

The mayor informed me that he sent an order to arrest some drunk and disorderly boys three weeks ago. The boys did not pay their fines. I asked to see the list, and it turned out the sheet did not include Luba's name. Mbomba's name appeared on the list; however, it was a different Mbomba. The mayor gave me a note to pass on to the soldiers. I found the soldiers and gave them the letter. They arrested the older brother of one boy who had not paid his fine.

I asked them, "Why did you arrest the brother since he has done no wrong? He should not receive a fine." The soldier responded, "We could not find the guilty boy. Since we arrested the brother, the family will pay the fine." I demanded, "Show me the law that permits you to arrest an innocent brother of a guilty person." They did not answer. I continued, "If you don't let the boy go, you are breaking the law."

They refused to let him go, so I returned to the city magistrate. He assured me he would set him free, and he did. Among the arrested boys, three were in the older prayer group, and one worked for Father Charles. I loaned the families money to pay the fines, and then I trudged home.

#

As I rested one evening, one of Luba's uncles visited me. We conversed about missionaries and how we lived. I explained that we received financial support from Christian friends and family. He replied, "White people are different because they share with others and send their children out to help the poor and tell them about Christ. God breathed on the whites and turned his back on Africans."

"But all of you have so many blessings. The forest, plenty of water, fish, game, and much more. If you cut and plant fields, your situation will improve." I don't know if I convinced him.

#

The next day, a lady arrived at the mission. It took one week for her to walk here from her village. The people measured distance by the amount of time it took to go from one point to another. Nine days before she came to the hospital, the woman had lower abdominal pain. She received treatment from a local medicine man. The pain continued, so she and her husband and mother headed for Pendjua. The woman walked part of the way. Her husband and mother carried her on their backs for the remainder.

When she arrived, the nurse thought she had a pelvic infection and gave her a penicillin shot without notifying the Sister in charge of the maternity. The next day, the woman had severe pain and had gone into shock due to blood loss. We found two people to donate blood, and we operated at once. There were at least three pints of blood in her abdomen. Then, we discovered that she had a ruptured tubal pregnancy, and we removed the ruptured tube and stopped the bleeding. The following day the woman could get up and about. Father Jeff called her the "miracle of 1985."

Afterward, I caught a cold, had a fever, and my arthritis returned. After a couple of days of rest and aspirin, I felt better. My minor illnesses were insignificant when compared to the great suffering of the people in Zaire. How they endured so much pain continued to amaze me.

### *Mbomba goes to Kinshasa*

Luba, Bola, Mbomba, and I left for Kiri. Luba and Bola wanted to see Mbomba and me off at the airport. At 1:00 p.m., they announced the flight could be up to a day late, or the plane may not come at all. Mbomba became nervous as this would be his first trip outside of Kiri. The aircraft arrived at 5:00 p.m., and we got on without any problem. When we took off, Mbomba had his face glued to the window. The panorama beneath him left him stunned. We arrived in Kinshasa after dark and took a taxi to Kimbanseke. The streetlights, trucks, cars, and buses amazed Mbomba.

The next day, we took a bus to see the University of Zaire. Then we went to the seminary for the Zairian confrères. The headmaster, a Zairian, remembered me from when I stayed there in 1980. He welcomed us and invited us to dinner. The Father showed Mbomba a television. This strange machine that showed people doing all sorts of things astounded Mbomba.

We also went to the city, which, like American cities, had many tall buildings and stores. The bus ride from Kimbanseke to the town created quite an experience for Mbomba. The people were packed in shoulder to shoulder, and we had to stand. Mbomba continued to be amazed at the cars and trucks and the constant noise of engines grinding away. He took in the sights and smelled the giant puffs of black smoke emitted from the poorly maintained vehicles.

One morning, we went to the Peace Corps. The director of health had left on vacation. However, the Director of Agriculture, whom I had never met, greeted us. When I introduced myself, the director said he knew my name because he remembered the health project I started. It surprised me that after eight years, they remembered my previous work. The agriculture director told me my plan became the model to begin other health projects in Zaire.

We ate dinner with the Sacred Heart Sisters, who did medical, educational and social work. They asked many questions about the relations between the Botoa and the Ekonda. At times,

Mbomba became embarrassed. Later, I talked to him about his feelings about being a Botoa. I encouraged him, "You should be proud of your origin and your people. If you spend your life denying who you are, you will be miserable. When you become a teacher, you will proudly represent your Botoa brothers and sisters."

"I do not know why I'm going through a denial crisis," Mbomba responded. "I am glad I can talk to you. If it weren't for Jesus and studying the gospel, I would be too afraid to continue. Prayer is vital to me." These words from a young follower of Christ encouraged me as we prepared to return home.

#

Once back in Pendjua, I talked with six men. One suggested, "When God created man, He put the white man first and the black man second." I asked him, "Why do you think that?" He replied, "I look at all the things the white man has discovered and all of the things white people possess. The whites run the only schools and functioning health programs."

Faced with these facts, I reflected before I replied. "God created all of us equally, and God gives everyone the capacity to develop and to work." Then I told them there were many ways to improve their lives. They could cultivate larger fields, put more effort into raising domestic animals, improve their home construction and water sanitation. It is also imperative to send their children to school. I knew the road to enhance their self-esteem would take time.

#

Mid-October began on a sad note, as Bola's mother died rather suddenly one night. I estimated her age to be in the late sixties. Last February, she fell and broke her thigh bone and stayed in the hospital for three months. The fracture healed without much deformity. When she returned to the village, she was afraid to walk with crutches because of the uneven ground. She stayed in her bed most of the time. I wanted her to come back to the hospital eight months ago for physical therapy, but her sister opposed the idea.

As Luba and Bola returned to the village, they stopped to talk to Bola's mother. They told her that their classes would start soon, and they had to study every evening. She advised them to go right home to their wives after their studies and not to linger in the commercial section at night. She did not give them any indication that she felt sick. Her sister, who lived in the same hut, woke at 11:00 p.m. to find Bola's mother mortally ill. She died minutes later. I suspect she had a blood clot dislodge from the veins in her legs that then went to her lungs.

I reflected on the life and death of the Botoa that I had come to know. To give some perspective, the number of Ekonda in the zone of Kiri approximated 100,000. However, in the collectivity of Pendjua, there were 10,000 Ekonda and 20,000 Botoa. Despite this difference, the Ekonda dominated the Botoa. Most people were hunters, fishermen, and farmers. The Ekonda were poor, but they were far better off than the Botoa. The Botoa were the poorest of the poor, so the mission spent more time and effort to help them.

At times, the Ekonda were envious, but they could not prevent our assistance to the Botoa. I continue to spend a few days and nights in the village to live in solidarity with the Botoa. I am passionate about this part of my missionary life. If I teach them agriculture and health education, I can improve their situation more than through medical work. By living in the village, I show them how much God loves them.

#

My time for reflection abruptly ended when they summoned me to the hospital. I treated one of the most astonishing patients I have ever seen. This man, a Botoa hunter, went into the forest two days prior when a sudden electrical storm approached. The man took shelter and sat down under a very tall tree with large, above-ground roots. The lightning struck the tree and followed the bark down to the roots to where the man sat. His buttocks, thighs, and legs received second and third-degree burns. Somehow, he managed to return to a Botoa village. When the people saw him, they fled into the forest because his skin allegedly shone white.

The man went into a house to lay down. The next day, the people returned, but they refused to help the man. They thought that evil spirits possessed him. His burn wounds filled with infection. By the time an Ekonda chief saw him, the man had become very ill. The leader transported the man on his bicycle for forty miles, and they arrived at the hospital on Monday. After I treated the man with antibiotics and provided daily wound care, he slowly recovered. I am thankful this good Samaritan came along and that the man continues to improve.

## *The Rich Man's Wife*

It seems that the worst cases always occur at midnight. The nurses called me for two patients in need of emergency surgery. The wealthiest man in Pendjua, who had six wives, almost had his right hand amputated by one of his wives. The other victim, his second wife, had a severe machete wound on her right arm. The machete had sliced the radius in two. Along with three Sisters, I worked non-stop until 2:30 a.m., sewing tendons, muscles, and skin back together. We sutured the cuts on her scalp, face, back, and abdomen.

Later, I learned that the rich man, a merchant, left for Mbandaka to buy merchandise to stock his store. Each Friday, he always gave his wives their soap, creams, and other items to make themselves up for Sunday. However, he only had enough soap for his first wife. He told the other wives that he would give them their soap on Monday. Well, wife number two became very upset. She retorted that if the rest could not have their soap, then the first wife could not have any. However, the man gave the first wife the soap and then left for Mbandaka. The second wife followed him to a village located about twenty miles away. She told him she would continue to harass him on his trip to Mbandaka.

The man then returned home with his wife. During the trip, he beat her. In the process, 1500 Zaires fell on the road and became lost. The man got angry and punished his second wife by refusing to sleep with her. In a polygamous marriage, the man took turns sleeping with each wife, done in strict rotation. On Monday, the man should have stayed with wife number two, but he stayed with wife number one. On Tuesday, the man called the village elders to judge the affair and determine whether he or his wife was at fault.

The elders ruled in favor of the man. Since he punished her by not staying with her on Monday night, it appeared that the affair ended. Now the man would have to be with her on Tuesday night. Tuesday night came, and the man again refused wife number two and went to his first wife's hut. Wife number two stormed in and jerked him out of bed. She yelled that he could not stay with any other wife if he did not stay with her.

The first wife grabbed a knife and slashed the second wife. Then, she left the hut and returned with a large machete about two feet long. She intended to cut off the second wife's head. When she swung the machete, the man stuck out his arm to protect her. The blade struck him on the right wrist, cut the tendons, the radius, and through the carpal bones. She then slashed wife number two with the sword, which sliced her radius bone in two. Then she grabbed a large sum of cash and fled to her family's village, fifteen miles away. Of course, the government officials did absolutely nothing because the man had money. Such is life in the Congo.

# Emergency Surgery
### *1986-1987*

The people didn't celebrate New Year's Eve, as their day began at daybreak and not at midnight. Since no one owned a clock or watch, midnight did not have any meaning. The celebration started at dawn with greetings of "Bonne Annee." The village musicians strolled through town, and they received a lot of local moonshine for their efforts.

Several days later, while I prayed at 5:30 in the morning, someone knocked on my door and disturbed the quiet. Much to my surprise, there stood Luba. He had just come from the maternity ward, as his wife, Ndongo, began labor at 4:00 a.m. Luba had brought her on the bicycle that I loaned him. Ndongo gave birth to a healthy baby girl. They had wanted a boy, but Luba reacted with joy to see this wonderful gift.

#

Then, I went to meet with the groups of young cultivators to discuss the problems they faced. I encouraged them to work together. I became a counselor and treasurer for the agricultural cooperative formed by a group of Ekonda cultivators. I agreed to the new tasks on the condition they accepted Botoa members. I always tried to find a way for the two groups to work together.

The meetings started to bear fruit. The men had built homes for the widows, and the youth helped the older people haul water,

71

and they cut wood for them. In addition to these meetings, I spent two afternoons and three nights in the village to share in their suffering and joy. Now, I am better able to encourage them and learn more about their beliefs and customs. I am always astonished by the people's deep faith and the depth of their prayers.

#

A bush doctor sees many things. Recently, I did emergency surgery on a woman who had an arrow stuck in her abdomen. She had wanted to go to a nearby village for a dance they held, and her husband refused. After a heated argument, she decided to go anyway. Her husband grabbed his bow and shot her with an arrow. Her intestines were not perforated, and I removed it and sewed up the wound. Her husband escaped into the forest.

A week later, I completed another emergency operation that turned into a challenging and frightening event. Two young men had fought over a woman, and one man beat the other with a large branch. The next day the young man came to the clinic with large bruises on his chest and abdomen. He had signs of a ruptured spleen, though his blood count appeared normal, so we kept him for observation. He seemed to improve as he ate some and walked around. One morning, he fainted and went into shock. A quick check showed that his blood count had dropped.

We took the young man to the operating room and found his spleen had ruptured and started to bleed. The surgery became more difficult as we struggled to make the repairs. I worried that the young man would die on the operating table as I prayed and pleaded with the Lord to help him. I completed the repair and tied the major blood vessels to stop the bleeding. I closed the surgical wound and went home, very tired after a challenging three-hour surgery. I looked forward to a much-needed break.

#

I made plans to go home and see my family in the fall. It refreshed me to be with them. In November, I arrived back in Kiri to see my faithful friends Luba and Bola, waiting to meet me. They rode their bicycles thirty-nine miles from Pendjua to Kiri. Tears ran down Luba's cheeks.

*The Christmas Tree*

After being back for a month, I had a joyful time as Luba and I went into the forest to cut a Christmas tree. Since we did not have pine trees, we settled for a tree with many branches from the ground up. We took off eighty percent of its leaves and returned to the village. Everyone stared at us as if we were crazy. We stuck the tree in a bucket of sand and put it in my hut's living room.

I opened the box of lights and ornaments. Luba helped me string three strands of tiny lights on the tree and put on tinsel and garland. Ndongo, Luba, their three-year-old daughter, Mputu, and an eight-year-old neighbor boy decorated the tree with ornaments. We sang Christmas hymns, laughed, and admired our creation.

Word spread that there was a "miracle," a "spirit," a "messenger from God" at the house. The people came and stared in silence. I also set up a manger scene and used black ebony carved statues I bought in Kinshasa. Some people knelt, and everyone blessed themselves and prayed. This moment is the first time since I arrived in Pendjua that I have felt the Christmas spirit of old.

On Christmas Eve morning, Luba and I cut African-print cloth to give to the widows. We distributed the fabric. Some older women only had a rag tied about their waist in front and nothing behind. Their faces lit up with joy when they received the cloth. They had hope for a better year ahead.

*1987*

At the beginning of the new year, I went on a retreat in Kutu. We met for finances and budgets and held a conference on the rights of Zairian citizens. Each mission had to look for ways to save money. At the meeting, I learned new ways to help the Botoa fight injustice. The timing could not have been better.

When I returned, the local county chief in Pendjua had ordered the Botoa of Ngondo Banga to cut a field for him. I informed them that no official could force them to do personal work unless they paid for it. As a result, no one went to cut the field. I imagined the chief's reaction and expected his visit.

The following day, we loaded the jeep and started a long journey to Imenge. Three adults and two kids piled in the front seat. The back held a trunk of supplies, a chest of the nurse's household goods, baskets, buckets, pots, pans, and the spare tire. Luba and two new nurses squeezed into a corner near the tailgate as their legs dangled outside. The numerous mud-filled holes and deep ruts made the road abominable. Everyone piled out at each mud-filled place in the roadway and walked until the jeep sat on more solid ground.

We traveled to Monio and Tweya and then went north to Zimbauli. We left the jeep there and boarded a twenty-foot-long dugout canoe filled with ten people plus all of our baggage. The trip took us on a winding river through the dense tropical forest. Once we landed, we walked for one hour before arriving at Imenge, where a crowd of over 400 children and adults welcomed us. The following day we were swamped as we examined and treated eighty patients. I looked forward to heading home.

### *Appendicitis Attack*

After we returned to Pendjua, I woke up one morning with abdominal pain and assumed I had amoebae. Laboratory tests showed I had some amoebic cysts, so I took medication and lay down to sleep for an hour. When I woke up, I had severe pain, a temperature, nausea, and vomiting. Based on my symptoms, I figured I had appendicitis.

Luba directed the prayer meeting that I usually lead. I asked Mbomba to bring me a bicycle, and I rode to the mission. I arrived in the evening and sent a note to Sister Elyse to ask her to come and examine my abdomen. She decided to get a white blood cell count. Mbomba went to look for the lab technician and arrived at the mission with him an hour later. The results showed an elevation in my white blood count. They contemplated whether or not to operate.

I said, "Sister Elyse, I think we should operate rather than wait until the appendix ruptures. If it isn't appendicitis, I will recover quickly." Sister agreed, and she set up the operating room. She gave me a spinal anesthetic. We did not have gas anesthesia or oxygen, just intravenous sodium pentothal, which I did not like. Within fifteen minutes, they began. Sister Elyse, a nurse, did the surgery. Sister Suzanne assisted Sister Wilhelmina, and they administered IV fluids. Luba monitored my blood pressure, pulse, and respiration. They prayed continually.

I wondered how many doctors had undergone abdominal surgery performed only by nurses. The operation went smoothly, and I did not feel any pain. My appendix had become swollen, red, and infected. At one point, Luba told Sister Elyse my blood pressure dropped to 90 over 60. So, I told Sister Wilhelmina to open the IV and run in more saline and administer an epinephrine shot. The next thing I remember is the nurse putting a bandage on my incision.

Little did I know the worst would be to come. Later, the spinal anesthetic wore off, and I realized how much pain an incision in the stomach caused. Luba gave me a shot of narcotics to take away some of the pain. He sat all night and read his Bible and prayed by candlelight.

### Lesson in Humility

During the first two days after my surgery, I could not do anything for myself. Here I lay, dependent on others for everything, even my survival. Lying there the first night, I groaned in pain. I thought about how fragile we are and how we depend on God and his goodness. When we are in positions of responsibility, and all is well, there is a danger of false pride. We tend to think we are doing everything by our power.

I act as the hospital director and organizer of seven rural health centers. I travel over nearly impassable roads, replace broken bridges, travel in dugout canoes, and walk miles to bring medicines to others. Also, I promote agriculture, cut brush and trees to make new fields, organize youth and adult prayer groups, and more. Now, I cannot even move one inch in bed without someone's help. A highly trained American abdominal surgeon did not operate on me, and that thought overwhelmed me. Instead, a Sister, who had taught herself surgery and saved hundreds of lives during the seven years when they did not have a doctor here, performed my operation.

I thought about Luba and how he prayed for me and sat by the bed the entire first night. I thought, "Who is he?" A priest with years of theology and education, prayer, and spirituality? No. A religious, who had years of training to build a sincere prayer and spiritual life? No. He was just a simple young man who came to know Jesus when he began to study the gospels in 1982. His faith in the Lord and love for the Lord likely exceeded our own.

In Pendjua, the Botoa Pygmies were considered low born and were despised. The intellectuals and even some Zairian priests thought them to be absurd and stupid. The Pygmies were counted for nothing by the local officials. Scholars and officials were the ones who were foolish and unwise because they did not realize Jesus manifested himself in the humble and the poor. I prayed, "Lord Jesus, make me humble and poor in spirit like my friend, Luba."

By mid-February, I recovered from the operation and returned to work. When I went to Ngondo Banga, the people were overjoyed to see me. Even the elderly, who never came to the mission, stopped by my hut. They entered, and stared in amazement, and praised the Lord to see me alive.

#

During my recovery, an older man, and a good friend of mine, died suddenly of an apparent heart attack. He was about sixty-five years old, powerful and wiry, a hunter, and the clan's patriarch to which Bola belonged. One morning, he had mild chest pain and asked Luba for an aspirin. The man died at home while everyone attended church. The people believed the ancestors were angry because the patriarch had sold some farmland to the Ekonda.

I recalled when he did this and how the young men were upset and angry. I did not like it because if the Botoa sold their land, they would become utterly dependent on the Ekonda. At the time, I spoke to the men to discourage them from selling any more of their land.

Luba's uncle became involved in the same land deal while I remained in the hospital. Afterward, he became ill from an allergic reaction. His face, neck, chest, and back swelled, and he could hardly breathe. He refused Luba's pleas to go to the hospital because he believed angry ancestors caused his illness. Instead, he went to a local witch doctor, but he did not improve. I gave Luba cortisone pills to give to his uncle, and in one week, he had recovered.

I share these anecdotes to explain how people's beliefs keep them from seeking modern medicine. The people are slaves to the fear of the spirits of dead ancestors. To add to the fear, our first AIDS patient, who lived in Kinshasa, came to Pendjua. We had no way to help him in his condition, and he died a few days later.

The people knew nothing about AIDS, so we held a conference to inform the nurses about it. As we met, I became concerned about the hospital's future. The medical mission Sisters will not send any new Sisters, and the ones here will eventually leave. The five Sisters here can stay as long as they want. However, they will hand over the responsibility for the hospital to another organization or the government. If the government takes over, it could end the health care in Pendjua. We planned to ask the bishop to take over the hospital and name the Sisters and me as directors.

A short time later, a 39-year-old woman became the next victim to die from AIDS. She and her husband lived in Kinshasa until her husband died last year of AIDS. When she became infected, the doctors told her they could not cure her, so she came home to die. She arrived in January but never sought treatment. I lamented that it would only be a matter of time before there were original cases of AIDS here. I told the Christians about AIDS and stressed that if married couples remained faithful, they had nothing to fear.

#

I needed a break from the hospital work, so Luba and I planned to work in the field early one morning. Our plans changed by the sudden death of our neighbor's three-year-old boy. In the afternoon, he complained of stomach cramps, and they took him to the clinic, where Sister Paula attended to patients. There, he went into cardiac arrest. Sister Paula did cardiopulmonary resuscitation but to no avail. She thought the child might have eaten a poisonous plant, as there were many in the area. This event brought heartache to everyone. Individual family members believed an enemy caused the boy's death. They wanted to perform a pagan rite that they called "lilako."

During the rite, the men marched while they carried the casket. They paraded before all the village members, who were obliged to be present. They believed the dead person's spirit guided them. The men with the casket ran until directed to stop in front of the person who caused the death. Often, this ritual caused animosity between the clans and resulted in battles.

Later, we called the Christians together, prayed, read Bible verses, and sang songs. We lowered the casket into the ground and prayed as we covered it with dirt. The family shared their gratitude for the Christian burial for their little boy.

#

A few evenings later, Sister Elyse and I did a cesarean section. Everything went well, including the incision in the uterus. Still, the baby lay in the wrong position, so we had great difficulty with the delivery. If I thought that this was the worst, I was mistaken. As we struggled to deliver the baby, the lights went out, and we were in total darkness. I could not see Sister Elyse across the table. We sent the nurse to get a flashlight. The lady's husband had a small kerosene lamp, which he held over the incision. I applied a pair of forceps to the baby's head and delivered him. The baby came out blue, but Sister Paula worked to get him to breathe.

The following day, the mother and child were doing well. Sister Elyse and I prayed a lot during those critical minutes. After the baby's birth, we closed the surgical wounds by the light of two flashlights. Later, we learned that the cable from the motor to the fuse box snapped. We fixed it the next day, and I prayed we would not have another nightmare like that again.

## The "Resurrection"

While in Imenge, I heard about a Botoa mother of ten children who died of chronic kidney disease in May. They described her as a charming and kind person, and everyone loved her. She had come to Pendjua in April for cortisone treatments. Since she did not improve after one month, she wanted to return home. The people said she claimed to have visions. She told the village that when she died, her body would resurrect in seven days. She stated she would return as a great medicine woman and cure all sorts of illnesses.

The deceased lady instructed her family to let her body rot for three or four days after her death. Then they should place her in an open coffin, lower the coffin into the ground and cover it with palm leaves. The leaves would allow her to leave the coffin without difficulty. She told them not to cry or grieve after her death but instead sing songs all night and day to help her awaken. While I worked in Imenge on June 10, it had been six days since she died, and everyone awaited her resurrection. The two young nurses believed she would come back to life. At the end of June, a nurse from Imenge came to pick up medications. I asked him if the lady had risen from the dead. He said, "No, but music is coming from the tomb, so we expect her to resurrect any day."

When I went to Imenge on July 8, the nurses and people said the deceased lady sent a message. The message stated she would resurrect on the night the doctor arrived. On the 9th, she still had not returned from the dead, so some people became discouraged and began to have doubts. When my jeep did not start, the deceased lady's sons said their mother prevented me from leaving until she resurrected. Once again, everyone believed and waited. On Friday, after we put the new battery in the jeep, the motor started. As we drove away, many people doubted the lady would resurrect.

#

Soon after our time in Imenge, we visited clinics in Ikoyo, Momboyo, and Bongolo. The people from Ikoyo continued to build dikes, so we drove the jeep within two miles of the health center. I doubt the levees will be stable enough to support the jeep during the big rainy season. We discovered a problem with the nurse in Ikoyo. He falsified his records and embezzled 4000 Zaires. When I confronted him with the facts, he denied them. However, the following day, he admitted he took the money and asked me for a second chance if he agreed to repay the funds. The man had six children, and I knew it would be impossible for him to find another job, so I gave him a second chance. I desired to help him change and become honest rather than fire him.

Once I returned, I filled medication orders from the health centers and made hospital rounds. The hospital overflowed with patients, of which five had AIDS. I fear this is the tip of the iceberg, and there will be many AIDS cases in the months and years ahead.

# Curses and Evil Spirits

## *1988-1989*

In mid-January, another needless, tragic death of a young man in Ngondo Banga occurred. The death certificate listed the cause of death as meningitis. The real reason is that the people's beliefs keep them from coming to the hospital for treatment. The people believed that one of three things caused illness and death. First, the evil spirit of a dead ancestor could cause a disease. Second, an enemy may cause a curse to befall the victim. Third, a witch could cause illness. They believed that to cure such a sickness, they had to use magic formulas and medicines. Some treatments killed the patient. They gave toxic enemas that caused severe inflammation of the colon and even perforated it. Sometimes I wondered if these beliefs and practices would end.

The young man had four children, and he had the flu before Christmas. However, his sister said their dead father's spirit had become angry, so she "treated" him. After the New Year, he had a fever, stiff neck, and weakness in his left arm and leg. After the enemas, he became dehydrated and comatose. After midnight on the 10th, the man's brothers asked Luba to examine him. Luba knew right away the man would die soon. They took him to the hospital. The man's sister objected all the way there and cursed at Luba. Upon hearing the story, I chased the sister out of the hospital. We did all we could to treat him with IV fluids and antibiotics for several days, but our efforts failed. He died just a few nights later.

The afternoon after his death, I went to the village for a Christian community prayer meeting. I talked about this incident and explained how people's beliefs prevented the man from receiving proper medical care. We talked about how they were captives and prisoners of fear of evil spirits and curses. I told them that Jesus wanted to liberate them from the fears and beliefs that prevented them from seeking medical care. I prayed that they would overcome their fear of curses and evil spirits.

#

The hospital remained hectic, as we had a new strain of resistant malaria appear. Children under five years of age could be in grave danger because this malaria rapidly destroyed their red blood cells. One day, a five-year-old Botoa boy arrived in a semi-comatose state from the loss of most of his blood. The boy's uncles refused to give blood, so Luba unselfishly gave some of his blood, and the boy survived. Luba's wife did not like that Luba gave blood. She reasoned that if their children ever needed blood, Luba would not have any to give them. I explained to her that 200 milliliters of blood were not very much, and if her children needed blood, Luba could provide some. I assured her I also would give my blood.

#

I prepared for a trip to Kutu. I did not look forward to the two-day boat trip under the blazing sun, though I had no other way to get there. Once in Kutu, I attended the regional meeting to discuss our projects, the new Constitution, and justice. We discussed how to help those who suffered injustice at the hands of government officials and the local police. Then, we decided to form a Peace and Justice Commission and teach the people their civil rights.

During my absence, two affairs occurred between the Botoa and Ekonda. The first one involved Mbomba. Last Sunday, Mbomba and some other boys were at the market. They drank some palm wine, which had a low alcohol content. A nineteen-year-old Ekonda girl asked Mbomba to buy her a glass of palm wine. When Mbomba bought her some wine, some Ekonda men became very angry. They exchanged words, and Mbomba went home without further issue.

A few days later, the police came and got Mbomba and held a trial in front of three judges. They charged him under the law that a Botoa man could not give an Ekonda woman a drink, not even water. Mfutu, the nurse supervisor, attended the trial, and he told the judges that no such law existed. Even if it had been a tribal law, they could no longer consider it a state requirement. A heated discussion ensued, but in the end, the judges dropped the charges.

The second event involved a Botoa nurse, Ndoba. He worked at the health center in Imenge. He did not have an internship in obstetrics, so I had him come to the clinic. Ndoba assisted with prenatal exams during my absence, but the Ekonda women refused to enter the clinic. The Ekonda village notables met with Sister Elise. They told her no Botoa male nurse could examine an Ekonda woman, according to an ancestral rule.

Sister Elise advised them the nurse would be present at the consultations. The following Thursday, no Ekonda women came for the prenatal clinic. I told the Sisters if the women did not attend, so be it; however, the nurses would be available to serve them if they came. The Ekonda notables wanted to meet with me. I planned to record the meeting and send the tape to the Governor because the Constitution forbade tribalism and racism.

#

Ten days later, a man and three boys from a nearby Botoa village went hunting. The man had the most respect of any person in the community. The group proceeded to hunt in the dense brush as the man went ahead of them. One eager boy saw the bushes move, so he let an arrow fly, and it entered the man's chest. The boys were afraid as they saw what had happened. The man told the boys to stand him up. Then, he grabbed the arrow and pulled it out of his chest. He advised the others that the boy who shot him should not receive punishment for an accidental shooting. The man said several prayers, blessed himself, and then he collapsed and died. However, the man's family did respect his wishes, and they beat the boy.

Sister Wilhelmina saw the crowd and demanded to know what they were doing. She ordered the people to let the boy go. She put him in the jeep and drove to the hospital, where he received police protection. The old law of an "eye for an eye" and a "tooth for a tooth" still ruled.

#

After a brief time back at the mission, I started a three-day trip to visit health centers. We went to Nzale and discovered the nurse could no longer work because of her illness. This realization made me sad. The nurse had six children. Her husband, a school teacher, and an alcoholic did not support the family. The nurse had heart disease, and one valve did not function properly. She had started the health center in January and valiantly tried to work. Now, her shortness of breath had become so acute that she could not continue. I had no choice but to close the center until we could train a nurse to replace her.

Luba and I took the Sister's large Toyota Land Cruiser on a mission of mercy. We went to Nzale to move the nurse, her six children, and all her belongings to Pendjua since her parents lived here. At least, they would be able to help take care of her. She required a heart operation to replace the mitral valve, but heart surgery did not exist in Zaire. I knew that it would be a matter of time before she had total heart failure.

#

After my return, I made hospital rounds and did outpatient consultations. When Luba came to work in the afternoon, he informed me about an immense tragedy. A friend of ours had died from acute alcohol intoxication. The man appeared to be about fifty years old. He and some of his friends went on a drinking binge one evening. When he went home, he collapsed on his bed. The following day, his wife could not wake him up. When Luba passed their house at 6:30 a.m., he told them to bring the man to the hospital. They did not follow Luba's advice because they thought an enemy placed a curse on the man. At noon, he died.

I went to the village in the evening. We held our community prayer meeting and reflected on what it meant to follow Jesus.

"What are your daily crosses?'" I asked. Some said, "Marriage." Others said, "Looking and working to find food for our family every day." "Raising our children." "Suffering and poverty."

This society was indeed a subsistence society because the people could not think about saving something for tomorrow, as one was fortunate enough to have for today. Matthew 6:34 says, "Never worry about tomorrow because tomorrow will worry about itself. Each day has enough trouble of its own."[3]

#

The congregation celebrated our 100th anniversary in Zaire. The first Missionhurst missionaries arrived on October 16, 1888. We held a celebration and the Zairian deacon preached on the importance of our missionary presence.

### *Mobutu's Anniversary*

The weeks passed, and we had a significant state holiday on November 24 to mark the 23rd anniversary of Mobutu's presidency, which I considered a dictatorship. The leaders organized a parade, made speeches, and held a dinner planned for the dignitaries of Pendjua. The chief had gone to Inongo, so his temporary replacement planned the celebration. Since the city treasury had no money, he canceled the dinner. The parade began at 10:30 in the morning. The mission nurses were furious since they had to march in the procession under the threat of stiff fines if they did not.

The nurses did not go to the event during the previous state holiday, and they were all arrested. I went to the parade to watch the school children file past. When I arrived, the dignitaries were seated on benches under a shady tree. They scrambled to find an oversized chair for me, but I declined, as I preferred to stand with the few Botoa there.

Everyone disliked the false praise given to a government that plunged the people deeper into poverty. The state administrators led the school children in songs to praise Mobutu, the supposed savior of Zaire. A line from one song stated, "Hardship and poverty do not

---

[3] Matthew 6:34 ISV

exist in Zaire." I hardly kept from laughing out loud when I heard this lie. Eighty-five percent of the population lived in poverty and were hard-pressed to find enough food to eat each day. We hoped for a better year ahead.

*1989*

In January, I remained hopeful with the start of the Botoa small farmer cooperative. This project took a lot of persistence to get started. Though it was a worthwhile project, it became clear there would be many challenges. Last year, the people were not enthusiastic enough, and I thought it would not have any chance to succeed. Recently, several men came and asked if they could start the cooperative. I said "Yes," and sent Luba and Bola to the five villages to organize the groups. They created nine groups of ten to thirteen men.

We met with 102 members of the small farmer's co-op and elected a board of directors. I would describe the process as an absolute riot. They had no idea what it meant to hold a ballot, as there were never any honest elections here. Afterward, everyone received their advance, and almost everyone seemed satisfied.

\#

After the meeting, I returned to the hospital to examine 16 new tuberculosis patients. This disease continued to be a real scourge. The people usually waited four to six months before they came to the hospital. Eventually, everyone in the clan became infected. The group patriarch, Papa Mbomba, had been sick for three months, and he suffered weight loss, anemia, and weakness. I thought he had terminal kidney disease. He did not cough much, but he cleared his throat often. Before we went on the road, I told Luba to examine the man's phlegm, which he discovered to be positive for tuberculosis. We put him in the sanitarium for four weeks. Everyone in the clan expressed their gratitude.

\#

I am happy to report that on April 20, Bola's wife began labor. We performed a cesarean section. However, there were a lot of adhesions, so we had a hard time delivering the baby. To add to the stress, we accidentally cut a small hole in her bladder. Then, making matters even worse, she had an attack of malaria and convulsions while we repaired her uterus. Sister Elyse and I prayed non-stop while drenched in our sweat.

#

A few days later, two soldiers came to help the village chief force the people to repair the roads. Then, an Ekonda man paid the soldiers a bribe to make 30 Botoa women transport manioc from his field to his home while he did not pay them. The Ekonda viewed the Botoa as either cheap labor or, even worse, as beasts of burden.

The man lived next to the mission, and when the women arrived with the manioc, they sang, "We are the slaves of the Ekonda." Luba came at that moment, and he became furious. I went and told the man he could not have slaves in Zaire. I declared, "I will report this to the county chairman in Kiri and the governor in Bandundu." Then, I invited the women to my office. They wrote their names and placed their thumbprint next to their name. I sent the reports and waited to see if the officials would act or not.

#

Next, the soldiers confiscated a large amount of rice from a distant village. They came to Sister Paula's rice mill to grind it, but she refused. The soldiers then rounded up six Botoa women to pound the rice by hand while refusing to pay them. I prepared a second report and decided to organize a Botoa justice and peace committee to report injustice cases. I realized that I needed to help the Botoa learn how to report abuses of power. Some days, I am not sure if anyone will ever resolve the issue of justice and peace.

# Crime and Punishment
## *1989-1990*

I traveled to the U.S. in the summer to spend time with my family. Once in the Congo in November, I left Kinshasa to go to Inongo, and I arrived at the mission where Father Jeff welcomed me. After we ate lunch, he informed me that it appeared that Mfutu, the supervisor, and Luba were involved in the theft of 900,000 Zaires from my office. I felt like someone hit me with a ton of bricks. Father Jeff did not know any details, so I had to wait until I arrived in Pendjua to find out the whole story. My despair overwhelmed me, and I prayed until 3:30 a.m. before catching two hours of sleep.

The boat from Kiri arrived on Sunday afternoon to transport me home. However, a heavy rain and wind storm whipped up waves on the lake, so we had to wait until the storm ended. The trip in the 16-foot aluminum boat took more than four long hours. I arrived in Kiri in the afternoon, and Sister Paula picked me up. Darkness had already come when we pulled into the mission. When I stepped from the Toyota, Bola, and Luba were there. Luba looked terrible, skinny, and worn. He said, "Brother, I am in big trouble."

"We'll talk about it tomorrow morning," I responded as I headed to my room. Thankfully, Bola was not involved in the affair, and he stood by his friend Luba.

The following day, I talked to Sister Elyse, Luba, Mfutu, and others. We were not sure of how many or who the thieves were.

Certainly, Mfutu, the supervisor, and Luba were involved. Luba had keys to the office, and Mfutu had the keys to the padlocks on the trunks with the money.

I learned that Luba had run to Sister Elyse while I was gone and told her to come to the office. Someone had forced the door open and stole the trunk. Sister Elyse noted that the back door remained open, but it did not appear to have been forced open. She said that someone removed part of the door frame that led to my office. She sent for the authorities, who came right away.

Thirty minutes later, some children saw the trunk in the weeds about three blocks away. Inside, there remained 78,000 Zaires in a small plastic bag. The chest had been forced open. Mfutu was not in Pendjua at that time. He had left for a nearby village several days earlier to preach at a Sunday service. The authorities took Luba to jail for questioning. He said he must have forgotten to lock the back door on Sunday after the prayer meeting. Later, the police arrested 14 Botoa boys and found each one with 300 Zaire.

#

Mfutu arrived the next day with the chief of the collectivity to inspect the door. Sister Elyse came to the office and expressed doubt that the lock could be forced open. Mfutu took out a machete and pried the lock open. Later, he filed an official report. He said an unknown thief forced the office door free and stole the trunk with 900,000 Zaires. Then, Sister Elyse looked through the papers scattered on my desk. She discovered several documents that indicated loans that the supervisor made to various people. Sister Elyse sent for Mfutu, who admitted he made them, but he forgot to enter them in the ledger. We realized that he might have made other loans he did not record as well. We may never know how much money the trunk contained.

#

Sister Suzanne sent Luba a note, and she counseled him that he must tell the truth. He wrote a letter back and said that he was the victim of a plot authorized by Mfutu to simulate a theft. Luba claimed that Mfutu told him he wanted to take the money and buy goods that his two older boys could sell. Afterward, they would return the funds. Luba said that he refused to go along with the plan. However, he noted that Mfutu threatened his life if he did not leave the back door open on Sunday. Luba did not tell this story to the chief until Thursday.

During this time, Mfutu continued to support Luba's first story that unknown thieves forced open the door. When he heard that Luba accused him, he thought the Sisters influenced Luba to change his story. He went to see the two priests and claimed that he would have Sister Elyse arrested. I found this activity to be odd for someone who claimed to be innocent. The chief questioned Luba, Mfutu, and his two sons. Then he sent a report to the county commissioner to judge the affair. Nothing more happened until I arrived in Kiri on November 21.

#

I talked to Luba, and he stuck to his story. "If you are the thief, you should admit it and return whatever money is left," I advised him. "Then they can judge the affair in Pendjua, and you will not have to go to the district court in Inongo."

"I am not a thief!" Luba cried. "I didn't receive any money."

Next, I talked to Mfutu. He declared his innocence and said Luba stole the money. Later, I received a copy of a letter Mfutu sent to the county commissioner. The letter accused the chief of the collectivity and Sister Elyse of influencing Luba to change his story. When I told the Sisters about the letter, they were infuriated.

The commissioner sent the police commander to do another investigation. He talked to Luba and Mfutu, and he never questioned Sister Elyse or the other officials involved in the initial review. Later, I heard that the commander asked Luba and Mfutu for 10,000 Zaires each. He threatened to beat them if they did not pay him.

Three days later, the commander left for Kiri with Mfutu and Luba on foot. Luba's father, mother, and wife went with them because the prisons did not feed the prisoners. Family members had to bring food every day. They scheduled the affair for judgment in Inongo on November 26 and December 3. I encouraged Luba to tell the truth and not make false accusations. Each time, Luba said that Mfutu committed the crime and that he did not receive any money.

As I thought about this tragedy, several things came to mind. Failures are not always bad. Disappointments make one humbler and more dependent on God. They take away false pride in the work we do and deflate our over-inflated egos. Jesus never promised His followers would have it easy, but instead, He said we would have crosses to bear. I kept the words of Mother Theresa in my heart, "Never let anything so fill you with sorrow as to make you forget the joy of Christ risen."

#

The past week had already been incredibly trying. Then the nurse from Imenge came to have his books reviewed. He picked up a supply of medications. There were problems with him since he embezzled in the past, but the amounts were small. This time, he stole 87,000 Zaires, which amounted to six months of his salary.

I suspended the nurse without pay until he reimbursed the health center, and then I told him he could no longer work there. "You will have to work at the hospital where the Sisters can supervise you. If you do not pay back the money in two months, you might go to jail." I felt exasperated that the nurse did not see the theft of 87,000 Zaires as being serious. I sent him to pick up the remaining medications, and I temporarily closed the health center.

#

The county commissioner sent me a message. He wanted me to come to Kiri to talk about the theft from my office. When we arrived at the mission, a teacher told us the police took Mfutu and Luba to a nearby sawmill to board a barge for Inongo. We jumped back into the jeep and raced straight to the mill.

As usual, they mistreated the "little people," and the so-called "important people" were allowed their freedom. Luba was a pitiful sight in his dirty clothes. They even made him stand in the sun with a guard nearby. Meanwhile, Mfutu stood under a large shady tree and talked with friends. Thanks to my intervention, Luba's wife and mother accompanied him to Inongo.

Later, I went to see the commissioner, the highest authority in the county, and a presidential appointee. I found him to be a kind person but not a very capable administrator. The commissioner thought Mfutu organized the theft and that Luba had been a pawn used by Mfutu. They believed that Luba did not get any money.

We stayed overnight at the mission. In the evening, a man came to the house to ask me to take his son to Pendjua. He told me that the boy had broken both bones in his lower leg. I went to the hospital and found him in critical condition. With the original fracture, the bones protruded through the skin. The local medicine man had set the bones without using sterile means, and the wound became severely infected. Three days had passed since the accident, and his whole leg remained swollen.

In the morning, we picked up the boy. I splinted his leg and placed cushions in the vehicle to make him as comfortable as possible. His mother sat on the floor and held his leg so it would not fall off the seat as we bounced along the rutted-out, bumpy road. I reassured him that he was a courageous 16-year-old boy. Even without any pain medication, he never cried out once on the long trip. We arrived and took him straight to the hospital, where Sister Elyse took over.

#

A few days later, I received a letter from Luba:

"Dear brother, accept peace and love from your brother Luba. I'm now in prison. Do not forget that I have never had anything like this happen to me since being born, but I'm praying to God that He will show me justice. Do not forget to pray for me. You must be patient with me. I want you to know it is painful for me to be in prison, but Jesus is giving me strength, consoling me, and filling me with His love. I know my suffering is nothing compared to what Jesus suffered for me. Amen. Luba."

*1990*

I continued to think about Luba's letter as I packed the jeep with enough supplies for three health centers. We went to Itendo and expected problems since the nurse did not send in any paperwork since November. When we arrived, the nurse seemed worried, and we asked him for the receipts from November and December. He avoided the question, and he talked about his family problems and the high cost of living. He complained that he could not make ends meet. "I want to transfer to another center where I can just be a helper to the nurse in charge," he pleaded.

I replied, "You will not receive the same pay as a helper because you will not have the same responsibilities." "Can I have the receipts?" I asked. He replied, "I only have half. I do not have the other half of the money. Please give me one month to straighten out the problems."

"If there is a large deficit at the end of January, I will suspend you for one month," I warned him. We finished our work and gave him a one-month supply of medicine.

### Kizitos

For some good news, we started a new youth movement called the Kizitos. The group consisted of youth between the ages of 12 and 15. The Kizitos are somewhat like the Boy Scouts but with an African orientation. There are ten boys in the group, and Bola is their leader. The manual is in French, so I first translate the lessons into Lingala every Saturday afternoon.

The name Kizitos came from St. Kizito, a 12-year-old African boy. A pagan chief killed him and a group of young African men and boys in Uganda in 1886. They killed them because they refused to deny Christ and worship the pagan ruler. So, the ruler marched the group for six days to a place where they burned them. They rolled each boy up in a bamboo mat and placed them on a large pile of wood. As the boys burned, one soldier laughed at and mocked Kizito, saying, "Man, you are going to burn now." Kizito responded, "This fire is not going to last forever, but the fire of hell does."

#

I received a letter from Father Jeff. He said Luba remained in prison while he waited for his trial. Luba wrote a letter to explain that Mfutu paid the judges a bribe. As expected, Mfutu remained free while Luba sat in jail. Luba could get out of jail on Christmas Day and New Year's Day. I waited for the trial to be over, so we would know what would happen.

The courts here are corrupt. I recall the time two years ago when the authorities accused Father Paul of selling bullets. The sale of ammunition is illegal, and everyone knew that Father Paul did not sell any, but they took him before the judge. When the provincial and Father Paul met with the judge, he told them to give him 10,000 Zaires to drop the affair. Father Paul refused. However, in the end, they declared his innocence. Father Paul said that if Mfutu were the thief and paid the judge a bribe, he would get off free of any charges.

Father Jeff told me that if I paid the prison director a bribe, Luba would be set free. He also informed me that whoever bribed the judge would win the case. I learned that the judge told Luba to give him 100,000 Zaires, and he would be declared innocent. The provincial and the other priests believe Luba spoke the truth and that he never received any money. They thought he left the office door open because Mfutu threatened to kill him. Since Luba was a Pygmy, he would be found guilty, and Mfutu would go free and never go to prison. Grief overcame me. I should not have allowed a Pygmy to work alone with a Bantu.

Although the circumstance caused great stress, I considered the event as a blessing in my spiritual life. This trial increased my faith and trust in the Lord. While it is easy to be joyful and love the Lord when all goes well, the real test is to see how we accept difficulties and failures.

#

Upon my return from Inongo, I went to Ngondo Banga. One man in the clan had a considerable cancerous growth on the lower part of his right leg. Last year, it was a small sore, and I told him many times to go to the hospital and remove it. Instead, the man went to a local witch doctor who told him the illness resulted from a deceased friend's spirit. Supposedly, the spirit became unhappy because the dancers had not yet held a dance for him. The man's three brothers urged him to go to the hospital. I even loaned them the money. The following day, the man still refused to go. I did not know what else to do.

#

The next day, word arrived that a little three-year-old boy had become lost in the forest for 24 hours. I knew that if they did not find him, the affair could end in bloodshed between the Botoa and Ekonda. The boy's mother had gone to the forest to cut firewood on the previous day, and she left the boy with her sister. The sister fell asleep, and the toddler went to look for his mother. When the mother returned, she asked her sister where her son was. They searched the surrounding area, but they could not find him anywhere.

The Botoa organized search parties, and they could not find him. The Botoa believed that the Ekonda kidnapped the boy, so they gave a call to arms. The men from seven Botoa villages grabbed their bows and poison-tipped arrows and machetes and surrounded the five Ekonda villages. They blocked all entrances and exits to each community. The chief asked everyone to remain calm. The next day, they organized a search party with both Botoa and Ekonda. That morning, an Ekonda woman found the little boy near a river, five miles away. Nobody had any idea how he got there, but everyone felt great relief to see him alive.

#

Sixteen barefoot doctors arrived for four days of training. We talked about the causes of disease and the traditional beliefs, and the scientific reasons for sickness. We also talked about how their ancestors searched for the sources of illness and death. Since they had no idea of germs, they concluded that disease and death came from evil spirits, ancestors, broken taboos, and witchcraft. I explained how the microscope's discovery led to the knowledge of germs and parasites as causes of disease and showed them pictures.

We began a three-day lesson on tuberculosis. To help with the assignments, we used flip charts with colored pictures. The pictures explained the symptoms and signs of tuberculosis. I told them how a person contracted it, how to diagnose it, treat it, and prevent it. On the last day, they packed some medicines in the containers I gave them, and they returned to their villages. It did my heart good to see their progress.

#

After weeks of waiting, I received a letter from Luba. He wrote that they acquitted Mfutu. However, Luba had to serve a two-year prison term, and he had to pay 800,000 Zaires. The Father provincial and everyone else believed Luba never received a single Zaire. They also thought Mfutu bribed the judges, which remained a prevalent practice. The Father provincial agreed to try to get Luba a pardon. Mfutu arranged to get a transfer to Kiri. In the meantime, as unfair as the circumstances were, all I could do was pray.

Luba's wife, baby girl, and parents were back home after five long months in Inongo. I had not heard any news during the past three weeks. One morning, I received a radio message from Father Jeff that said they transferred Luba to Kiri's prison. Luba had boarded a barge that left Inongo for Kiri. Imono, the mission handyman, and I went to Kiri. The rainy season started in full swing, so the roads were almost impassable. One 45-foot-long bridge had rotted out. The logging company based in Kiri had placed six large tree trunks across the river, but they did not place planks across the bridge.

When we got there, I did not think I could cross over on the bridge. The distance between the two logs was a greater width than the space between the wheels. I approached the bridge until the wheels touched. Then, I got out to see if we could cross on them. I cut a length of stick equal to the distance from one front wheel to the other. Next, I walked the bridge to make sure the gap between the logs was not too much for the jeep. Though it would be risky, we decided we had to try to make it. Imono stood on the other end of the bridge and directed me as I inched across. I could hardly breathe, and by the time I reached the other side, my legs were trembling.

### Luba's Homecoming

We arrived in Kiri, and I sent Imono to the prison to check on Luba's situation. The chief judge in Inongo decided to let Luba out of jail on parole to work in Pendjua. I learned that I would be responsible for him. I would have to take Luba to Kiri every Saturday to sign in with the prison director. The director said it might not be necessary for Luba to come to Kiri after a few months. Everyone sighed relief, and they were thrilled that this ordeal would come to an end.

No one complained about the jeep being overcrowded. Imono, Ndongo, Luba's mother, two babies, and I rode in the front seat, and Luba, a cousin, and ten cartons of medicines somehow fit in the back. The second baby was the child of a woman who had been killed by lightning last week. Fortunately, the bolt did not strike Luba's mother, wife, or child, though they had been standing right next to the woman who got hit and killed.

We had a joyous trip back home. When we got to the large bridge, I made everyone get out of the jeep and cross on foot. We arrived at the mission after the sun had already set. I took them home, and what a homecoming they had, as no one knew Luba would return with me.

At the first Ekonda neighborhood, which was next to the mission, even the Ekonda rejoiced and yelled to Luba. We arrived at the five Botoa villages. Luba was unable to stay in the jeep because the people pulled him out of the window. I stopped at each community, and Luba and Ndongo got out of the vehicle as the people hugged them and yelled, "Luba, Luba!" Tears of joy tumbled down everyone's cheeks. Tears ran down my face as well when I saw how much the Pygmies loved their brother.

They arrived at their hut, unloaded their meager possessions, and I returned to the mission. I did not think a single, solitary Pygmy thought Luba committed the theft at the office. I told Luba to take some time with his family, especially his other two daughters, who had not seen him in six months. On Sunday, many Ekonda parishioners had not yet seen Luba. After church, they came over and shook his hand.

Later, when I wrote to the judge in Inongo, I did not write that I thought Luba was innocent. That would place the judge's ruling into question, and he would never consider my plea to liberate Luba. Therefore, I wrote that after some reflection, I have decided to pardon the restitution of the money the court obliged Mr. Luba

Etofi to repay. I asked him to consider the possibility of releasing Luba on parole and cited several reasons for clemency in his case.

#

At the end of May, Luba went to Kiri for "physical control," which meant he had to sign in with the prison director. Luba had to do this every Saturday. I wrote to the director and asked if he could do the control in Pendjua. The director agreed, so I hoped that Luba might not have to go to Kiri anymore.

#

A new group of barefoot doctors came to the mission. Ninety-nine percent of the people still retained their ancestral beliefs and did not know germs caused diseases. I talked about conditions such as measles, whooping cough, colds, gonorrhea, syphilis, and others. I showed them photographs of bacteria and malaria, and intestinal worms to help them understand. They were astonished to learn that these tiny organisms caused all those illnesses.

Little by little, they understood the need to disinfect a wound and place a gauze on it to protect it. I believed that with more lessons, they would accept modern health care and teach their people these new concepts. On Saturday, they received their first aid kits and medications and proudly returned to their villages.

#

After the sessions, I went to Ngondo Banga for the night. Belipe, one of my good friends, had terminal cancer. I previously wrote about him and how he had a small tumor on his leg a year ago. However, he would not let me take it off. When I returned from my vacation, the cancerous tumor had grown to the size of an egg, and I did not doubt that it was malignant. I tried to convince him to let me operate, but he refused. He believed the tumor resulted from an evil spirit of a man who had died last year. The cancer had spread through the entire leg, and he lay at death's doorstep. Belipe would leave behind three wives and twelve children.

Luba had left to do a medical census in five Botoa villages, but his trip got cut short by the death of his uncle, Belipe. I sent Bola to inform him, and they arrived back in time for the funeral. They were all saddened by Belipe's death. I knew that his beliefs kept him from allowing me to remove the skin cancer when it first began, making it even harder for me.

#

Several days later, Luba and I went to Kiri to check in with the prison director. We first met with the county chairman and the doctor responsible for county health. The zone's commissioner is a presidential appointee, not an elected official, but he has total power over the territory. A few months ago, he asked me to supply the hospital in Kiri with medications. I told him I would agree to his proposal if he guaranteed payment.

Then, Luba and I went to the prison director's office. The director usually acted reasonably. However, this time he said, "I might keep Luba in prison and not allow him to return Pendjua for the work release program." Well, I had been around long enough to know he wanted a bribe. I told the director I was hungry and wanted to go to the mission to eat. The director said he would keep Luba in prison until 4:00 p.m. When the time came, the director sent Luba to ask me for 10,000 Zaires, the equivalent of $15.00. I almost gave him the money, but then, I decided that two could play this game.

I went to the county commissioner and explained the problem. Then, I informed him that if Luba could not return to Pendjua and work, I would never supply Kiri's hospital with medicine. The commissioner sighed and said he would take care of the problem. Later, when I returned to the prison director's office, he acted as pleasant as he could be. The director said, "I am glad to inform you that Luba can return to Pendjua."

#

Luba and I went to Kiri again in August to check in with the director. Luba returned to the mission and informed me the director wanted to see me. He said that he required part of Luba's salary. With that, we went to see the county commissioner. He told us that usually if a prisoner is on a work-release program, part of the wage went to the prison director. I told him that I would agree to that if they signed papers to make it official. I feared that Luba would have many troubles until the end of this process in October of 1991. I contacted the Arch Bishop of Mbandaka and asked him to use his influence to obtain Luba's parole.

#

Back home, I made hospital rounds. When I went to my office, several Botoa men were waiting for me. They told me the collectivity chief had arrested their wives, and each one had to pay 2,000 Zaires. He fined them because they did not sow seeds in the field that he had forced the Botoa to cut in May. An official could not legally force the people to cut an area and then plant the field for his profit. When the chief's secretary came over to buy paper and supplies in the afternoon, I refused to sell him any items.

As my throat tightened, I said, "Tell the chief I will send a letter to the county chairman concerning his illegal activities." With that, the secretary left. The next day, I wrote the letter and sent a book on the rights of Zairian citizens. Afterward, the chief of the collectivity came to my office to inform me my letter hurt him. He explained that the Botoa agreed to cut and plant a field for the community. In return, he said that the Ekonda would construct the shelters for the open-air market. "Even so," I told him, "you have no right to levy heavy fines on the poor Botoa women, and if you do not change, you don't need to come and ask for office supplies."

He thanked me for my advice and left. Two days later, the chief went to Sister Elyse and asked for tax money. Sister Elyse told him to get lost as she did not like how he persecuted the Botoa women and did not make the Ekonda do any work. He retorted that the Ekonda were building shelters. After Sister Elyse informed me of the encounter, I went to the market to see for myself. I was not surprised to find that the only workers were 30 Botoa men and no Ekonda. I stormed over to the chief's office and congratulated him on his lying. "Don't bother coming to my office anymore." He did not respond but put his head in his hands as I strolled out the door.

#

At the end of November, I went to Kinshasa. Attempting to get something done by the government in Kinshasa could be very frustrating. The congressman who promised to take Dr. Ewusu and me to the Department of Health did not show up until noon. By then, it was too late. Almost no government workers worked in the afternoon, even though they were supposed to work until 3:30. The congressman said he would be there the following day. The time came, and the man did not show up the entire day. I became frustrated as we had wasted a whole day as we waited for him and could not leave and visit other places.

On Thursday, we went to the office of the program to control sleeping sickness. This disease had increased at a rapid rate in certain areas. The Zairian doctor who directed the program told us they had enough medications for four months. He did not know where to get more because Mobutu had expelled the Belgian government workers. The Belgian government had helped Zaire fight tuberculosis, leprosy, and sleeping sickness. Now, they no longer provided funds.

#

When I returned home from Kinshasa on December 1, I found a stack of letters and cards dated September through November. When I read the letter dated October 23, I discovered that my dad had multiple myeloma cancer. I sat on my cot in shock. My mom wrote that their faith would carry them through this dilemma. I wrote a personal message to my mother and father.

#

The following week, Luba and Bola went on a worm treatment trip to three Botoa villages. They completed a population census. On Thursday morning, they returned and came straight to the hospital because Bola had fallen quite ill. It turned out he had severe pneumonia in his entire left lung. The following day he had shortness of breath and a temperature of 102 degrees.

By Christmas, Bola remained in the hospital with staphylococcal pneumonia and fluid in-between the chest and lungs. I continued to treat him with antibiotics, and I performed a chest tap, which helped him feel somewhat better, though he was depressed about the length of his recovery.

The people celebrated Christmas and packed the church on Christmas Eve and Christmas Day. Bola continued his stay in the hospital. Ten days ago, I thought he would die. The prayer group wondered how God allowed Bola to be so sick. After we prayed, they agreed they had to put their faith and trust in the Lord.

# Justice and Peace
*1991-1992*

In February, I went on a retreat in Kutu. Afterward, I left for Inongo and arrived after a 10-hour trip across the lake. The heat and humidity made for a sweltering day. Shortly after my arrival, Father Jeff and I went to see the prison director. Father Jeff said that on November 24, President Mobutu pardoned all prisoners with less than two years left to serve. Father Jeff could not believe that Luba remained in prison. The director in Inongo expressed surprise, and he said the blame fell on the Kiri prison director.

We left Inongo for Kiri. The weather cooled, and we had a pleasant 11-hour trip. I went to see the prison director. "You were supposed to have given Luba his freedom on November 24 of last year," I informed him. The director squirmed in his chair as he looked very nervous. "I did not receive the declaration from Inongo," he replied. I knew he was lying. He just wanted to continue to receive the 10,000 Zaires Luba paid him each month. After more discussion, he promised to come to Pendjua in one week to give Luba his documents. I again felt that he lied, as usually, Luba should have to go to Kiri.

#

Once back home, I made hospital rounds with Dr. Ewusu. We discovered eight more AIDS patients in the last two weeks. Dr.

103

Ewusu did not like to tell the patients they had a fatal disease, so I talked to them and their families. I feared that within another year, the hospital would be half full of AIDS patients. Nurses from ten different health centers arrived for a one-week continuing education session. We devoted three days to lessons on AIDS.

The discussion on AIDS prevention became a lively topic. The primary means of prevention required marital fidelity, which rarely happened in this culture. The people with AIDS here were heterosexual, and the number of women infected equaled the number of men. In Kinshasa, a research team tested 1,000 prostitutes, and 800 tested positive for AIDS. The nurses believed AIDS would be a terrible problem if people did not change their sexual habits. The young people were the hardest to convince that AIDS would be a significant killer among them.

#

After the AIDS sessions, I took a trip to a new region I had not visited before. A tribe to the north of Pendjua requested me to open health centers in their area. First, I had to ask permission from the medical director in Mbandaka, as these tribes were in another region. I received approval and scheduled the trip. The people opened 51 kilometers of road and built 20 log bridges, which allowed us to visit the whole area. They did an impressive job, and that increased my willingness to help.

The nurse supervisor, Bola, Luba, and I headed north and arrived at Befili. We received a warm and noisy welcome from the Bom Baj tribe. The people were not Ekonda; instead, they were Mongo. The Mongo people are a Bantu ethnic group and the second-largest ethnic group in the Congo. The region also has many Botoa villages. The Mongo treated the Botoa here the same way the Ekonda treated the Botoa in Pendjua.

We stayed in Befili, and the following day we took a trip through 12 villages. At each community, we stopped and talked to the people about the health program. The visits gave us an idea of the number of people in each place. Luba and Bola recorded the number of huts.

At Betsimbola, the Protestants built an elementary school and a high school. American Protestants from Disciples of Christ had evangelized this region. American missionary doctors and nurses once staffed this largest hospital in the western part of the area. The Americans left in 1975 and turned the administration over to the Zairians. The hospital went broke in 1978 and never reopened. For over ten years, the whole area did not have health care. To make matters worse, the state hospital located 70 kilometers further west no longer functioned.

We continued our trip. The village of Boyera sat on the bank of a beautiful river. This village had a Catholic elementary school and church. The nearby river fed into the Momboyo River, where the mission Imbonga was situated. I visited this mission in 1989, and CICM hoped to staff Imbonga in a year or two.

### Trip to Rome

In April, I traveled to Rome to attend a conference on social ministry. The topics included justice and peace, rural development, and promotion of self-development. We also learned about the culture and its influence on development, non-violent means to change dictator governments, the church's social doctrines, and liberation theology.

Confreres from each country reported on their work. They shared about the problems of justice and peace they confronted. It surprised me that the countries in Latin America and Africa were going backward instead of forward. Poverty, disease, and oppression were worse now than 30 years ago. They blamed most of the misery on corrupt dictators who were kept in power by the countries in Europe, the U.S., and Russia.

During the last week of the conference, we had group sessions. We made proposals concerning the following issues: development, human rights, non-violence, justice and peace, and popular movements. Each group proposed a plan related to their subject. The one-month conference moved and touched me. Now, I knew a lot more about development work and justice and peace. I also felt energized to continue the work of justice and peace.

#

On my return from Rome, I stopped in Kinshasa. The prices shocked me as they had gone up 25 percent in one month. The people of Kinshasa suffered a lot as most families only ate one meal a day. An ordinary worker received 150,000 to 200,000 Zaires a month, which would be the equivalent of $30-$40 a month in the U.S. A sack of manioc cost 100,000 Zaires. One bag fed a family of four for three weeks. I could not imagine spending one-half of my monthly salary on food. Many strikes took place throughout the city, and the post office and university also closed as a result.

#

In June, my team and I left to visit the land of the Bombomba tribe. We traveled on a dirt and gravel road through the forest and swamp and crossed 40 log bridges and did not fall through a single one. I appreciated that the people worked very hard to replace them. Also, they had constructed a building for the health center and a home for the nurse.

We were amazed to see three thousand people waiting for us to arrive. In the evening, they performed traditional dances and served us dinner. We arose early the following day as we had a full day of work ahead of us. We explained how the center would function. I advised them that the center's success or failure depended on the people and their health committee.

We loaded the jeep and headed for the second center in Betsimbola. This location had the largest village and the only high school in the area. We arrived in the afternoon, and after a short rest, we watched a soccer match between the Bantu and the Pygmy teams. I gave each village a soccer ball. After we examined 30 patients, we left for Befili.

Another large crowd awaited us. The county councilman gave a speech, and he used a parable to explain the people's responsibilities. He started by saying a boy became a man when he took a wife. The man had certain obligations. He built a home and cut and cultivated fields. Then, he had to go to the future wife's father to ask for her hand in marriage. The councilman asked, "Would a woman want to marry a man who did not have a house?

106

Would a woman marry a man who did not have a field and who did not hunt game for her?" Everyone responded, "No, never!"

The councilman continued, "Well then, a man who wants a wife will build a hut, cut fields, and hunt game. You see, the health center nurse is like a wife. We have to construct a center and a home for him. We have to repair the roads so that his father, Dr. Jerry, will bring him here. You have done this, and now we have a nurse and medications. But the work is not finished. Suppose a married man became lazy and drank all the time and gambled. Then he no longer cut and planted fields and stopped hunting. Would his wife's mother be happy? Would his wife be satisfied? Would his wife want to stay with him?" Everyone exclaimed, "No, never!"

He added, "Well, if you do not maintain the roads, then the doctor cannot deliver medicines. If you do not maintain the health center building, and it begins to fall, will our wife, the nurse, want to remain with us? Will our white father, Dr. Jerry, want to stay with us?" They responded, "No, never." The man ended by saying, "Well then, we have to fulfill our obligations forever if we want the health center to remain." Everyone agreed.

#

I am happy to announce that on July 3, Luba's wife, Ndongo, gave birth to a baby girl. They now had four girls. Luba accepted the birth of a girl with joy. It feels good to share some positive news.

### Bombomba Region

Last month, we had opened three new health centers in the Bombomba area. We left early Monday morning to return to this area. Upon our arrival at the first village, we encountered the new commissioner for the zone. We stopped to talk with him, and he became upset. He demanded to know who gave us the authority to open health centers in his area. I informed him that his predecessor authorized the health centers. The commissioner continued to be very sarcastic and antagonistic.

"Look," I told him, "if you do not want us to work here, just say so, and we will close the centers and return to Pendjua." Then, his tone changed, and he said, "I do not want to deprive the people of health care. You have my permission to keep the centers." Well, I did not need his permission, as the governor and the medical director authorized us to open the centers. However, it helped to know that the commissioner wouldn't cause any more trouble.

We climbed into the jeep and continued to Boyera. However, Luba and the nurse supervisor, Bitumba, were upset and angry after the encounter and wanted to return to Pendjua. I told them the people were not at fault for having an unfit commissioner. We treated 35 patients in Boyera and then continued to Betsimbola, where we encountered the commissioner. Once again, he confronted us.

"You must pay a tax of 1,000,000 Zaires," he demanded. I knew they could not legally charge the tax, as the health centers were state-owned, and the missionaries were tax-exempt. "I don't have 1,000,000 Zaires with me," I stated. "Then you can pay me next month," he replied.

After we left, we decided to close the centers. The people in the villages were agitated and told me they would beat up the commissioner. Once home, I wrote to the governor and the medical director and informed them about closing the health centers. I refused to return there until the authorities cooperated and canceled the tax. I knew the governor would be furious and order the commissioner not to interfere with the health centers. I hope and believe we will go back there in the future.

#

Upon my return, I learned that the civil unrest in Kinshasa continued. Trouble also occurred in Kiri. A gang of 30 men broke into a missionary storehouse and stole various items. We met with the people of Pendjua. We warned them that if anyone took medicines from the hospital, they would be the ones to suffer. Each clan agreed to provide a night security guard. From that night forward, ten men with bows and arrows and shotguns guarded the mission hospital.

I received a letter from a medical student I helped support in Kinshasa. He felt discouraged that the university would not open this year. He wrote how downtown Kinshasa was a disaster, and the rioters ransacked every store. Thirty square blocks were devastated by the riots. They even raided the factories, and now thousands of people were unable to work. All the European and American business people and government workers left. Only the missionaries remained.

#

I was not surprised when a delegation from Bombomba arrived to talk to me. They requested we reopen the three centers we closed on October 1 due to the issue caused by the commissioner. The people had sent a delegation to the commissioner's office to insist he cancel the tax. He wrote me a letter and asked me to reopen the health centers. The three nurses also arrived to pick up their equipment and medications. I am glad that it appears the commissioner has seen the light.

#

The bishop came and encouraged us to stay and help the people. His visit lifted our morale. The bishops in the country criticized Mobutu and called for him to step down. Mobutu seemed bent on destroying the country. He had raised all salaries by 1,000 percent in October. The hospital nurses who earned 400,000 Zaires a month now received 4,000,000 Zaires. However, the bank in Inongo did not have any money, so the hospital nurses had not been paid for two months.

In December, the nurse's October salaries arrived. The delay resulted because the government needed to print more money to pay the increased wages. The price of all goods went up 1,000 percent overnight. A chicken that cost 20,000 Zaires now cost 200,000 Zaires, and soap went from 10,000 Zaires to 100,000 Zaires. No one gained anything.

Everyone rejoiced when they received a large amount of money. However, it would only be a short time before the people realized the new currency had very little value. There would likely be riots in the cities again. I encouraged the people to spend their money and not save any, as it would soon be worthless.

*1992*

Early this year brought great sadness. Luba and Ndongo's six-month-old daughter died of pneumonia and malaria on February 11. She had been sick for three days and then became short of breath on Monday night. By noon on Tuesday, her condition was critical. After I gave her a transfusion, she seemed in less danger; however, she died at midnight. Over 300 people attended the burial, and Bola led the prayer service.

In the villages, the people buried the dead in the yards of their homes. They dug the little girl's grave in the front of Luba's house. Luba and his brother Mbomba lowered the casket into the ground. Then, Ndongo and Luba covered the coffin with dirt.

### *Kiri Hospital*

While sadness prevailed in February, by early March, Zaire continued toward total economic ruin. For five months, the medical, teaching, and government personnel did not receive any pay. The schools closed, as well as the two largest hospitals in Kinshasa. The regional medical director asked Dr. Ewusu and me to take over the Kiri hospital and two health centers. The former doctor transferred to another health zone. Dr. Ewusu wanted to go to the Kiri hospital as long as I helped him with equipment and medications.

We went to Kiri to talk to the commissioner and to inspect the hospital. We met with him and his department directors and discussed their request to take over the Kiri hospital and the functioning health centers. The commissioner said everyone believed I would take over the hospital and live in Kiri. I interrupted him, "No, I will not be the one coming to Kiri. It will be Dr. Ewusu."

The commissioner fumed, and he asked his secretary to read the regional medical director's letter. Since they could not find their copy, I gave them mine. He read it aloud three times before agreeing that Dr. Ewusu had been named director. I assured them I would do all I could to make their hospital like the one in Pendjua.

We visited the buildings and made an inventory. The condition of the building's interior shocked me. They were the dirtiest places I had ever seen. In the operating room, layers of dirt covered the boxes of medical instruments and the operating table. I could not imagine how the previous doctor even thought of operating in that filth. Twenty rusty metal beds without springs and mattresses sat among the five pavilions, and broken, dirty equipment filled the lab.

"Are you sure you want to work here?" I asked Dr. Ewusu. "I'll work here, but not without your help," he responded. I filled a notebook with a list of equipment they needed. Now I had to wait to see if the Father Provincial would allow me to write a budget.

I often wake up at night and ask myself if I want to get involved in this endeavor. The answer is always "yes." The people in Kiri have not had good health care since 1974. The seriously ill patients come to Pendjua, which is a 63-kilometer walk.

When we returned home, we brought five patients with us. More than 20 other patients wanted to come with me to Pendjua. The sad state of health care in Kiri gave me greater motivation to help them.

#

As each week passed, the political and economic situation deteriorated further. In Pendjua, the people suffered less than in other places since they had animals, fish, manioc, rice, and cornfields. Of course, they did not have running water, electricity, or other items. The small projects also helped. They had the co-op, a country store, a silk-making enterprise, road crews, and a store run by the Ekonda. These projects kept money in circulation.

We no longer sent the excess Zaires to Kinshasa because the money would run out if we did. No new cash entered Pendjua since the state had not paid salaries, and no trucks came to buy agricultural products. Each county had become an island unto itself. Even the local governments could not function, so authority began to return to the village chiefs' hands.

#

The Father Provincial arrived in Kiri. I met him, and we talked about the hospital project and the plan to reopen the 20 health centers in the area. The people had cut the weeds around the building and scrubbed the hospital's walls and floors. Another group of young men recovered 50 metal hospital beds that the state officials and military personnel confiscated and used in their homes. These young men entered every house in town to search for the beds and tables stolen from the hospital.

#

On Easter, we had a feast for the 54 Kizitos and their leaders. There was a similar organization for girls, ages eight to twelve, and they were called Anaritas. Saint Anarita, a 19-year-old Zairian Sister, died after being shot by soldiers in 1965. They killed her because she refused to take off her clothes and give in to their sexual advances. The Botoa did not have an Anarita group yet. We planned to begin one later in the year. Ndongo and Mboyo, the wives of Luba and Bola, agreed to help.

#

After Easter, I took a six-day trip to visit six health centers. Many of the female patients had secondary infertility problems. After two or three births, they were unable to get pregnant. In Africa, the women wanted five to eight children since three or four died before adulthood. They wanted adult children who could care for them in their later years. They also believed that a dead person remained "alive" if they still had living descendants born before their death. Once there were no more living descendants, then the deceased was deemed to be dead. So, this belief increased their desire for more children.

The most significant cause of secondary infertility was chronically infected tubes, which would cause them to close. I had a device to help open the fallopian tubes that worked for some women. If a wife could only have two or three children, then many men married a second wife. The first wife usually grieved when her husband married again. I believed it was essential to help infertile women have children.

#

Sister Elyse and I prepared instrument trays, obstetrical delivery sets, bandages, medications, laboratory items, and clinical supplies. These items were necessary to reopen the hospital in Kiri. Dr. Ewusu appreciated our efforts. He said he felt fortunate to have our help; otherwise, he would not go to Kiri. Sister Elyse was excited the Kiri hospital would reopen since the medical missionary Sisters started there in 1958. She participated in the first group to go there. The Sisters left in 1974 when a Zairian state doctor pushed them out. Within four years, the hospital no longer functioned. The people of Kiri have suffered much since then.

#

In June, I again returned to Kiri to appoint Dr. Ewusu as the medical director. I made a round trip to Pendjua with the Kiri mission's pickup truck, as my jeep could not haul everything. The nurses and janitors spent the entire day scrubbing the walls, floors, and beds. Many people came to cut the weeds and grass. Knowing that the hospital would function again as it had in the years when the Sisters were there made everyone happy.

When I arrived home, some sad news confronted me. Four soldiers had severely beat Luba just two days earlier. He and a friend had left Liamba on Thursday to buy salt at the store. They encountered four soldiers who blocked their path. When they went to pass, one soldier struck Luba's friend for no apparent reason. Luba went to his aid when the soldiers began to beat him. They took him to jail, took off his clothes, kicked him, and stomped on him. The sergeant arrived and yelled at the soldiers. He commanded the soldiers to give Luba his clothes and sent him home. This news outraged me, and I went to see Luba. He had many wounds and bruises on his back and chest. I sent a report to the county chairman.

After several inquiries, I discovered the soldiers had stolen money from at least seven other people. The Justice and Peace Committee will make a report on each case and send it to the authorities. I suppose the mayor of Pendjua is the real culprit because he called the military to force the people to work on the roads and state grounds. I realize there is a real danger that law and order will break down because the central government is in crisis.

#

In July, I had altercations with the military twice in the same week. They arrested the mission janitor for no reason other than to get back at me for the report I sent to the county chairman. The janitor's wife came to the mission, screaming hysterically. She said the soldiers hit her husband and even hit their son and took them to prison. Father Paul and I immediately went to the chief. I told him if he did not do something, I would go to Inongo to talk to the governor. The village chief sent the chairman to release the janitor and his son.

Two days later, the village chief came to inform me the four soldiers were leaving. He added that they were going to a hearing and were taking Luba with them. The chief and I went to talk to soldiers. "Why are you taking Luba?" I demanded of them. "He has accused us of torture," they responded. "If there is going to be a trial, we will accuse Luba of resisting arrest."

I borrowed the Sister's Toyota and took the group to Kiri to see the county chairman and their commander. We were halfway to Kiri when we encountered a county Land Rover. When we stopped, Dr. Ewusu, the assistant county chairman, and the commander got out. It turned out that Dr. Ewusu had made an official complaint against the soldiers. In retaliation, the soldiers arbitrarily arrested the three health care personnel.

We turned around and returned to Pendjua. The four soldiers in my vehicle were terrified of what would happen. I said, "God hears the cry of the poor and the persecuted, and He is just."

#

The assistant county chairman, Dr. Ewusu, the commander, and I met. The assistant chairman said he would judge the affair. He said, "I will leave with Luba and the soldiers, and Jerry can come tomorrow morning, along with the three witnesses and the chief." I argued, "I don't think Luba should go with them." However, the chairman insisted and promised that Luba would stay at Dr. Ewusu's house and not in the military camp.

I went to Kiri, and Father Louis met with me. He told me that Dr. Ewusu had an altercation with the soldiers. Luba and Dr. Ewusu came and told me what happened when they arrived in Kiri last night. They went straight to the county chairman's home. When Dr. Ewusu and Luba began to leave, the commander said that Luba must stay in the military camp. Dr. Ewusu stated that he would not allow Luba to remain with those beasts. The soldiers became angry and threatened to beat up Dr. Ewusu.

When the commander and the chairman did not move to stop the soldiers, Dr. Ewusu became irate, and he accused the commander of being incompetent. He told them he would go to Inongo and charge them before the governor. Then, Dr. Ewusu called the county chairman the country's biggest coward because he broke the promises he made in Pendjua. The commander stormed out. The soldiers began to depart with Luba, and Dr. Ewusu told them he would stay in prison with Luba. Dr. Ewusu went to his home to change his clothes.

Luba had been in prison for 15 minutes before the county chairman arrived. He told Luba to gather his baggage and come with him to Dr. Ewusu's home. When they arrived, Dr. Ewusu had already gone to the prison. He had dressed in a tattered pair of shorts and a T-shirt and carried two blankets. The county chairman asked the doctor to return since Luba could stay at his home. Dr. Ewusu replied, "No way, it is too late; I will stay in prison with Luba."

The county chairman pleaded with him not to stay at the prison, as it would embarrass him if a county medical director were in jail. The doctor relented, and he and Luba spent the night at his house. "I think the chairman and assistant chairman are afraid of the commander and his soldiers," Dr. Ewusu told me. His observation would be confirmed later.

#

The chairman sent us to the assistant's office since he gave him the responsibility to judge the affair. The assistant asked everyone to leave except for Dr. Ewusu and me. He turned to me and said, "You are a foreigner, and you have been to school. You have come to live among the poorest of the poor and to bring them health care and education. You must try to understand our difficulty. The country is in chaos. There is no respect for law and order. Many officials are corrupt, our commander is uneducated, and you claim he is a criminal. He is responsible for our security; he has guns and bullets, and he is a delinquent. What can we do? I ask you not to press charges and let us deal with these men. There are no charges

against Luba. If you press charges, I don't know what will happen."
We decided to let him handle the affair in his way and agreed not to
press charges against the military.

#

I left for Belgium in mid-September, and from there, I went
to Chicago to see my family. When I arrived, I found my dad to be
seriously ill. We celebrated my parent's 60th wedding anniversary
on Thanksgiving Day. Otto Galloway died on December 13, 1992.
I spent Christmas with my family as I wanted to be with them during
this bittersweet time.

# Missionary Life
*1993-1995*

I left the U.S. for Africa on January 23 and arrived in Kinshasa two days later. Soldiers were everywhere in the airport, and I felt the tension in the air. The soldiers opened everyone's luggage. Somehow, I managed to leave the airport without them searching my bags. From there I went to a large store to shop. When I arrived, the three white owners stood out in front of the store. They had backed up a large truck to block the door. "What's happening?" I questioned. "We expect trouble from the soldiers, and we won't be opening the store," they told me. My shopping trip abruptly ended.

The problem with the military resulted from the soldiers not getting their pay. The government issued five million Zaire bills, but the prime minister declared them illegal and worthless. The shopkeepers refused to accept the currency. However, Mobutu paid the soldiers with these five million Zaire bills, so the soldiers were angry that they could not buy anything with them.

As I walked the streets, suddenly, I heard gunfire coming from two blocks away. By evening, the soldiers were shooting everywhere, so I headed to the conference center. I felt safe here because the American embassy sat just across the street. A group of Marines guarded the embassy, and the Zairian soldiers were afraid to walk down that street. A twelve-foot-high block wall surrounded the conference center yard. I heard gunfire all night, and the next day, because soldiers fired rifles, machine guns, and bazookas. They looted stores, private homes, and many convents and parish houses. Mobutu's special presidential guard got the upper hand by nightfall and drove the regular army back to their two military camps.

On February 9, I found myself still in Kinshasa. I waited for the barge to be loaded to leave for Kutu and eventually to Inongo and Kiri. Kinshasa had been calm for several days as the last fighting took place at the city's edge. Soldiers attacked the Zairian radio and TV station that night. The presidential guard drove them back onto their encampment.

I went to the place I used to get vaccines. However, no one worked there since the trouble started in January. Next, I went to the Youth and Children's Fund building to see some health officials. The building was in the area where looting occurred. Looters had broken into all the stores. They even smashed into and looted the Youth and Children's building. They left nothing behind as they took the light fixtures, toilets, sinks, and other items.

The looters took a large stock of medical supplies for the 14 health zones. Now, many hospitals would be without medication. Looting of pharmaceutical companies and many dispensaries and hospitals occurred. I heard stories about soldiers who took patients from their beds, laid them on the floor, and took their mattresses. At one maternity ward, the soldiers took the babies out of cribs and incubators, put them on the floor, and took off with the cribs. Many parish homes and convents fell victim to looting. The priests and nuns escaped with only the clothes they were wearing.

#

I will provide some context. The U.S., Belgium, and France asked Mobutu to transfer power to the transitional government. Of course, he said he would not do that. Mobutu blamed the prime minister for the trouble, and he fired him. He then asked the high council to appoint a new prime minister to form a "government of salvation." The fired prime minister refused to step down since Belgium, France, and the U.S. supported him. So now they had a standoff. Mobutu held all the power and the only capable army. So, if he did not want to give in, the opposition could do very little.

#

I boarded the barge for Kutu on the 11th. Though I did not look forward to the long trip, I enjoyed the sights along the Congo River, as I had never traveled on it. The barge did not have a cabin, so we slept under the stars. A shelter with a rusted sheet metal roof protected us from the scorching sun and the heavy rain. They lowered some canopies during a driving rainstorm. The first night, we slept on the barge in the port because the boat captain wanted to leave early in the morning. I didn't get much sleep as dozens of boats anchored in the harbor, and people talked and sang all night.

We left the port very early and began our five-day trip to Kutu. Everyone read magazines or books as we had nothing else to do but talk, read, sleep, eat, pray, and look at the scenery. We ate fresh fish twice a day. There were always fishermen who were willing to sell their catch. At night the barge pulled over to a riverbank, threw out the anchor, and everyone slept.

The barge departed at 4:30 each morning. We laid seven mattresses out side-by-side at night and then stacked them up in a dry place each day. There were no private rooms or bathrooms on the barge. At night, we put on our shorts and plunged into the river for a bath. After two days on the Congo River, we came to a large village called Kwamouth, where the River Kwa joins the Congo River. The early CICM missionaries had opened their first mission here in 1888. However, an outbreak of sleeping sickness occurred, and over half of them died within the first three years.

We entered the Kwa River and continued our trip to Mushie, and arrived at noon on Monday. There was a mission house, so we ate dinner there before we continued our journey. A few miles upstream, we entered the Fimi River, which originated at the end of Lake Mai Ndombe (Inongo). We arrived in Kutu on Tuesday afternoon and stayed there for five days before departing for Inongo for the final day of our long voyage.

#

I arrived in Pendjua on February 23, after being in Zaire for one month. Everyone was thrilled to see me. I received an update that Luba and Ndongo had a baby girl born on December 24, 1992.

They named the girl Rita after my mother. I went to see the baby and showed them a picture of my mother.

Later, I went to Ngondo Banga to see everyone. On my way, I passed through three villages. The women and children stopped me and swarmed all over me. Being back home made me very happy.

#

Now, I had to get up to speed on recent happenings. I learned that the AIDS problem increased in the zone of Kiri. Though we have education programs about AIDS, most do not accept the truth and will not change their ways. Fortunately, there are no Botoa with AIDS since the two races rarely mix. There are a few Botoa prostitutes with Ekonda clients, so it will only be a matter of time before the Botoa become infected. The young Botoa men know which Botoa women practice prostitution. They also know which ones visit the Ekonda. They pass the word to refuse the prostitutes who sleep with the Ekonda.

#

The new Zairian doctor, Dr. Botuli, arrived. His birthplace was Kiri, and he had studied at a university in southern Zaire. He finished his studies in 1991 and worked in the Congo Republic because he could not find work in Zaire. When the state health system had collapsed in 1988, doctors had no way to be paid. The villagers could not bear the salary of a doctor.

I made hospital rounds with Dr. Botuli. Then, I met with Luba and Mbomba's family. We discussed the opportunity to send Mbomba to a new teaching college in Inongo. The priests in the parish there promised to help Mbomba find room and board. Mbomba had a wife and one child, with another one on the way. After much discussion, they gave their approval.

*Currency Exchange*

A new crisis came to Zaire in late October when the government decided to change the money. One new Zaire equaled three million old Zaire. The people had until November 21 to exchange their money. The closest bank was in Inongo, which would require a two or three-day trip without a vehicle or boat. In my opinion, this new plan felt no different than legalized stealing by the government. The health project would lose thousands of dollars since we could not stop treating the people. We agreed not to close the hospital and health centers.

During the next week, we dealt with the exchange of money. The government issued new money, and the people exchanged their old money for the new currency. The process seemed to be an impossible project for people in the interior. After service on Sunday, we told the people to bring their money to the mission. We sent men on bicycles out to the villages to inform everyone.

By Monday, many people arrived and left their money. The next day I took three trunks and two boxes of cash to Kiri. The remaining amount got counted and packed into boxes, and sent to Kiri. The bank in Inongo then received the currency. We waited for the new money to arrive.

The total funds collected were 6 billion Zaires, or $2,500. This total amount of money for a population of 35,000 people showed their extreme poverty. For now, no one had any money, so the people returned to the barter system. All stores closed, so the people had no way to buy soap, salt, and other necessities. The new money had already devalued by 500 percent. The mission provided health care for almost free as the people had no way to pay for it. A few years earlier, I thought the situation in Zaire was terrible. In comparison to today, those were much better years.

At month-end, the health workers received five months of back pay. The total did not equal one month of what they now received. The value of their salary in October 1992 equaled $19.00. The new amount had an equivalent value of $1.33.

#

I have to admit that I often reflect on how I ended up here in the rainforest. I know if it were not for Jesus, I would not be here. I could not suffer the trials and tribulations of life and work here if it were not for the Lord's grace. However, no amount of suffering can take away my joy and peace.

As Christmas approaches, the people rejoice even though they have nothing to celebrate in the eyes of many. They are more impoverished than ever before. There will be no clothes, toys, or candy this year. The children do not have stockings to hang on the mud walls of their huts. Despite the poverty, the people rejoice and find happiness in the little things.

The Kizitos wore the one pair of shorts they owned, sewn by my sister-in-law, Sonya. The high school boys wore pants they had received two years ago. The children would be happy if their fathers killed an antelope or monkey to have for Christmas dinner. One Kizito said, "Jesus' mother, Mary, did not have anything to clothe Jesus in. Our mothers don't have anything to clothe us, so we're more like Jesus."

*1994*

In early January, Luba, Bola, and I left for the mission in Beronge. We used Father Andrew's 15-foot-long wooden boat. With only an eight-horsepower motor, the trip took nine hours. The mission staff hired an experienced fisherman as a guide. The floodwaters inundated the forest, so we could not see where the banks of the river were. The river had so many twists and turns that our experienced guide became lost two times.

We left Beronge and stayed the night at the rectory of an old mission site in Ireko. This mission was the first in the region, but they relocated it to the more central village of Beronge in 1963.

#

Once home, I spent the day packing for my trip to Kutu. It will take two days to travel to Kutu by boat. When we arrived at the dock, at least thirty people wanted to board the vessel. It would be impossible to take all these people. I allowed the ten people who already asked permission to board, and then we left for Inongo.

When we arrived at Lake Mai Ndombe, a violent wind and rainstorm came upon us. The waves were so high that we docked on an island for one hour. When it seemed to calm down, we started again, until another massive storm began. The waves were so rough that the cable attaching the barge to the tugboat snapped. I rode on the barge, and I thought for sure it would turn over in the waves. The tug pulled up alongside, and we struggled to tie the barge to it. Then, we retreated to the nearby shore and anchored there for two hours.

During the storm, Father Antoine smashed his right thumb in the cabin door when the cable snapped. Blood poured out from a deep cut, and his thumbnail had torn off. I took gauze and tape from my bag, bandaged up the wound, and managed to stop the bleeding. After the wind died down, we continued to Inongo.

### *Lutoy River*

In March, I went on the road to Beronge, and the trip took longer than anticipated. If I thought that was the only issue we would face, I was mistaken. We arrived at the Lutoy River. Someone had pushed a homemade ferry onto the bank. The chauffeur forgot to bring the ropes used to tie the boat to the post, so he improvised with vines. I knew I should not try to drive the jeep onto the ferry, but we were behind schedule. When the front wheels mounted the planks, the vines broke. The boat moved away from the bank, and the jeep, with me in it, plunged into the river.

By the time I opened the door and got out, water poured in through the windows. The murky water rose to my shoulders. Luba and the others were in shock. The jeep settled into the river until only the upper half of the back door stuck out of the water. We opened the back door and unloaded our luggage and the five cartons of medications. We got out the block and tackle and managed to pull the jeep up on the bank. Afterward, we chose to cross the river in a dugout canoe and stayed the night at the old mission in Ireko.

The chauffeur rode a bicycle to Beronge to get the jeep. I did not sleep well for several days as I worried about how to have my vehicle repaired. The chauffeur arrived, and we went on to the village. The people were anxious for us to come, and they were grateful I did not drown.

#

I went to the health center to examine 25 patients. Father Daniel arrived in the morning and began to work on the jeep. He could not get it started. We thought it would be best to return to Kiri and send a tractor to tow the vehicle there. Several mornings later, the driver took us to Pendjua. A massive crowd had gathered at the mission before our arrival. Stories traveled like wildfire, and many people heard rumors that I had drowned. They were thrilled to see me alive. I received a good dose of humiliation and a lesson that haste makes waste.

#

After being home for one night, Mfutu, the nurse supervisor, and I left for Kiri by boat the following day. The chauffeur from the mission went with us because the river passed through the rainforest. There were many large creeks, small streams, and lakes, and one could quickly become lost. The first day, we went to Ilunga, and the entire village waited on the bank to welcome us.

The following day, many people lined up to see me, and I did my best and checked 50 patients. We ate a quick lunch, loaded the boat, and headed for the next village that bordered a small lake. We entered a small creek filled with dead trees, stumps, and logs. When we arrived at the bank, a women's dance troupe met us. A half-mile trail led from the lake to the village. The women danced and sang all the way there.

There were hundreds of children in the community. Everyone looked well-nourished, as their diet consisted of fish, turtles, and alligators. We met with the health committee and then with the villagers. The following day, I saw 40 patients. After lunch, we headed for Ibeke, the location of the first mission in the lake region. It began in 1908, and in 1950, the missionaries left and moved to Kiri. The brick school, the convent, and the dispensary still stood and were usable.

#

I visited Luba in July, and I talked to him and Ndongo about Luba's drinking problem. He had become an alcoholic. When he became drunk, he turned very mean and beat Ndongo. While I was in Beronge, Bola told me that things had become worse due to Luba's drinking. I knew I had to do something before anything worse happened. So, that morning, we had a long talk. We talked about the reasons why he drank so much. I learned that the problem started in

1984 when Luba went to prison. Then in 1991, their six-month-old daughter died.

"Luba, you have to stop, or you will risk losing your job, wife, and even your life," I told him. He broke down in tears. "I want to quit, but I do not know how to, and I am afraid to."

Together we prayed and asked God for strength to help Luba stop. I placed Luba on heavy sedation. The next day, Luba, Ndongo, and I talked about how the family could improve the situation. I learned that Ndongo drank a lot as well. She and Luba both agreed not to keep any alcohol in the house any longer. I planned to continue to talk to Luba to help him surface his problems. Luba also harbored much-suppressed resentment against his father, who had abandoned his family when Luba was only ten years old.

The following week I went to Luba's for dinner. We ate wild boar, manioc greens, and roots. I could not believe the change in Ndongo and the four girls since Luba had quit drinking. The girls told me they now had joy and happiness. I never missed an opportunity to talk against alcohol and the misery it caused. If I were the chief, I would arrest the people who made alcohol. Then, I would destroy the stills because it was illegal for them to make whiskey. Since only the Ekonda made whiskey, I was not very popular with some of them.

#

Several days later, Sister Elyse had a severe malaria attack, and she recovered very slowly. Three weeks prior, she fell off her bicycle and hurt her back. Instead of improving, her back became worse, and she could barely walk. I decided it would be best for her to go to Europe for a thorough checkup. Her absence would put another burden on me because only Sister Elyse knew the accounting for the hospital. Before she left, I spent an entire day learning her system.

#

The provincial council decided not to renew Dr. Ewusu's contract and the Kiri hospital project. Dr. Ewusu came and told me my superiors were his enemies. However, I believed that he brought the problems upon himself since he rarely went to the hospital.

Unfortunately, this meant that most people in Kiri came to Pendjua for health care.

Each afternoon before Christmas, we made holiday preparations. This year we were able to give each boy a pair of shorts. The shorts we gave them three years ago were threadbare. In the village, the boys wore shorts filled with holes and tears or wore breechcloths.

A group of 138 lekis (little brothers) came to the mission. They were between the ages of seven and twelve years old. To receive the shorts, the boys went into the conference room ten at a time. The big brothers helped them find a pair that fit. The boys, soaked in sweat, crowded into the doorway as they pushed and screamed. I feared that some might suffocate. The boys were worried there would not be enough pairs of shorts to go around. When we finished the distribution, we had a few pairs left. The boys were happy to have shorts for the new year ahead.

### *1995*

One night in early January, I listened to a program about foreign aid on Voice of America. I will use this opportunity to share my reflections. I agree that much international help goes to waste, but that does not justify a lower support level. When the African countries became independent in the late 1950s and early 1960s, an ideological battle to win their governments' hearts took place. The U.S. and western Europe were on one side of the fight, and the communist countries were on the other side. Dictators received support if they agreed to join either one or the other of the ideological camps.

Zaire is a good example. Mobutu came to power in a military camp in 1965. He immediately aligned himself with the West. Two neighboring countries, Angola and the Congo Republic were on the communist side. The U.S., Belgium, and France poured money into Zaire to keep Mobutu in their camp. These countries also armed Mobutu. They gave him millions of dollars, much of which he used for himself and his supporters. The countries that supported Mobutu seemed to turn their backs on the human rights violations in Zaire.

In my opinion, Mobutu does not care if the health care and education systems collapse. He is not concerned if anyone receives wages or that the people suffer. Mobutu and his supporters appear to be living the "good life." In my view, they received these riches in the name of anti-communism. So, who is to blame?

I feel that the poor African people are powerless to change their governments. I think many conflicts in Africa resulted from tribalism, and I believe that the inter-tribal issues started during colonial times. During this era, the colonial powers divided Africa into countries and did not consider tribal boundaries. For example, they split the Bantu tribal lands between Zaire, Angola, and Zambia. This division caused problems because the respective chiefs did not recognize these false divisions.

What is the solution? I don't claim to have the answers. However, I believe foreign aid should go to non-profit, non-governmental organizations (NGOs). These organizations can be held accountable for the assistance they receive and their results evaluated. I believe it is essential to develop and handle the projects with the local people.

#

When I first came here, I learned that the Botoa men had to cut the forest to make fields for the Ekonda. The Botoa women had to plant, weed, and harvest the fields. They received corn and cassava as payment. They did not have farms because the Ekonda convinced them that God would not give them a harvest. If a Botoa hunter killed an antelope, he had to give half to his master. Any intermixing of the races was forbidden. If they caught an Ekonda man with a Botoa woman, they banned him from his village. Then they made him live with the Botoa, and they considered him to be one of them.

This total separation has spared the Botoa from sickle cell anemia, a hereditary blood disease of the Ekonda. A Botoa man cannot greet an Ekonda woman or give her a drink of water. If he does, he receives a severe beating. When Ekonda men and Botoa women encounter one another on a path, the women enter the forest.

127

Then the women turn their backs to the trail until the men pass. An Ekonda man cannot eat food cooked by a Botoa woman.

The hospital even has separate wards for the Ekonda and the Botoa. There are very few Botoa children in school because the Ekonda children taunt them and call them nyama (animals). Discrimination exists even in the church. The Botoa sit on one side of the aisle, and the Ekonda sit on the other side.

One Ekonda catechist taught the Botoa they were descendants of Canaan. He told them Noah had cursed them and made them slaves of Shem (see Genesis 9:25-27). Therefore, they are to remain slaves of the Ekonda, who are descendants of Shem. This story reminded me of a Baptist newspaper I read in Georgia in 1967. The article cited the same Bible passage to explain why black Americans should remain slaves. I found it strange how two different people, thousands of miles apart, used the same Bible passage to justify slavery and discrimination.

\#

When I arrived in Africa in 1981, the racism and discrimination that I witnessed horrified me. Years earlier, I had been a civil rights worker in the battlefields of the South. Then I moved to the Congo to live with the Botoa and organize them and fight for their rights. I befriended a group of ten young-adult, Catholic Botoa. After a few months, we built a mud hut in a neighboring Botoa village, where I stayed on the weekends.

I spent months listening to their history, stories, grievances, and struggles. Little by little, I learned their language, Lotwa. I came to know and love these marginalized people. We formed a Christian community and met to reflect on the gospels. The group came to learn that God never intended anyone to be the slaves of another.

\#

I believe the first step in their liberation is for them to become self-sufficient in food production. So, I motivated the Botoa to clear and plant fields for their use. Eventually, I convinced three young Botoa to cut an area with me. We had an abundant harvest. However, the young men said God gave them a plentiful harvest because I was white. Despite these obstacles, the young men cut their fields. Fourteen years later, most of the Botoa in this area have farms. They no longer share the fruits of their hunting with the Ekonda unless they receive payment.

Naturally, there is opposition from the Ekonda. However, the local congressman supports my efforts. Many of the Ekonda are my friends, and they agree the discrimination must end.

#

It made me happy when Sister Elyse returned. When the Toyota was at least 15 miles away, the "talking drums" (drums used to send messages) sent word of her pending arrival. Over 1,500 people gathered at the hospital and convent before she arrived. We had a joyful and tearful reunion. We met on Friday to plan for the last eight months the Sisters would be at the mission.

The chief of Pendjua published a list of taxes due for the bicycles, temporary workers, soap-making projects, and other items. I informed him that missionaries were tax-exempt. Two days after Sister Elyse returned, he went and asked her for taxes. They argued for two hours. He would not leave, so Sister Elyse gave him 240,000 Zaire's, or about $60. This act agitated me, and I told Sister Elyse she should have summoned me since she knew we never paid taxes.

I wrote to the county chairman and the governor and asked their opinion on the matter. The chief became afraid and angry because he knew he had acted illegally. Then, he dared to send his secretary to ask me to pay taxes on the bicycles we used to transport vaccines. I lashed out at him, and he fled from my office. I was still upset. Then, I read in the Gospel of Luke, where Jesus said we are to love our enemies, do good to those who hate us, and pray for those who mistreat us. "Jesus," I prayed, "It's hard at times to carry out Your teachings, but I will try to do what You say, and I will pray for the chief."

#

I taught 20 barefoot doctors this week, and I tried a new technique developed in South Africa for illiterate adults. I presented a picture of a specific health issue. Then I asked a group of four or six people to discuss their answers to the following six questions: 1) What is happening in the picture? 2) What is the main issue or disease? 3) Why is this happening? 4) Does this happen in your village? 5) What causes the problem? 6) What can we do about it?

The first picture showed a dilapidated house without an outhouse. One child had intestinal worms while another made a bowel movement in the bushes next to the house. The following picture showed a creek near the village. One person washed his clothes in the stream while another boy urinated into it. Downstream, a woman filled a water jug from the creek. The pictures provoked much discussion. Each group drew up a plan to solve the problem.

By week's end, we discussed 32 different problems depicted on the charts. The topics ranged from health issues to agriculture, money, housing, and education. The barefoot doctors were anxious to return to their villages and use the charts to teach the people.

### The Imposter

At the end of May, I left for the U.S. to spend time with family and friends. On September 9, I arrived in Kinshasa and hoped to go to Inongo within a few days. When I arrived at the airport, I encountered a problem. The driver who always picked me up and helped me through immigration and customs had died two weeks prior. The new driver did not know the process. He did not meet me at the gate and instead waited outside the airport. The driver waited a short while, and then he left. When I got off the plane, a well-dressed man approached me. He claimed the procure sent him, and he would help me through immigration and customs. It turned out the man was an imposter and a thief.

I became suspicious when he did not take me through immigration. The man escorted me to the VIP lounge. I never went there before. The man wanted my baggage claims so he could get the bags. I told him we would wait until immigration returned my passport. Then, we would go together to pick up the baggage.

I picked up the suitcases, hired two porters to help, and went through customs. There I encountered a problem. I thought everything seemed to be in order, so one porter and I went through the gate. Then the imposter and the other porter left in the opposite direction. I quickly followed them. After some discussion, they agreed to follow me. Once outside, I discovered no one waited there to meet me. I found myself stranded with my suitcases, three shady characters, and no taxis. I thought they would steal my luggage.

Just then came an answer to prayer. Two English Baptist missionaries appeared in a Land Rover. They stopped and asked me if I needed a ride. We loaded the suitcases and left. I could not wait to get back to Pendjua.

#

After I arrived home, the Bishop of Inongo came to celebrate a Mass of thanksgiving. He thanked the Sisters for their service and said goodbye. I decided not to accompany the Sisters to Kiri, where they would take a private plane to Kinshasa. I believed that the people's emotions, especially the Botoa, would run high. Hopefully, my presence would have a calming effect.

The Sister's departure marked the end of a vital era at the mission. Before they left, I ate dinner with them, and we prayed and reminisced about our many years together. The Sisters had been at the mission since 1958 and left behind a well-equipped and well-run hospital. Though they were sad, the people did not overreact to the Sisters' departure. I believed the transition would be smooth. My role would be more of an administrator than a doctor. I hoped a second doctor would arrive by early November.

After a four-month absence, it was so good to be back in Pendjua. A large crowd of Botoa came to greet me a few days later. Luba and Bola and their families remained in good health. The people were quite sad the Sisters left. There were four African Sisters to take their place, and I believed they would do a good job.

#

In the past few months, a terrible dysentery epidemic (bloody diarrhea) broke out, and many people died. This disease resulted from contaminated drinking water. I knew we had to make a considerable effort to improve the water quality. Each day, one or two more people died from the horrible epidemic, despite treatment with IV fluids and antibiotics. The outbreak hit the Botoa hard as 20 to 30 deaths occurred in some villages. Many Botoa believed that dysentery was either a scourge from God or a curse from their dead ancestors. Therefore, few came to the health centers for treatment.

The four new African Sisters adapted well to the demands. Two employees worked at the hospital, and two worked in the agriculture project and at the social center for the Botoa girls. One new Sister, Sister Augustine, previously worked in youth ministry. She wanted to take over the girl's Christian youth group. Sister Augustine was an answer to my prayers, as I always wanted to do more for the Botoa girls.

I prayed for an end to the epidemic of dysentery. Not only did it not relent, but some cases were also resistant to the available antibiotics. I knew that newer medicines existed in the U.S. and Europe. However, they were costly, so I planned to ask the provincial if the congregation could buy some. I asked everyone who received my letters to pray for the suffering people and the epidemic to end.

#

The new doctor, Dr. Bakoko, arrived at the mission. Since we had two doctors, I went back to doing administrative work. However, I kept an eye on the Botoa patients who had dysentery. Currently, there were 20 dysentery patients at the hospital. It saddened me to see them on their bamboo beds with a bedpan underneath and almost continuous diarrhea. Many family members who cared for the sick also contracted dysentery.

Father Joseph, the Inongo district superior, told us to spare no cost, as the congregation will give us funds. We talked to the procure in Kinshasa by ham radio, asking him to order more potent antibiotics from Belgium. I noticed that some Ekonda nurses did not give the Botoa patients good care. I met with them and reminded them of their moral obligations to provide proper treatment to everyone, regardless of race or beliefs.

New dysentery patients arrived each day. I visited them in the afternoons and helped the mothers give young children oral rehydration solutions. Some children refused to drink the liquid because it tasted salty. Many children did not have clothes, and the rags they wore were so filthy they were in shreds. I took new shorts and shirts to them, and it brought smiles to their anguished faces.

The doctors and nurses did not have gowns and gloves to protect against contagious diseases because they were too expensive. We saved our medical gowns and gloves to use solely in the operating room. I did not worry about getting infected. The best prevention was the continuous washing of one's hands after caring for the patients. Since Friday was a holiday, the cleaning man did not work. I grabbed a mop and bucket, went to the Botoa ward, and cleaned it with a disinfectant solution.

# Photographs of Dr. Jerry

*Jerry studying while in Peace Corps*

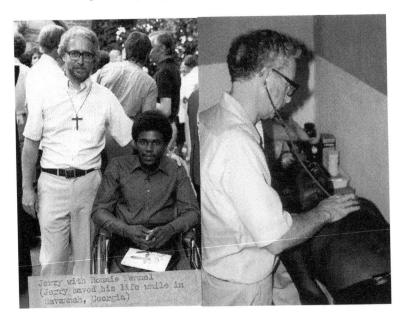

*Jerry with Ronald*      *Jerry treating a patient*

*Jerry's ordination as a Brother with CICM*

*Jerry at home with his mother, sister, and brother*

*Jerry examining a child*

*Hazardous road conditions*

*Boys with a pig for pig raising project*

*Dinner time at the boarding home*

*Jerry with "barefoot doctors"*

*Jerry tutoring students*

*Jerry with a local clan of Pygmies*

*Luba (right) with one of his daughters*

*Repairing a log bridge*

*Mealtime*

*Young men's prayer group*

*Jerry in his hut in a village*

*Bola (left) with his son*

*Possibly a village clinic*

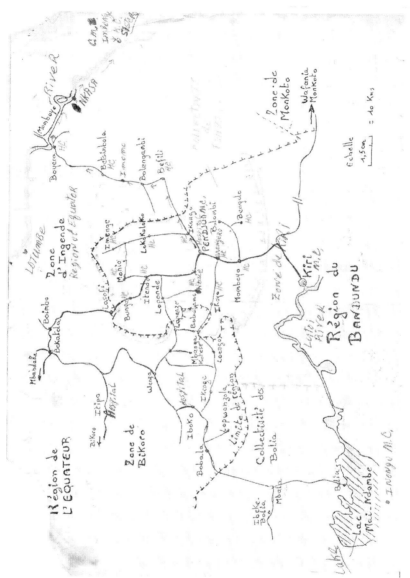

*Hand-drawn map of region Jerry worked*
*(HC = health center)*

# The Great Rainforest
## *1996*

At the start of the new year, the dysentery epidemic continued to decimate the Botoa Pygmy villages. During November, the number of cases diminished, but now they started to increase again. The two Botoa wards were full of patients. I took 15 bamboo mats over to the hospital to use for beds. With the new antibiotics for the resistant cases, I believed that the cure rate would be higher.

One morning, a young Botoa woman, half-naked, came to my door and wept. Her husband had dysentery, and his pair of shorts had been so stained that he laid naked on a mat. I gave her shorts for him and a half sheet to wrap around his waist. We did not supply hospital gowns for the patients because we did not have the budget for them.

#

Though the need in Pendjua was great, Dr. Botuli and I had to travel to Kinshasa. Our three-day trip covered almost 1,000 kilometers or 625 miles. We visited the Ministry of Health office to talk about taking over the Kiri hospital. We received a favorable response. Now we had to put our proposal in writing and wait for an official response. Next, we went to see Dr. Mputu, the leprosy program director. He promised to give me three bicycles for the three nurses responsible for the leprosy program. Next, we stopped at the procurer's office to pick up 10 million Zaires to return to

Pendjua. Without the funds, we could not pay the hospital staff. The currency had become even more worthless. The value of the 10 million Zaires equaled $400.

The return trip took four long days. Upon arriving, I learned that dysentery continued to move from village to village. Fortunately, we now had enough medicine to treat the people if they would come to the health centers. Nurses visited each community. Luba and Bola visited three villages a week to give health education and inspect the outhouses and water sources. They also took a supply of medicine. Almost all dysentery cases were among the Botoa. Their sanitary conditions were far worse than the Ekonda.

#

After a brief rest, I visited the village of Benge Nkelete, a small community of about 100 people, consisting of only eight adult men and many widows and small children. I had not been to this village in over two years. Of the 21 households I inspected, only four had latrines. I gave them a spade to dig latrines for each home. I planned to organize the men to cut a large field so the women and older children could plant manioc, rice, and corn.

My next stop was Lokula, where only nine of 35 households had outhouses, and in Liamba, only eight out of 55 had them. I spent two hours talking about dysentery, its causes, its treatment, and prevention. In Ngondo Banga, I found only 22 of 86 households had latrines. I knew I must spend more time with the Botoa, so I planned to adjust my work schedule.

### *Father Daniel Londrioor*

Amid the bad news, I will share something good and introduce Father Daniel. He has worked in Beronge, Kiri, and Pendjua for the past 25 years. His specialty is road construction. In the 1970s and 1980s, Father Daniel built a 152-kilometer-long road to connect the parishes of Kiri and Beronge. He has lived in Kiri for the last five years and joined the missionaries here in Pendjua in December 1995. During the two prior years, he repaired the road, dikes, and bridges to connect Kiri and Pendjua. The repairs allowed us to transport medicines, supplies, diesel fuel, and kerosene from the river port to the mission with greater ease.

Father Daniel planned to repair the roads connecting Pendjua to the surrounding villages. These repairs would allow the farmers to transport their grain and produce by truck to Kiri's port. He also built a grain storage bin to provide a way to buy and store the farmer's grain. We believed this would improve the economy for the people in the future. The mission now had two four-ton trucks to haul rock and gravel, two tractors and wagons, and a five-ton vehicle. Father Daniel received funds from Belgium and Europe to support his efforts. He employed 50 road construction workers, and he opened a small store for the workers and villagers.

## The Rainforest

In late March, I made an eight-day retreat in the forest. I felt a real need to get away and spend time with the Lord. I went into the dense rainforest and pitched my tent on the bank of a beautiful, white sand-bottomed creek. Luba and four youth helped me get there and cleared a place to set up camp. Then they left me. A rainforest is a beautiful place, even though it is also hostile. There are many inconveniences. It is hot and steamy during the day and cold and damp at night. The forest is so dense that I could become lost if I walked more than 25 yards from my tent.

Thick underbrush consists of all kinds of thorny bushes, and vines are everywhere. One vine has a fuzzy coating. If you brush against it, it leaves a stinging rash that lasts ten days unless you have cortisone cream. One type of grass has a blade so sharp that it leaves a clean-cut if you brush against it, like a razor blade. Appropriately, it is called razor grass. There is another vine with short branches, filled with sharp thorns that tear at your flesh if you brush against it. In the past, the Botoa used the thorns as fishhooks.

In the rainforest, there are millions of insects. By mid-morning, the mbengele come out. They are a little larger than gnats and are attracted to sweat. They always come in swarms of hundreds and cover your body, hair, eyes, and ears. Once you can no longer tolerate them, you have to look for the shadiest, darkest place to escape or plunge into the nearest creek. However, when you emerge, they are there waiting for you. Sweat bees also come in swarms.

Many different varieties of ants exist in the rainforest. There are three types, in particular, I did not like. First, we have red army ants. They make the ones in the U.S. look small. These ants are carnivores, and they pinch very hard. The only way to get rid of them is to throw hot coals on them. There is another variety of red ants with pincers. Food attracts these ants. Large black ants that are venomous make up the third type. If you get stung by one, the pain lasts for 14 hours. I only got bitten by one during my eight days in the forest.

The rainforest has six kinds of poisonous snakes: two vipers, two cobras, and two deadly water snakes. Each year, seven or eight people in the area die from snake bites. I did not dare venture from my tent after dark. I am vigilant when I walk in the forest or wade in the creek.

The rainy season came in full force. I dug trenches around the tent to allow the water to run off. I considered these inconveniences as nothing, compared to the many blessings and graces I received from being in solitude for eight days. During the last three days, I read all four gospel meditations and fasted and never sensed any fatigue or hunger. Dry periods and times of desolation came, and sometimes I wondered if I could persevere until the end.

## My Testimony

During these days of solitude and meditation, I reviewed my life. I reflected on how God spoke to me through others. I remained astonished at how I ended up as a missionary in Africa. While I attended medical school, I intended to become a cardiologist and move to Denver, Colorado. I visited with a good friend when I went to the U.S. on vacation last year. Our conversation seemed more like an interview. He asked me many questions. At one point, he asked, "Jerry, do you feel trapped there and that there is no way out?" I said, "No, I have a calling to this life." He responded, "Really, you feel called?" I hesitated, and then I said, "Yes."

I thought about the question and my response. I found it hard to go into detail about my past and my call to missionary life. During my retreat, I decided maybe my crisis of faith and my spiritual journey might help others who faced such a situation.

While in college, my friend and I discussed whether a "call" to religious life really could happen. The sister of my friend's wife had entered the Dominican sisterhood, only to leave. My friend and I had decided there was no such thing as a calling.

In those days (1958-1965), my only ambition was to be a medical doctor, go into private practice, and live a comfortable life. I was a staunch Republican and dead set against Medicare. I saw Medicare as the opening of a door to socialized medicine. In 1966, I joined the U.S. public health service. They sent me to Savannah, Georgia, to work in the County Health Department. My assignment for the next two years focused on the tuberculosis control project.

While there, I encountered the civil rights movement and my first experience with segregation. To my dismay, I discovered discrimination also existed in the church. Growing up in Mendota, Illinois, I never knew of these things. While at Marquette University, my studies did not allow me to get involved in the movement. However, I followed the civil rights movement and Dr. Martin Luther King on the nightly news. While in Savannah, Georgia, three of my best friends were priests. They belonged to a society of African missionaries who worked in two Afro-American parishes and a small Catholic high school. They were very active in civil rights, and one had a popular Saturday night radio program.

Through these priests, I met a paraplegic, 10-year-old Afro-American boy named Ronald. This encounter changed the whole direction of my life. Ronald belonged to a family of 12, and they lived on a plantation in almost slave-like conditions. He had fallen from the roof of a tobacco barn and broke his back. A priest took him to the University hospital. He paid the bill since the family had no insurance and only received slave wages. The priest visited the family until the plantation owner ran him off the land and forbade him to return.

The NAACP then moved the family to Savannah, Georgia, and asked me to take care of Ronald. Ronald never complained and always had a broad smile on his face. One night they called me because he had become seriously ill. When I arrived, he had a very high temperature, a urinary tract infection, and septicemia. I went to a public telephone and called some of my doctor friends since I did not have staff privileges at the city hospital. One by one, each friend gave me an excuse for not accepting Ronald as a patient.

As tears filled my eyes, I asked God to help me, and if He did, I promised never to go into private practice. Instead, I would serve the poor. I marched out of the phone booth, picked up Ronald, put him in the car, and drove to the hospital. I carried him into the emergency room and promised to pay the bill. They found a doctor, and God spared his life. Years later, I learned that Ronald graduated from high school and worked at a dental drill-making company.

In 1968, I received another shock. The diocese had asked the three priests to leave and then sent replacements. The three priests made many enemies in the Priest Senate who did not like their civil rights engagement. At this point, I experienced a crisis of faith. I left the church and became a socialist and an atheist. I decided I did not need God or the church to do humanitarian work.

I returned to Marquette in 1968 to begin an internal medicine residency. There, I joined the Students for a Democratic Society (SDS). This group was a student activist movement that represented the views of the New Left political movement. The organization developed and expanded rapidly in the mid-1960s before it dissolved at its last convention in 1969. This student organization had an anti-capitalist and anti-war agenda.

At the same time, I joined the medical committee for human rights. This group opposed the American Medical Association since they supported socialized medicine. They ran free medical clinics in the intercity to help the oppressed.

I interrupted my internal medicine residency in January 1971 to be the medical director of a comprehensive health service program. This program served 50,000 rural, poor Afro-Americans in South Carolina. The project director, Thomas Barnwell, had a tremendous effect on my life. He had great enthusiasm for helping the poor develop themselves and pull themselves out of poverty. He was renowned for his civil rights work and his promotion of economic development.

Three years later, I remained a socialist and an atheist. However, I became restless to go to work in Africa. I joined the Peace Corps, and they sent me to Zaire. I insisted that they did not assign me to a missionary hospital. However, my plea did not change their decision. They sent me to a hospital run by Canadian Sisters in Mwene-Ditu. The Sister responsible for the hospital patients and I did not get along. I did not like the way she treated the Africans, so I left after six months. Then, I went to a nearby hospital run by Africans. Two Missionhurst priests and a brother stayed at a nearby mission. Though I was anti-missionary, we became friends without discussing God or the church. By 1977, I had completed three fulfilling years of work in Zaire. Afterward, I returned home.

I became the medical director of a comprehensive health program that served the urban poor in the Quad City area of Illinois and Iowa. In this place, God sent His messenger to me to bring me back to Him and the church. Joyce, an auxiliary nurse at the clinic where I worked, was an evangelical Protestant. She carried her Bible to work and read it every day at lunch hour. I would ridicule her and tell her that the book was simply fiction. I told her that it was a hoax on ignorant people. "Do you believe what's in that book?" I asked her one time. Joyce just smiled and said, "Of course I do, and you know it is true."

One day Joyce looked at me and said, "Jerry, Jesus loves you and is following you, but you keep running away. Why don't you stop and listen to Him?" I am sure that the deep roots of faith planted in me by my parents and Catholic educators had never really died. I bought a new American Catholic Bible and read the New Testament in the evening. When I read about St. Paul's conversion in the Book of Acts, I experienced deep sorrow. I asked God to forgive me. Only then did I experience God's love and tenderness, and forgiveness. I felt like the prodigal son who returned home to his father.

The parable's central figure is not the son but the father who so loved his son. Even though the son refused him, his father forgave him and celebrated the son's return. It is the same way with God. God so loves us that He is always prepared to forgive us. He rejoices more from one repentant sinner than over 99 virtuous people who do not need repentance.

Being a Catholic, I sought out a sympathetic priest and made a general confession. The priest had to be a strong-hearted person to sit quietly and listen to me because I had committed almost every sin known to humankind.

In December of that year, I went home to Mendota, Illinois, to celebrate Christmas with my family. During the Christmas Day Mass, I experienced my call to the religious missionary life. Just after communion, I looked up. Light streamed through the beautiful stained-glass church window. In a flash, I saw the visage of the crucified Jesus on a pillar. I closed my eyes and thought I had lost my mind. I opened one eye, looked up, and He remained there. "Lord, what do you want me to do?" I cried out to Him.

"Follow me, and I will make you a channel of God's love, compassion, and healing to the poor," He responded. What? He must be thinking of the wrong person. "Are you sure you know what you are doing, Lord? I'm one of the worst sinners of all time. I even denied Your existence and have been against your missionaries." He said, "Trust Me." I replied, "Yes, Lord." Then He was gone.

The rest is, well, history. I joined Missionhurst, and now I am a religious missionary doctor in the middle of the equatorial rainforest. I try to be a channel of the Lord's love, compassion, and healing to the Botoa Pygmies. They are some of the most destitute and despised people in Zaire. Yes, there is such a thing as Jesus calling one to the religious life. I know I needed an authentic calling and a real relationship with Jesus to endure the hardships, disappointments, and failures I encountered in this hot, steamy rainforest of Zaire.

I did not write about my testimony and spiritual journey for my glory, as I do not have a glorious past. Instead, I wrote about it for the glory of God, who never abandons us, even if we leave Him.

My prayer is that my testimony will help someone who has gone through a crisis of faith or abandoned God or the practice of their faith. I pray that he or she will return to God and the way of their faith.

#

After my retreat, I am sad to report that the epidemic of dysentery continues. In May, we had 67 new cases in 27 villages. The number of new cases and deaths continued to increase. In one of my books on infectious diseases, I read that an epidemic could last three to five years in an affected area. This outbreak had already been going for over one year.

The mothers come to the mission every morning, and I give them a large pot of rice and dried fish to cook for the noon meal. In the afternoon, they bring firewood. I pay them for the wood so they can buy food for supper at the outdoor market. One little child only had his grandmother take care of him since his parents had died of dysentery. At the end of the week, the grandmother died, and the villagers now have another orphan.

More problems confronted me. First, lightning struck the solar panels for the refrigerator with the vaccines and destroyed four solar panels. Secondly, the administrative bookkeeper embezzled money from the health project. He stole $160. I discovered it by accident. I felt very disappointed, as the bookkeeper had been an excellent worker. He also had a severe handicap due to polio he had contracted at age two that left him paralyzed. He used a wheelchair. I showed mercy and did not fire him, but I sent him home for one week without pay.

#

Though I recently had a retreat, I looked forward to time to rejuvenate with family. In June, I went back to the U.S. and returned to Kinshasa in August. While in Kinshasa, I received a radio message from Dr. Botuli informing me the epidemic of dysentery had come back in alarming numbers. He asked me to buy IV fluids and antibiotics, so I went to Memisa, a Belgian foundation, who kindly gave me the medicines.

The director for sleeping sickness control also obtained some medications for me. I learned that the director, a young Belgium doctor, and his wife, a Dutch woman, recently came to Kinshasa. The return of some Belgians may help the health care programs. Previously, they operated on projects for tuberculosis, leprosy, sleeping sickness, and cholera. I obtained the vaccines and packed them in an ice chest for my trip to Kiri.

I returned to Doctors Without Borders and received more antibiotics, IV fluids, and oral rehydration solutions for treating dysentery patients. Next, I went to the center for disabled children. I talked to them about buying two artificial limbs for a 10-year-old boy who had his legs amputated due to gangrene this past March.

When I left for the airport, I had 200 pounds of medications and vaccines. The plane, a twin-engine, fifteen-passenger, Russian plane, had two Russian pilots. There were only six passengers, and the rest of the airplane contained baggage. I remained grateful when these overworked planes got off the ground.

While in Kiri, I visited the hospital and had quite a surprise. They had scrubbed the walls and floors, painted the metal beds with white enamel, and placed new screens on the windows. The hospital looked much better, and I enjoyed seeing the many smiling and grateful patients.

#

December arrived, and I made plans to build a boarding school for the 31 Botoa students who attend the junior high school. The students did not get enough to eat; they were always sick, missed school, and were unable to study. They usually only had one authentic meal in the evening. It was unreasonable to expect them to stay in school and attend the two-hour study in the afternoon when they were weak and hungry.

We decided to make bricks to build six more dwellings, of which some will house two women and a cook who will live on the premises. The students will cut firewood, cut the grass, plant a large garden, wash the dishes, and clean the dormitories and houses. The large dining room will double as a study hall. We have a solar panel to charge a battery to provide light for three hours at night. There is

153

also a two-room apartment with running water, a shower, and a toilet. I will stay there at the beginning to make sure all goes well.

#

One plan that did not go well occurred with the shipment of vaccines to the mission. The procure sent enough vaccines for 5,000 children in an ice chest for air transport. They did not use the two large ice chests I specifically bought to transport them via the barge. The vaccines must remain at a temperature between 2 and 8° C. When the container arrived, the temperature registered 25° C, and all the vaccines had spoiled. It infuriated me that the procuring department made the same mistake twice. A measles epidemic recently broke out north of Pendjua. I had planned a measles vaccination campaign, and now I am very concerned many children might die.

### The "Miracle Boy"

It is a miracle of Christmas to see people rejoice and hope for a better tomorrow, despite their poverty, misery, and subsistence. The people are an inspiration for us at the mission, who have all we need. People prefer to live better, and they also wish to be able to eat better. They continue to place their faith and hope in Him.

We had a three-year-old boy in the hospital who arrived on December 21 in critical condition. His parents had given him an enema of traditional medicines to treat a respiratory infection. The boy had a distended abdomen and did not pass any gas or stool. He was very short of breath. I gave him IV fluids, antibiotics and then inserted a gastrointestinal tube. His condition was so desperate that I was sure the boy would die.

However, the following day, his abdomen was flat, and he was breathing better. On Monday, he had bowel sounds and passed gas. At noon, the nurse called me to come because the boy was short of breath. They had let a liter of IV fluids run for over three hours. Now, we faced a crisis as the little boy had heart failure and water in his lungs. I immediately started to treat him, and he began to get better. By Christmas Day, the boy ate and smiled, and I was pleased, though that would change.

Several days later, the nurses called me again because the boy had shortness of breath and wheezed like an asthmatic. I treated him with three asthma medicines; however, he did not improve. The next night, I told the nurse we already given him all the medications we could. I did not think the boy would live through the night.

In my prayers, I said, "Lord, I have done all I can. This little fellow is in Your hands." The following day the little boy breathed as usual, and he ate. I could only shake my head and say, "Thank the good Lord." I called him my "miracle boy."

#

Later, I thought about the little boy and the treatment he would receive if he were in the U.S. He would have been placed in intensive care. The boy would receive oxygen, have monitors attached to him, and have had X-rays and lab tests. However, we had nothing, no oxygen, no X-ray machine, no way to measure electrolytes or do other tests. We only have our ears, eyes, and hands to make a diagnosis. We do not have modern equipment or skilled technicians to run them. I believe that it is better to spend our limited resources on village health centers to impact people's health significantly. I hoped and prayed for more help.

# Refugees
*1997*

New Year's Day came, and the people were not in the mood to celebrate. Maybe, in part, they were too poor to buy much local brew. Or, possibly, they were just tired, frustrated, and did not have hope for a brighter future.

However, I am happy to report that the Kiri hospital has become a great success. Patients now fill the hospital, and the hospital will likely need to purchase more beds. A foundation in Belgium gave me money to buy a generator, electrical wire, and light fixtures. We hope to have lights installed within the next six months. I also expected to receive funds from another foundation to renovate the four buildings on the hospital site.

\#

Progress on the boarding home continues. Each Saturday, the boys cut the grass, spade the garden, dig latrines, chop firewood, and clean their rooms. Sister Pascaline gives the boys lessons in manners and proper eating. Before that, they always stood to eat and gulped down the food as fast as they could.

The boys have many problems, and I often take on the combined role of mother and father. We just hired a director for the boarding home. He will not start full-time until we complete the house for him. There are always repairs needed for the solar lights, water pump, and other items in the boarding homes. I know the boarding homes are beneficial. I have already seen an improvement in the boy's nutrition, health, and performance in school. It only costs $15.00 a day to feed and lodge the boys.

One night, the housefather knocked on my door and told me that one boy went wild and beat on the ground and the trees. They grabbed the boy, led him to the meeting shelter, and threw a bucketful of water on him. Smoke started to come out of his chest. The house father wanted to know how this happened and how to treat it. Their belief in curses made them think the boy was cursed, which caused smoke to come from his chest. I realized there were always smoldering logs in the middle of the shelter with benches around it. I am sure that when the boy sat down by the fire, they saw smoke rising from the fire. They threw water on him. The smoke they saw came from the smoldering logs. With reluctance, they accepted my explanation.

#

In addition to their beliefs about curses, the Botoa boys and girls suffer from horrendous inferiority complexes. I want them to be proud of their heritage and free from oppression. On a recent visit to the boarding school, the boys related a horrific event that took place during my absence. Eight young Ekonda men got drunk one night, entered the dorms, terrorized the students, and stole their clothes. The school director filed a complaint with the authorities; however, they did nothing about it. The ringleader's father and I were friends. I asked the man to come and see me. The man apologized for his son's behavior, and he said he would replace the stolen items. I asked the boys to forgive the Ekonda for their actions.

## Mobutu's Era Ends

On April 27, I heard that Kabila's rebel army had gathered north of Pendjua and headed toward Mbandaka. For now, we still had peace here. Each mission used their ham radios for one hour, three times a day, to keep informed of the Zairian soldiers' whereabouts. Many were armed, and they pillaged missions and villages when they passed through. Everyone would panic and flee into the forest. We were fortunate that most soldiers were not on the main route from Kinshasa. I hoped the war would end soon, as our medication stocks were low. The procure did not think it would be safe to send the barge from Kinshasa. There were at least 400 cartons of medicine that had not shipped.

I made sure to have my radio on most of the day. Mobutu and the rebel leader, Kabila, were meeting on a South African ship off Angola's Atlantic coast. According to the radio, Mobutu agreed to resign. They made plans for the transition of power. I prayed it would be peaceful and that Kinshasa would not see any fighting. If there were a peaceful transition, then transportation in and out of Kinshasa would resume, and I could receive my medicines.

#

As of May 18, we have a new "president," Laurent-Desire Kabila. Kabila led the rebel army to overthrow Mobutu. Kinshasa fell into the rebel army's command. The country has a new name, and it is now called the Democratic Republic of the Congo. The people are no longer Zairians but are Congolese. I thank God that Kinshasa did not experience a blood bath. I pray the new government will bring justice and peace to this beautiful country.

#

The past week included tension and fear for the people, the Sisters, and the missionaries. Group after group of armed Zairian soldiers and miserable Rwandese refugees arrived every day as they fled Kabila's advancing army.

The chief came to the mission with a letter from a nearby village. The letter said ten armed soldiers and 22 refugees were there. They requested the mission truck to pick them up and take them to Kiri. I agreed with the idea so that the soldiers would not stay here. The transport left and returned five hours later with no problems. Father Daniel arrived in the afternoon. In the evening, 15 more well-armed soldiers arrived.

The soldiers were very unfriendly, and one of them even threatened to throw a grenade at the crowd gathered around them. The chief allowed them to stay in a house he owned, and the villagers had to bring them food. We could not wait to evacuate these 15 soldiers tomorrow.

The following day, the soldiers strode into the mission. Father Daniel told them to wait since five more soldiers and 32 refugees would arrive soon. He explained that we would transport all of them at one time in the truck. The soldiers were upset.

When the group arrived, the soldiers refused to allow the refugees onto the truck. The mission team began to treat them since so many were sick. The refugees were Hutus who had fled to Zaire in 1994. They had to escape to many places during the past few years. They wanted to go to Kinshasa, but I knew they would never reach there. The rebel soldiers killed every Hutu refugee that they encountered. The villagers were afraid to give them lodging at night.

I learned that the group of refugees who went to Kiri earlier did not get to enter. They fled toward the Zaire River, where they hoped to cross over to the Congo. This second group also left in the direction of the Zaire River. I felt so sorry for the women and children. Most of the men were murderers who had killed the Tutsis in 1994. They had paid dearly for their sins. Thirty-seven more refugees arrived, and they were hungry and sick. We fed and treated each one and then lodged them for the night.

Later, 15 soldiers and 26 more refugees arrived, and the next day 11 more soldiers came. The truck left for Kiri with the soldiers and returned Saturday morning. A group of 26 more well-armed soldiers had arrived and demanded to go to Kiri. Their commander threatened to kill Father Daniel if he did not agree to transport them.

The next evening, the 22 refugees who had passed through earlier returned. They were desperate and did not know which way to go. The Hutu did not speak Lingala or Lokanda, so they were unable to communicate. However, two Hutu women spoke French, and I could talk with them. The two women had three children, and they said they were tired and preferred to die rather than continue to flee. The mission lodged and fed them. In the morning, the 17 men left in the direction of the Zaire River. The two women and three children stayed at the mission. I hoped Kabila's soldiers would not harm them when they arrived.

#

I packed a trunk with my tent, sleeping mat, matches, candles, and clothes. I sent the chest to Luba's house in case we needed to flee into the forest. The mission received a radio message that two hundred Hutu soldiers of the former Rwandese army, along with 150 Hutu women and children, had arrived in Kiri. They blocked the roads and occupied the airport and state buildings. They asked for a boat to transport them downriver. These were the same Hutu soldiers who killed the Tutsis in Rwanda during the genocide.

We received a report of 30 armed Zairian soldiers in a village 17 kilometers north of the Pendjua mission. The soldiers pillaged the people's homes. The group arrived at noon. However, there were only seven soldiers and seven women and children. Three came to the mission. They were polite and asked for transportation to Kiri. The mission truck took them. Everyone lived in terror, and they could not wait until Kabila's soldiers arrived. The mission in Beronge radioed that 500 Hutu soldiers, women, and children were 240 kilometers away and headed toward Kiri. We radioed the new government in Kinshasa and asked them to send soldiers there.

#

Seven soldiers arrived on a Tuesday night, and they did not bother anyone. The mission truck took them and their wives and children to Kiri the following day. The mission received reports about 60 soldiers who were only 30 kilometers to the north of us all week. They were armed, mean, and they stole household goods. On Saturday, fourteen soldiers arrived along with their wives and children. Two were very ill, so I treated them at the hospital.

"Where are the other forty-six soldiers?" I asked them. "There are only thirty soldiers," one responded, "And sixteen are headed west toward Mbandaka."

Later, we heard that 300 Hutu Rwandese armed soldiers roamed the woods to the east, but they would bypass the mission. I hoped so because these soldiers were mean and dangerous. They were like trapped animals who could not escape Kabila's army. The army consisted mainly of Tutsis, who hated the Hutus.

160

Kiri had 250 Hutus arrive during the past week, and the situation there became terrible. The soldiers broke into the pharmacy and stole a large quantity of medicine. They threatened to kill Dr. Botuli because he looked like a Tutsi. Dr. Botuli paid them 25 million Zaires ($150). The priest in Kiri hired a large barge to evacuate the soldiers to a village 100 kilometers downriver. There, they would cross over to Congo Brazzaville.

#

I contended with all the Zairian soldiers who passed through to the port in Kiri. The soldiers wanted river transportation to be able to return to Kinshasa. All this chaos and danger prevented the mission barge from bringing much-needed antibiotics. The health center pharmacy shelves were almost empty, and we were out of antibiotics. The hospital in Kiri had depleted nearly all of its medicine. The war caused much suffering.

I still did not know if I could return to the U.S. There were no flights to the interior. The mission experienced the effects of war. Hundreds of Rwandese refugees passed through Pendjua, hoping to reach the Zairian River to cross to Congo Brazzaville.

There were 500 armed Hutu militiamen, only 10 miles to the north, at Ikongo. They stole everything in sight. Everyone thought they would come on the road through Pendjua, and they panicked. People took their belongings and animals into the forest to hide. At the mission, we had a large cellar in the workshop, so we put our valuables there. We pushed a large cabinet in front of the door so no one could see we had a cellar.

#

I went to Kiri to work on bookkeeping. Dr. Botuli continued to do better after his harrowing experience with the Hutu soldiers. For two nights in a row, they threatened to kill him. The losses at the hospital totaled $1,800. They pillaged several health centers, and we still did not know the total losses.

I returned home, and that night, Dr. Bakoko awoke me. He had arrived with a team from the High Council on Refugees from the United Nations. They brought two jeeps and two large trucks to be able to evacuate the Hutu refugees. The group included a French woman, an Italian man, and five Zairians. I talked with them until the early morning hours.

There were groups of refugees in the forest five miles from here, and when the refugees saw the trucks, they fled. They could not follow them because they were armed. The team returned to Mbandaka in the afternoon.

Later, four young Hutu refugees hobbled up to the mission. They had tropical ulcers on their feet and were in terrible shape. We set the refugees down in the dining room and gave them water, sardines, and rice. We boiled water and then added disinfectant for them to soak their feet. They took showers, and I bandaged their sores and gave them injections of penicillin. They had arrived dressed in dirty rags, so we gave each one a new pair of shorts and T-shirts. We housed them in the tuberculosis center.

For now, things were relatively calm, as only one group of soldiers passed through. Nine more Hutu refugees arrived, along with a 10-year-old orphan boy, who had been found in the forest by hunters. The boy had sores all over his body, and he could not sit down. Every day we soaked him in a large tub filled with warm water and disinfectant. The boy improved a lot during the last five days, though he remained acutely malnourished. We gave him three meals a day.

A 20-year-old man arrived on Tuesday. Scabies covered his body. We treated him each day, and by the end of the week, he improved. A man, two women, and four children arrived. They were in better condition than the previous group, as they had stayed in a nearby village where the villagers fed them. I hoped the UN Council of Refugees would come and pick up the refugees.

Another group of soldiers arrived. They had been in a nearby village. Three soldiers got drunk and planned to rape a young woman. The men knew the soldiers were out of bullets, so they beat them with clubs and shot one soldier in the head with an arrow. Dr. Bakoko removed it and sewed up his wounds. The other soldiers were terrified and did not cause any trouble.

*Kinshasa*

The airlines began to fly to Inongo. I planned to go to Kinshasa at the end of June. With all the recent events, I needed a vacation. These were trying and tiring times. I knew I endured them by the strength of the Lord. I went home to the U.S. until mid-August and then returned to Africa.

My process to go through immigration, customs, and baggage check occurred without any harassment from government agents looking for a "tip." However, the good news ended there. The economy had become dysfunctional, and the government seemed incapable of addressing the problems. The Belgian confrères were pessimistic that things would improve. The political opposition who opposed Mobutu since 1990 now opposed Kabila. Kabila did not include any opposition party in his government. Also, Rwanda had a lot of influence, as they supplied many soldiers, who were Tutsi people. The Congolese people in Kinshasa did not want the Rwandan soldiers there. I wondered if there was a peaceful solution.

I went to the office of the new timber company that started up operation in Kiri. However, I discovered they no longer had offices in Kinshasa. I went to the former owners to ask what happened. The director told me the new company did not have confidence in the new government, so they pulled out. The withdrawal came as terrible news. We would not have free airplane transportation between Kiri and Kinshasa and no satellite phone or fax service.

The war in Brazzaville on the other side of the river continued to rage on. Throughout the day and night, the air filled with the sound of artillery bombardments, rocket grenades, and machine guns firing. From my room at the procurer's building, I could see the river. I observed 30 wooden boats laden with women and children cross over to my side each day. It broke my heart to see so much suffering.

#

Before leaving Kinshasa, I also saw certain events to indicate the new president would be a dictator. Every cabinet minister had a general as a vice minister. The generals were always present when the minister spoke in public. The government took control of the radio and television. The military attacked the headquarters of the largest political party, and all political meetings were banned. Hundreds of people went to jail without due process.

The president also had a problem with the international community. The Tutsi soldiers who fought for Kabila were the ones who slaughtered the Hutu refugees. Kabila delayed the United Nation's commission responsible for investigating the massacres. When the commission arrived, Kabila obstructed their work because he needed the Rwandese soldiers who did not want the investigation. If he stopped the process, he would not get financial aid from Western countries. If he went ahead with it, then his army might overthrow him.

#

I felt like I took my life into my hands as I boarded the plane to Kiri. The aircraft, a Russian military cargo plane, had folding benches along the sides. Last year, two of these planes crashed, so I felt uncomfortable about going on them. However, I had no other way to get back home. The aircraft stopped in Inongo and loaded several tons of food, including vegetables, smoked fish, monkey meat, alligators, and tubs with live fish. The odor sickened me, and I smelled the stench on my clothes as I exited the plane.

## The New Government

I received the following updates once I returned to Pendjua. During my vacation in the U.S., more Hutu refugees arrived in Pendjua. A large group of 43 refugees stayed in our tuberculosis sanitarium. A troop of Kabila's soldiers had a station in Kiri. One day, they came to the mission, fired their AK-47s into the air, and threatened to throw grenades. Fear gripped the people. The soldiers left without doing any harm.

The more I heard and saw what the new government did, the more it seemed another dictatorship would occur. The agents called themselves AFDL (Alliance for Democratic Liberation), and they were a long way from creating a democracy. They forced the people to work for the state each Monday and Thursday morning. The hospital and health centers had to give the AFDL agents and soldiers free health care.

One morning, I went to the hospital, and none of the personnel were there. All the nurses and workers were required to cut grass at the government center until 8:30. I could not believe they had to abandon the patients because of state requirements. The government's disregard for the patients made me furious. I marched over, and I told the AFDL how unfair they were being. The people also had to attend a 10-day indoctrination course, and I thought this practice leaned toward communism.

Luba and Bola informed me that only a few Botoa barefoot doctors came to pick up medicine because they feared the AFDL. Three weeks ago, the AFDL beat a Botoa night watchman with clubs and ruptured his spleen. The local doctor did an emergency operation. They clubbed the man because a prisoner had escaped. They also beat one nurse because he got drunk, and he spent two weeks in the hospital.

The more I learned about the new government and the AFDL, the less optimistic I became for the Congo's future. The government held indoctrination sessions in the villages to explain their ideology. I received a copy of their 20-page brochure, and it read like a form of Marxism and included many contradictions.

The AFDL came and asked for diesel fuel, and Father Daniel refused to give them any. They sat in front of his room all day. The situation angered Father Daniel, but, at the same time, he felt nervous. I told him to stay calm and not give in. The agents left without any fuel.

Next, the AFDL came and took ten mattresses from the hospital. They incurred 15 million Zaire in medical bills that I am sure they did not intend to pay. The previous government never took anything from the hospital. I advised the provincial in Kinshasa and asked him to invoice the government for the medicine they received.

The AFDL president and secretary came and met with Father Daniel, Father Paul, and me. They explained the party ideology and all they intended to do. At the end of the meeting, they asked for the mission's collaboration, which meant they wanted bicycles, kerosene lamps, plates, water jugs, paper notebooks, and pens. I responded, "Our congregation already helps you with health care by supporting hospitals and health centers, and we cannot do anymore."

Father Daniel added, "I have built over fifty bridges and have maintained the roads, which is what the government is supposed to do, not me." To appease them, we gave them some paper, notebooks, and pens.

Five days later, I received a letter from the AFDL president in Kiri. He asked me for financial and material aid to propagate the party ideology. I am amazed at their audacity. They asked for help from the church when, in fact, they opposed the church. I wrote a polite letter to the president to explain all we did for the government through health care.

#

Then, on October 4, a man arrived, and he had a wound in his abdomen from a metal arrow. The man did not look like he would survive, and Dr. Bakoko had doubts about operating. African doctors normally did not do surgery if they thought the patient might die on the operating table. They were afraid of the repercussions of the family. I encouraged him to do the operation, and fortunately, the man lived. The arrow penetrated the small intestine but did not touch any major blood vessels. The wounded man, an Ekonda from the Mongo tribe, lived north of here. He got in an argument with his neighbor, who then sent his Botoa slave to shoot the man with an arrow. The Botoa must obey their masters, even if it meant killing another person.

#

I was thankful to have Dr. Bakoko at the hospital so that I could attend to other needs. My next trip required me to return to Kinshasa. The plane had four seats with one engine, and some American Protestant missionaries owned it. The pilot, a white man named Daniel, had been born in the Congo. It rained very hard all morning, and the plane made three stops. The trip took six hours, and we did not have anything to eat or drink all day.

I went to Kinshasa to meet with the provincial finance committee since the economy remained at a standstill. We discussed the budget for the Kiri hospital and the 24 health centers in the territory. The international community did not send the promised aid because President Kabila had not allowed the United Nations to investigate the Hutu refugees' massacres.

Meanwhile, 45 million people suffered, as there were no schools, health care, civil service, road repairs, or transportation. The road between the ocean port in Matadi and Kinshasa washed out 30 miles from Kinshasa. Trucks could not get through to or from the docks. Over 1,500 containers remained stacked up at the port, and none had the medicine I needed.

Everywhere I went throughout Kinshasa, thousands of people just milled around. I wondered how they survived, as no factories functioned. They had closed due to the looting by soldiers during the past few years. The priests and brothers who lived and worked in Kinshasa called the people's survival the "African miracle."

The political and military situation continued to deteriorate in Kinshasa. The president arrested and imprisoned the military commander, who led the rebel army to victory over Mobutu's army. The president thought that he would plot to overthrow the government. I wanted to leave Kinshasa because some soldiers fired at passing cars at night. I hoped a civil war would not break out. In Brazzaville, they did not have electricity, and the whole city went dark at night.

### Boy Soldiers

On November 30, I arrived in Inongo and tried to get back to Kiri and then Pendjua. I left Kinshasa the day before on a cargo plane to fly direct to Kiri. However, the schedule changed since I was the only passenger going to Kiri. I became very concerned because I had an 80-pound ice chest with vaccines for 2,000 children. Fortunately, the refrigerator at the parish house in Inongo functioned, and the freezer had nothing in it.

On the day I planned to leave Inongo, a massive storm rolled in, and the lake became very rough. We loaded the boat onto the trailer and prepared to take it to the beach. Two 16-year-old soldiers arrived, armed with submachine guns. They asked me if I spoke Lingala. "Yes, I speak Lingala," I replied. "What do you want?"

"We are going to Kiri in that boat," one stated. I said, "I have one hundred pounds of medicine and vaccines on this boat, plus a teacher and a chauffeur. There is no room."

"If we are not allowed to go in the boat, then we will not let the boat leave," another stated. The soldiers fingered the triggers on their guns. "The vaccines are for the children, and if I don't go now, they'll spoil," I explained. "We are more important than children," they responded.

I realized that it was useless to talk to them, so I said the boat would not leave, and I took my bags back to the mission. The bishop's assistant went and convinced the soldiers to let me go, and the boat left at noon. The trip to Kiri required a 100-mile-long journey by river, and upon my arrival, I stayed at the mission for several days. I departed for Pendjua by jeep, and all the dikes and some bridges were under two feet of water. Everyone got out and stood on the wooden bridges, so the driver knew where to place the jeep's wheels.

#

By December, I had returned to Pendjua. One morning, the soldiers were at the Kiri port when Father Daniel arrived. Father Daniel yelled at them because they were whipping two young women. The soldiers also made them roll around in a giant mud puddle and then forced them to eat dirt while they called them pigs. Father Daniel advised the boy soldiers that good soldiers would never do such things. When they attempted to arrest him, he told them they needed to learn to respect their elders. The soldiers reluctantly let him go.

Later, after they had loaded the mission truck and parked at the mission, two AFDL agents came. They said we had to pay a 50 million Zaire tax. I told them, "We are a non-profit organization and have tax-exempt status." I added, "If I have to pay the fee, I will close the Kiri hospital." The agents excused themselves, and then they left.

I prepared a report on all the violations of human rights that I had seen. I plan to send it to the U.S. Ambassador in Kiri, the Secretary of State, the Senate chairman of the Committee on African Affairs, Amnesty International, and the African Justice and Faith Network. I cannot remain silent in the face of these rights violations.

# Congo War
*1998*

In mid-January, I arrived at the provincial house in Kutu. The house sat on the bank of the Fimi River. It had a panoramic view of the river, the surrounding marshlands, and the forest. The beautiful setting provided me a place to pray and meditate in the midst of all that took place around me.

We met for two days about justice and peace. By the year 2000, we would staff only two missions – Pendjua and Beronge. Most activities of the procure would transfer to the diocesan procure. Likely this will be the last year we will support the hospital in Kiri and the health centers in the Beronge and Lutoy parishes. I arrived back in Pendjua after taking a two-day boat ride and a three-hour jeep ride from Kiri.

#

The boarding home director came to tell me the boys planned to return home. Last week, the principal and some teachers admonished a group of Botoa students who they thought were proud and arrogant. They told them if they thought their education would change their social status, they were dreaming. They said the Botoa were inferior to the Bantu and would always be servants, even if they had an education. The boys decided they did not have a reason to stay in school if the principal and teachers were against them. My blood pressure rose. I went to the boarding home and told the students that no one could keep them from advancing. I urged them not to quit just because some people were jealous. As I tried to sleep, I reminded myself to keep the faith.

#

The good news is that the state salaries arrived for the nurses. The bad news is they expected to receive four months' pay, but the governor stole a large sum of money. The Inongo and Kiri health zones were to receive 24 billion Zaires ($10,000); however, the governor in Bandundu took 22 billion Zaires and paid his civil servants instead. I knew that the governor would not face arrest since he was one of President Kabila's men.

A week or so later, the people celebrated the anniversary of Kabila's defeat of Mobutu. Joseph Kabila came to power on May 17, 1997. The school children, hospital personnel, and others were required to march and sing songs of praise to the AFDL and President Kabila. Mobutu had the exact requirements when he took power in 1965. I did not attend the festivities.

#

Despite all that was happening, I left for Chicago, Illinois, and spent two months with family. In August, I stayed at Scheut, the CICM main house in Brussels, for 12 days. I waited for the war taking place in the Kinshasa region to end.

The people in Kinshasa supported Kabila because they did not want to be ruled by the Tutsis. Many ex-Mobutu soldiers joined the rebel army. The people were angry because the rebels cut off electricity, and they did not have running water. The people in Scheut had email and phone contact with the provincial in Kinshasa. All of the missionaries were safe, including those in the rebel-held territory. They had chosen to stay in the Congo to be with the people.

I wished that I were in Pendjua to help the people during this time of crisis. I received news that Tutsi rebels in Kiver slaughtered 600 Congolese, including a priest and two Sisters. Many feared the insurgents would resort to genocide, especially if they began to lose the war fought in the eastern section. I prayed the chaos would not prevent me from being with my Botoa brothers and sisters.

## Mission Work

I used my free time to write a summary of the mission team's activities. The group consisted of two priests and me. Our territory covered 4,000 square kilometers. The 40,000 inhabitants consisted of two races or tribes - the Bantu of the Ekonda tribe and the Pygmies, called Batwa. As I call them, the Botoa (or Batwa) made up the majority as 25,000 lived in 76 villages.

The Botoa are victims of discrimination and oppression. They are the most impoverished people in the Congo and are marginalized and relegated to an inferior social status. Since 1981, the mission team has made special efforts to help the Botoa liberate themselves. We did this through evangelization, adult formation, health care, economic development, and education.

Currently, we have 30 Botoa catechists who share the gospel. Thirty-five villages have built clay chapels. I organized the African Christian Youth of the Light. When I started in 1981, there were nine boys in the group, and now there are over 400 members. For health care, we have a 100-bed hospital. Until 1995, the medical mission Sisters from the Netherlands administered the hospital. Now, I am the medical director and the only foreigner at the mission.

Preventive health care or rural health care did not exist in the Pendjua territory until 1982. With the help of Missionhurst and our benefactor's donations, we opened 14 rural health centers staffed by African nurses. The nurses provide primary health care, well-baby clinics, vaccinations, and health education.

Since few Botoa participate in health care services, I started the barefoot doctor program in 1983. The people in the villages choose their barefoot doctor who engages in six one-week training sessions a year. We now have 76 Botoa barefoot doctors. They provide first aid, treatment of malaria, intestinal parasites, lice, and burns, along with primary health education.

Father Daniel is primarily responsible for economic development. He promotes agriculture, maintains the roads, and supplies transportation for agricultural products to Kiri's river port. The economy of the farmers has improved due to these efforts.

Education is the key to improved health and economic status. In 1981, only 20 Botoa children attended the four primary schools, and none attended high school. Over the years, we convinced the Botoa parents of the importance of education. We help pay for school fees, notebooks, pens, and uniforms. Today, 407 Botoa children attend mission schools. Local schools exist in 26 villages, with grades 1-2 in the Botoa villages. They are not yet accredited since most teachers do not have diplomas. Today, 1,040 Botoa children attend village schools.

In 1996, I opened the first boarding home for Botoa high school students. Their living conditions had made it difficult to study and learn. The boarding school provides a healthy environment for the students and a venue for moral, social, spiritual, and character building.

My life and work with my Botoa brothers and sisters have been the happiest and most rewarding years. All of our work has been made possible by the Lord's grace.

#

On September 12, the plane landed in Kinshasa. The full flight included at least 40 missionaries, all anxious to get back to their people. I bought two newspapers to get more information about the war and the economy. It appeared Kabila and his allies were making progress in the eastern part of the Congo. The economy had fallen into chaos, and no one received their pay. The money devalued drastically. The country faced a food crisis, as many raw food staples were exhausted, and Belgium began to airlift rice and beans to Kinshasa.

Kabila is a popular hero because of the war. The people rally behind him because they are angry that Uganda and Rwanda sent troops to fight on the rebels' side. They felt the U.S., and especially France, supported Uganda and Rwanda to destabilize Kabila. The people do not understand why the U.S. and the United Nations have not condemned Uganda and Rwanda after they invaded the Congo.

I believe Kabila wants to install a dictatorship, even though the people recognize him as president. He has the right to ask other countries to help him. As a result, the governments of Angola,

Namibia, and Zimbabwe station soldiers in the Congo. The war caused the Congolese people to suffer. It did not resolve the Tutsi-Hutu problem existent in the Congo, Rwanda, and other places.

The problem will only worsen for the Tutsi Congolese, who have lived in the eastern Congo for over 100 years. When Kabila won, it seemed the Tutsi Congolese would not be allowed to live in the Congo. Everyone hated them and wanted to kill them. No one knows how many Tutsi civilians have already died. They were rounded up and put in military prisons at the beginning of August when the war started.

As of September 20, I remain in Kinshasa. Immigration still has not given me a residence visa. I also hope to see the assistant secretary of education about the Botoa schools' accreditation.

I left Kinshasa on October 2. I received my visa last week. I could not meet with the secretary of education after I had wasted all that time. However, my old Toyota jeep, which had been in Kinshasa, received a complete motor and brake system overhaul. The vehicle could ship on a barge, along with the other supplies.

### Brutal Soldiers
When I arrived in Kiri, there were soldiers everywhere. They opened and searched through my luggage. I came home to a big welcome. The following day, three soldiers accompanied the lieutenant governor to Inongo, armed with semi-automatic rifles. Even though I only permitted them to borrow our bicycles, they went to the convent to take the Toyota by force. The vehicle had a broken spring, but the soldiers refused to believe the Sisters. I went and told the soldiers that they could not take the Toyota. They left and found Father Paul and forced him to give them the jeep.

The authorities in Inongo used the mission truck to take the ten soldiers stationed in Pendjua to Kiri. We thought we were finally rid of the soldiers until eight new ones arrived several days later. I did not understand why soldiers got stationed here, as I could not see anything strategic about Pendjua. Kiri, however, had an airfield and a river port.

The new group of soldiers acted brutally, and they arrested the mission's high school principal. They stopped everyone and checked their baggage, which the soldiers had a right to do since the country remained in a "state of war." However, if they found any food or money in anyone's luggage, they confiscated it for themselves. They tried to take some items from the principal, and when he resisted, they arrested him.

The following week the soldiers returned to their brutal ways. They beat up the director's brother and took a bicycle that belonged to the water project. A few days later, I hired someone to buy a crocodile for the boarding school students. As the young man brought it to the boarding school, the soldiers beat him and took the crocodile. We had to hospitalize the young man. Dr. Bakoko and I wrote a report to the military court in Kinshasa. The following day, the soldiers withdrew, but replacements will come. No one wanted the soldiers here because they took their goats, chickens, and ducks.

\#

I went to the village to visit my friends and to practice Lotwa. When I arrived, a lady sat on the ground and cried. A young man stood over her, yelling. I asked my friend why the man treated the woman this way. The woman, a widow of the young man's older brother, had lost her husband four years prior. When a man died in the Congo, his wife or wives then belonged to his living brothers. The young man wanted to "play with her" (they never said "have sex"), and the woman did not want to. He accused her of insulting his dead brother because she would not "play." I told him maybe the woman may be having her period, and she did not feel well, and he should let her go. The man agreed, and the grateful woman departed.

\#

A few days later, the barge arrived, and there should be over 100 cartons of medicine on it. I left to receive them as we had run out of many medications. Unloading the barge became hot and heavy work. The temperatures reached 95 degrees, and the humidity had to be higher. Only 80 cartons arrived, and they weighed a total of 500 pounds. It took us 6 hours to unload the packages, barrels of fuel, food, and other supplies onto the beach. We then started loading the truck. I climbed onto the truck bed to help place the cartons in order. As I did so, soldiers arrived and demanded we open every container.

"Your commander told me we do not have to open the cartons," I responded. We continued to load the truck. They spewed insults at us, which I ignored, and then they left. However, the soldiers soon returned and ordered the workers to unload the truck, or they would whip them. I got off the vehicle, climbed into my jeep, and drove straight to the hospital. I picked up Dr. Botuli and went to the military camp to see the commander. "I don't understand why the missionaries who help the people are always bothered by the soldiers," I scolded him.

The commander got into the jeep and returned to the beach. He bawled out the soldiers and told them to stop interfering. The soldiers were furious, but they left and did not come back.

# Life in the Congo

*1999-2000*

I went to Kutu in January for our annual meetings. We completed a questionnaire about whether the work we did met the criteria of working in "frontier situations." We all agreed that work with the Botoa remained a frontier situation and a priority. We decided that I would not work for the hospital in Kiri and the health centers in Lutoy after this year. My primary focus would be on the barefoot doctor program, the water project, education, and the farmer's cooperative, which had slid backward. We recommended that CICM keep a missionary presence in Pendjua for at least another ten years.

While I was there, we received terrible news from the procure. The bank did not have enough new money to replace the old currency. The mission had sent over $4,000 of old bills to the bank in Inongo. The government promised to continue to exchange the money until June 30. If the mission refused to accept the old currency, then many people would go without health care. The situation discouraged me, and I wondered how much longer we could operate here. The people suffered one hundred times more than the missionaries did.

#

Once I returned, I talked to the students about studying hard and preparing for semester exams. "If you fail, it will be your fault,"

I warned them. They responded, "You are wrong. If we fail, it is because our enemy has placed a curse on us." The belief in sorcery still dominated their lives, and they believed their enemies caused their suffering and failures. They feared retaliation and curses caused by their enemies. As a result, they never turned a cheater, thief, or another wrongdoer into the authorities. Fear dominated their lives. I realize that it may take several generations before these beliefs disappear.

#

In mid-April, I went to Kiri. I worked two twelve-hour days on the bookkeeping for the hospital. It became clear that the bookkeeper and possibly his assistant had embezzled money. Somehow, I stayed calm, though inside, I felt anger. Dr. Botuli and I met with the bookkeepers. After I exposed proof of the embezzlement and asked for explanations, they remained silent.

After they left, I told Dr. Botuli to hire a new bookkeeper, and if he did not, I would no longer assist him. Dr. Botuli agreed that we needed to find a new bookkeeper. In the meantime, we decided the current secretary would be responsible for the money.

I arrived back home, and as I corrected the nursing student's exams, the timber company Toyota pulled into the driveway. Out stepped Dr. Botuli, and he appeared worried. "Well, to make a long story short, I discovered the billing clerk did not keep good records, and they could not prove all the bills were correct," he said. The hospital stood to lose 30-40 percent of the amount they had billed. Dr. Botuli wanted to resign. I told him we have to accept the bad news and carry on from there.

### The Pharmacist

Father Andy arrived for a three-day visit. I worked in meetings with him in between teaching classes. He informed me Father Yves would get his assignment to Pendjua in six months. Father Yves currently worked in Beronge, and we looked forward to having him here.

After Father Andy left, I took a summer trip to my home in the U.S. I could not recall a worse week after returning from a vacation. Upon my return, I found a note under my door. The letter said that small stores in the area had an ample supply of medications they received from the pharmacy. I asked the pharmacist for his stock forms and found he had destroyed the paperwork for 72 different medicines. I reacted in anger and suspended him on the spot. After more investigation, we found the pharmacist had stolen several thousand tablets of aspirin, chloroquine, and antibiotics. I felt sick to think that he would do such a thing.

I spent most of the week in the pharmacy since I had fired the pharmacist. The chief of police arrived from Kiri to do an investigation. He arrested the ex-pharmacist, and he believed there might have been others involved, as well. The affair upset me, but I knew I had to carry on for the patients' sake.

#

Once again, I became the only hospital doctor. Dr. Bakoko returned to his village for a ceremony for his recently deceased mother. The hospital filled with patients and many had respiratory infections. We also had several cases of malnutrition, which we did not often see here. Most of them were Ekonda infants. The Ekonda depended on the Botoa for fish, wild game, and caterpillars. However, the summer fishing season had been lacking. Therefore, the Botoa kept most of the fish for themselves. The Ekonda relied on leafy greens and manioc roots, which were low in protein.

#

In December, ten soldiers arrived and stole chickens and ducks, including two ducks, from my secretary's house. She had paraplegia and used a wheelchair. I stormed to the mission in a rage, and when I found the army captain, I lashed out at him. The captain then asked Father Daniel to transport him along with seven soldiers to Kiri. I told him no, and I took the truck keys. The secretary recovered her ducks, and Father Daniel wanted to take the soldiers to Kiri. I relented and had the chauffeur take them.

## The Rest of the Story

On Christmas, the mission was quiet, so I wrote a letter to confide some personal things to my good friend, Joyce:

"I cannot imagine what my life would be like if you had not entered into my life. I would probably be in prison or dead. You see, I was a member of a terrorist group, the Weather Underground, a branch of the students for a "democratic" society. In 1968 after the assassination of Martin Luther King and Bobby Kennedy, we decided that the non-violent movement was useless and that we could make changes only through violent action.

Huey Newton founded the Black Panthers, and white liberal college students founded the SDS. One of our slogans was the only good capitalist was a dead one, and we put Christians in the same category. Oh, I never planted any bombs, only because they did not ask me. We took care of the medical needs of the demonstrators.

I joined the Peace Corps and came to Africa in 1974, hoping to sort things out. I returned still anti-Christian and communist, and then you entered my life and 'spoiled' everything. You turned me toward Christ, and the rest is history. He made me His channel of love, compassion, and healing for the poor of Africa. It is almost like Paul's story - the persecutor becomes the evangelizer."

## *2000*

The new year arrived, and in early January, Luba, Bola, and I traveled to Beronge. The trip covered 133 miles and took us 10 hours. Three Filipino confreres at the mission house, two priests, and an intern welcomed us. Even though I discovered a supervisor and two nurses were stealing and selling medicines, we had an enjoyable stay. This past year I had such a difficult time with people involved in stealing. I have not decided whether to fire the supervisor and nurses. In the meantime, I suspended them. The graduate nurse surgeon, the midwives, and the nurses at the health center all did an excellent job, and that made me happy.

#

In early March, a new group of six soldiers arrived, and they were awful. They went to a Botoa neighborhood and entered homes, stole chickens, and threatened the people. The soldiers entered the home of a Botoa teacher, who tutored the sixth grade and made advances on his wife. The teacher pushed the soldiers out of his house; however, they arrested him. They took the teacher and his wife to their military camp and locked him in a separate room. He protested that his wife must be allowed to stay with him. After a certain amount of time, he did not hear his wife, so he started to scream and kick the door. We do not know if the soldiers raped her since she would not say a word.

The following day, I sent a message to Kiri's military police commander to come and arrest the soldiers. He arrived, and after he heard the teacher's story, he had the soldiers rounded up and hauled off to Kiri. I vowed that I would not let the soldiers harm the Botoa.

#

In May, I went to Kutu for a retreat. I received messages from Kasai and Bas-Congo, where both sides looted many missions in the war. At a mission in Kimpango, the soldiers killed eight patients and ransacked the hospital. The priests and Sisters buried the dead and then left. They were now in Kinshasa and hoped to return when the area became safe again. I felt blessed that we were not directly in the war zone and that our mission did not get looted.

#

In early June, terrible battles took place in the Kisangani area between the Ugandan and Rwandan armies and the rebels. The people saw the Ugandans and Rwandans as invaders even though they fought for the rebel army. The troops looted gold, diamonds, coffee, tea, and timber in the northeast region. I regretted the Hutu massacre of 800,000 Tutsis in Rwanda in 1994, and I did not understand why the U.S. helped to build up the Rwandan army. That did not give the Tutsis the right to invade and kill Congolese people.

#

One day, in mid-June, Mbomba, Luba's younger brother, arrived at school five minutes late. The principal got angry, insulted him, called him stupid, and said his college diploma had no value. Mbomba felt so humiliated that he went home. The principal turned to a group of Botoa students and told them they were non-educable and that Brother Jerry wasted his money on them. He added that they were lousy Batwa and would remain Batwa and that washing the face of a monkey was a waste of soap.

I became distraught. I decided not to react until the report cards got sent out. Then, I planned to write to the priest who oversaw the diocesan schools and ask him to remove the principal. The Botoa students were hurt and angry, and if it were not for me, they would have beat the principal. I had worked with him for six years and liked the work he did; however, we could not have a racist at the school. Father Yves and Father Paul also agreed he must go.

## AIDS Crisis

I have not provided an update on AIDS recently. The international conference on AIDS held in South Africa released some reports. Africa's results were bleak, with the average life span expected to drop to 30 years in some countries by 2015. The conference projected there would be 10 million orphans in Africa because of AIDS. We have given many conferences on AIDS to the people, but I do not know what effect they have made.

My three priest confreres and I agreed we could not hide our heads in the sand when it came to the issue of AIDS. We decided to give sessions on AIDS prevention in high schools and villages. We would more aggressively treat sexually transmitted diseases that predisposed people to HIV infections. We would make prophylactics available. However, we needed more HIV test kits to screen blood donors and do random testing.

The soldiers who frequented the Botoa villages tried to entice or even force the young girls to have sex. Last week, I filed another complaint against a soldier who terrorized the girls in one village. The girls fled and hid in the forest for the night.

#

Later in the summer, while I was in Kinshasa, I went to see the USAID director. He was an African American who worked in the Congo for 16 years before he left in 1996. He expressed amazement that I remained in Africa, despite the mutinies and wars. He promised to do all he could to help.

The following day, I shopped for the boarding school students and the Botoa store. I bought bowls, pails, and cloth for school uniforms. Then, I went into a store that sold African-print material for women. I bought 150 pieces. Several of the women there sold fabric. After negotiating the price with one and choosing the cloth, five other women insisted that I also buy from them. The first lady did not want any part of that, and they all broke out in a huge argument. The women threw pieces of cloth at each other. They finally agreed that the first lady would sell 60 portions, and the other five women would each sell me 18 articles.

It is hard to admit that I only have $1,087 in my account, and I still have not received any grant money for the new school year. I have no choice but to step out on a "wing and a prayer" that provision will come.

#

The second round of the anti-polio vaccination program took place in mid-August. The mission sent out 19 teams of two persons each. The World Health Organization paid each worker $5.00 a day. The nurses were happy to earn $15.00 for the extra work since their monthly salaries were only $14.00. My bookkeeper and I compiled the statistics for the World Health Organization. I received $8.00 a day for my work, which I contributed to the boarding school.

#

Father Paul and I were upset with the bishop. Father Paul sent him a project for the Botoa grade schools. The bishop needed to sign it since the church in Holland that promised funds required his signature. He wrote a letter to Father Paul and stated that the Botoa school project seemed to be a shameful waste of money and was not formative. I suspected the bishop reacted out of jealousy because the mission received money for the projects. We decided to send this and any future projects to Cardinal Etsou in Kinshasa since he felt we did marvelous mission work.

There are days when I ask myself how much longer I can keep going. Then, I think of my students and what would happen to them if I left.

#

Again, I temporarily became the only doctor in the region, as Dr. Bakoko left for Brussels for a ten-month public health course. He promised to return in July of 2001. A doctor friend of his agreed to come to Pendjua and will hopefully arrive in September. On the four days before Dr. Bakoko left, he did non-stop surgery, and I took over the internal medicine and pediatrics.

Being the only doctor in Kiri's zone, with a population of 120,000 people, has stretched my abilities. The past Sunday, Dr. Botuli arrived from Kiri and announced he got accepted for a public health course in Belgium. I advised him he had a responsibility to stay in Kiri until he found a replacement. However, he left the next day on a flight to Kinshasa.

The new week brought more unfortunate news. The four soldiers stationed in Pendjua were terrible as they beat people and stole from them. They stopped one of Father Paul's school teachers and took his books, chalkboard, and money. Then they tied him up and beat him. When Father Paul went to his aid, the soldiers threatened to beat him. "Go ahead," he said, "but I will stay until you free him and return the things you stole." The soldiers relented, freed the teacher, and gave back all except his money.

#

Later that week, we had four AIDS patients in the hospital. We did not have any medications to treat it. We only managed the complications and then sent the patients back home. The big dilemma always turned to whether or not to tell the patients they had AIDS. The African nurses did not want to tell the patients, but I thought we should advise them to protect others. I also knew the patients would go from clinic to clinic, hoping to be cured and spend money uselessly.

#

For some good news, the boarding schools opened in September. However, we started on faith, as we had not received any grant money. Three days a week, we would only have manioc greens for lunch and supper.

#

By mid-September, the war heated up north of Pendjua. Twelve deserters from Kabila's army passed through the mission. They were armed, and they were obnoxious. The mission truck transported them to Kiri that afternoon. The soldiers reported that the rebels captured 2,000 other soldiers, 2,000 had died, and another 2,000 fled. There were supposed to be 50 more soldiers coming, but we were relieved to learn that they took another route to Inongo.

#

In late October, the mission barge still sat in Kinshasa. For two months, they have not found any available gas or diesel fuel. I waited for three medication orders. The mission had 400 liters of diesel fuel left, so Father Daniel stopped the road work and laid off the workers. We had enough manioc to last one month. If we could not get fuel to drive to get food, we feared we would have to close the boarding school. In the 21 years that I have been here, we have never run out of diesel fuel. If the war continues, then the conditions will worsen.

With the fuel crisis in Kinshasa, very few planes were flying. In early November, the barge still waited to buy fuel. The hospital no longer had gasoline for their generator. The mission had just 200 liters, and we had electricity, but only for two hours each night.

#

I arrived in Kinshasa on November 13, and Dr. Bakoko, whom everyone thought went to Belgium, came to see me. He did not get his visa by October 31, the last day he could enroll. He agreed to return to Pendjua, and his decision made me very happy and gave me hope that I could hold on through the end of the year.

# Arrested!

*2001*

January 14, 2001

Dear Mom,

I sent this letter to Bonnie as I thought you might be upset when you read it, and I didn't want you to read it alone. I had a new experience in my missionary life. The government security agency arrested me on December 29, and I was a prisoner until January 13. I never feared being harmed, nor did I fear for my life. My only fear came from the possibility of being expelled from the country. I could not imagine what would happen to my Botoa brothers and sisters, especially my dear students.

On December 21, I received a message from Kiri that the administrator of the territory (A.T.) and an ANR (a government security agency) agent were coming to see me. They arrived that afternoon and went to Dr. Bakoko's house. At about 5:00, they arrived at the mission with Dr. Bakoko. I escorted them into the living room. After we sat down, they gave me two radio messages from the ANR in Kinshasa. The first one, dated December 12, asked the ANR agent to spy on my activities. The second one, dated December 13, instructed the ANR agent to arrest me and bring me to Kinshasa.

They gave no reasons, and they wouldn't tell me anything. The agents asked for my passport and permission to inspect my room. They collected letters, pictures, my camera, video camera, radio, and videotapes. They also gathered my tent, .22 bullets, my .22 rifle, raincoats, put everything in boxes, and said they needed it for evidence. They put the boxes in a spare bedroom, locked the door, and kept the key. Dr. Bakoko became upset and afraid. I told Fr. Paul and Fr. Daniel about the events that took place.

In the meantime, the A.T. and the ANR agent told Dr. Bakoko if we gave them $500, they would not take my things to Kinshasa. Dr. Bakoko wanted us to pay them money, and we almost gave in. However, when the ANR agent said he would still have to take the boxes to Kiri and hide them, I decided they were looking for a way to steal them. So, I refused to give them money and told them to take the things to Kinshasa.

At 7:00 p.m., the agents returned to Dr. Bakoko's house. Later, Dr. Bakoko came and informed us that they would take me to Kiri. The agents arrived to get me and my things. Fr. Daniel angrily told them that he refused to let them take my stuff. The A.T. threatened to call the soldiers to arrest Fr. Daniel, but Fr. Paul and I calmed everyone down. I insisted they make a list of everything they were taking and sign it. Afterward, we loaded the jeep and left at midnight. We arrived at the edge of Kiri at 3:00 a.m. when the transmission went out. We walked an hour to the parish house, and then they agreed to let me stay there under house arrest.

On Friday, the ANR agent and his secretary arrived to interrogate me. I soon discovered why they arrested me. A group of Ekonda had always been against me because of my work among the Botoa. They asked many questions and made accusations. They inquired about the "Pygmy Project" and where I got the money for the barefoot doctor program. They asked the same question about the Batwa education program, the boarding homes, and the Batwa country store. Then they questioned me about my relations with the chiefs and village elders. The agent said I caused a conflict between the Pygmies and the Bantu, and the Pygmies no longer obeyed their

Bantu masters. He accused me of encouraging the Pygmy boys to date Bantu girls.

They claimed to have information that I went into the forest with the Pygmies one week at a time. Next, they said they knew that I went into the woods and stayed by myself for three days every month. They wanted to know what I did in the woods. They added that every time I left the forest, I went to Kinshasa.

The agent continued, saying I went into the woods with the Pygmies to dig diamonds to sell to finance my projects. I laughed, as this rumor had spread among the Ekonda back in 1994. I asked, "If this were true, wouldn't every able-bodied Ekonda be in the forest digging diamonds?" I continued, "Why don't you go and inspect the rainforest yourself instead of taking me to Kinshasa?"

In the end, they said they had information that Luba caused conflicts between the Pygmies and the Bantu. They added they had information that he organized secret meetings with the Pygmies to incite them to revolt against the Bantu.

After their last comments, they left. I sat in my room, half amused and half angry. I thought to myself: *the Ekonda know 80% of the patients at the hospital and health centers are Ekonda. They know 70% of the students at the high school where I teach are Ekonda, and all the nurses at the hospital and health centers are Ekonda, except for six. They are willing to risk losing all of this because I work for the liberation of the Botoa.*

The following day, many hospital personnel came to find out why they arrested me. They were all Ekonda, and they were distraught and vowed to find out who my accusers were and punish them. When they threatened the ANR agent, his attitude changed a hundred percent. He became nicer and promised to write a report to defend me and state that all the accusations were false.

On Sunday, no planes were available, so I celebrated Christmas with the three Congolese priests and five Congolese Sisters. I will be forever grateful to them for their kindness and support. They did everything possible to make my stay pleasant, given the circumstances.

The whole week went by, and no plane. I left in such a hurry I didn't even bring any books to read. I spent my time in prayer and receiving visitors. The airline agency said there would be a plane Saturday morning, so we notified Kutu, who notified Kinshasa. On Saturday morning, they said the flight would not come, and there wouldn't be another flight until after New Year's Day. I sat there in disappointment, as I wanted to get this whole thing over.

In the morning, the ANR agent came to tell me there would be a plane at noon and to prepare to leave. The priests and I were a little worried about my trip because they did not have a way to notify Kinshasa when I would be arriving. Nobody operated their radios on Sunday.

The plane arrived at 4:00 p.m., and we left for Kinshasa. When we landed, my guard took me to the ANR office at the airport to arrange transportation to the prison. One hour after another went by, and no one showed up to take us. At about 11:00 p.m., the agent said we would have to sleep in the office. At midnight, we went out to the parking lot where the police and airport personnel celebrated New Year's. We sat on empty beer crates. I bought my guard a beer, and I drank a Coke. An hour later, we returned to the office. I slept on a wooden bench, and the guard rested on a table.

With the windows broken out, there were hundreds of mosquitoes swarming in the room. My rain poncho covered most of me, so I didn't get too many bites. Another agent arrived in the morning and took us to the ANR prison and office. The director wasn't there, so we sat outside under a shelter. At 10:00, the director still hadn't arrived, and none of my confreres knew my whereabouts. I did not have anything to eat or drink since the New Year's "party."

One guard offered to go to the provincial to tell him that they had me at their office. I gave him the fare for a taxi. At noon, the provincial and another confrere arrived with coffee and sandwiches. The guards wouldn't allow us to shake hands. They asked the guards if they could bring me a mattress and chair as the prison cells had no furniture. As they left, the director arrived. He told them I could stay at the provincial house and report back on Tuesday morning. That news made me one happy jailbird as I didn't relish staying in those dirty cells with no toilets, running water, or electricity.

When we got to the provincial house, the five confreres asked me about my ordeal. I didn't know it then, but since no one knew where I went, it caused a panic. Emails flew back and forth from Missionhurst, the Vatican, Belgium, and Kinshasa. Everyone asked where I had been and how long had I been missing. Even the Doctors Without Borders in Belgium wanted to know where I had gone. Tuesday, we sent out emails that I got to go to the provincial house, safe and sound. The only thing, I couldn't leave the house.

The provincial and I went to the ANR bureau and waited. Finally, they told us to leave and come back on Thursday. The provincial contacted his friend, the second-highest official in the ANR, and asked him to intervene. He checked into the matter and said they had no proof in these accusations and that I should be free. Thursday, we went back, but they hadn't finished the report and said they would call us.

On Monday, the ANR agency called the provincial to come to his office without me. Later, he came and told me I would be free on Friday. They told me who my primary accuser is. He is a misfit who has a hut on a piece of the mission lot. We built two houses near him for the principal and a math teacher. He claimed that the land belonged to him. We had a court hearing, and the judgment ruled in our favor. His older brother is a judge in Kinshasa, so my accuser and his friends wrote a letter to the ANR in Kinshasa. Now the ANR director is embarrassed, and he apologized for my arrest.

On Friday, they brought my passport and a document that declared my innocence. God has reasons for allowing things to happen in our lives, even if we don't understand the purpose at the time. Before being arrested, I spent three days in the forest, praying. I read a little book called "Abandonment to Divine Providence."[4] I have had this book for over twenty years and never read it. The advice that I received helped me during my ordeal, even though I had difficulty with one chapter on accepting humiliations.

---

[4] Written by Jean-Pierre de Caussade

As a prisoner on the plane and at the airport, everyone stared at me, and some probably wondered how they could arrest a white religious. What had I done wrong? What criminal act had I committed? I have a prayer that I prayed every morning for years, asking God for the grace and strength to support humiliations, adversities, and controversies. Little did I know that one day, I would be humiliated and mocked.

I thought a lot about our parishioners in Pendjua. Are we truly Christians? Are we, indeed, followers of Christ? God didn't create humans to dominate other humans, and He didn't create humans to be the property of other humans. He also didn't create humans to be the owners of others as the Ekonda consider the Botoa to be "their Batwa." They think themselves superior and masters of the Botoa. The intense hatred for the Ekonda strikes each missionary who lives here. I worry that if attitudes don't change, there could be a blood bath like the one between the Hutus and Tutsis in Rwanda.

My prayer is the Ekonda will change and consider the Botoa their equals and treat them as such. I recalled what Dr. Martin Luther King said. "We don't want to be victorious over the enemy, but we want to convert them."

Love and Prayers,
Jerry

### Back Home Again

I was relieved to be back in Pendjua, and in late January, I moved into my new mud hut in Liamba. The people were delighted that I returned as it had been eight years since I last lived there. I furnished it with a bamboo bed, a small table, two chairs, and a bookcase. The clan there consisted of seven families. There were seven men, seven women, and many children, and we conversed about illness, daily life, and family history.

I used Mbolia, a sophomore, as an excellent source of information. One night, he talked about his aunt, who had chronic stomach problems. Mbolia said his aunt's dead sister, who appeared from time to time at night, caused the problem. The Botoa believed their dreams were real, and if they dreamt about a deceased relative, they thought that their spirit was present.

One night, they talked to me about the tensions my arrest caused between the Botoa and the Ekonda. The Botoa believed the Ekonda wanted to get rid of me because the Botoa were becoming more educated and independent. In truth, the Ekonda were also upset by my arrest. Mbolia told me that recently an Ekonda woman bawled out all the Ekonda at the marketplace. She said, "We have good health care because of Brother Jerry, and if I find out who accused him, I will chop off their heads." That is why I would not name who accused me.

The report cards were issued, and it appeared my arrest hurt the students. In early January, we were in the middle of the semester exam period. Father Paul told the director and students that he doubted that I would return. The students went wild and started breaking things. Then, they all left and returned to their villages. It took the director and his assistant more than a day to round them up and convince them to return to school.

#

It was not until late February that I met with the boarding school students. They wanted to know about my arrest and what happened in Kinshasa. When I finished telling them, I said that I forgave my accusers and the police. The students disagreed and said that I should not have forgiven them. I quoted Jesus' speech in Luke 6:27, "But I say to you who are listening: Love your enemies. Do good to those who hate you."[5] "That is just a story," the boys retorted. "No one can forgive and love his enemies." I replied, "Forgiveness is a primary condition to be a Christian. Jesus mentioned forgiveness many times in His teaching."

#

We continued to have problems with the soldiers. Three students informed me that a soldier beat up the Botoa high school teacher. I got on my bike and headed to where they held the teacher. As I rode, I prayed that I would stay calm. When I arrived, I saw that

---

[5] Luke 6:27 ISV

the teacher had large welts on his cheeks. The soldiers were drunk. "Why did you arrest the teacher?" I asked them. "We did not arrest him," they replied. I demanded, "Then, why did you hit him?"

They said, "We did not like the way he talked." The soldiers were illiterate and did not like that the teacher spoke French to them. "Since you did not arrest him, then I am going to take him home," I said. They allowed him to go. The boy's home director was furious, and he filed a complaint with the commander. The commander had the soldiers tied up and thrown into jail.

Two days later, the police chief and two associates stopped and fined three barefoot doctors because they didn't have the proper ID papers. The irony was that ID cards had not been printed or sold since 1980, so there were no ID cards to lose. This law was just a way for local authorities to collect money from people. The health personnel had ID cards, which indicated they were health personnel. However, the chief of police said that their ID cards had no value.

Dr. Bakoko, Sister Mary Emiel, and I decided to close the outpatient department in protest. This decision caused quite a reaction. The police chief and the military commander invited the "important" people of Pendjua to a meeting. They received many complaints and agreed to accept their cards as legitimate.

### The Soldier

Early the next week, a young soldier with an AK-47 rifle came to the mission. The boy soldiers often caused trouble, and this one was no exception. He demanded that the storekeeper give him an axle for his bicycle. The storekeeper told him the price, and the soldier said he should not have to pay. So, the storekeeper refused to give it to him. Suddenly, the soldier threatened him, and the shopkeeper fled through the back door, which opened into the missionary yard. The soldier knocked on my door and told me that the storekeeper had made him angry. Not knowing the situation, I took him to Father Daniel, who oversaw the store, and then returned to my room.

A few minutes later, I went out the back door and saw the workers gathered together. They told me they saw the soldier stalking the storekeeper and that he planned to shoot him. Just then, the storekeeper ran toward me, and I locked him in my room. Then, I returned and blocked the soldier from advancing. Father Daniel, the soldier, and I arrived at the same spot at the same time. Father Daniel yelled at the soldier to leave and made a motion to push him.

The soldier put his finger on the trigger of his rifle. Father Daniel sent a worker to get the commander. The soldier moved toward my room, and I again stepped in front of him and told him, "If you pull the trigger, you will go to jail. We are not at war, so put down your gun and leave." The soldier and I just stared at one another as my adrenaline flowed. He turned and left.

I got on my bike and raced to inform the village chief and the chief of police. Both leaders were afraid to do anything. The commander came and disarmed and arrested the soldier. They made a preliminary investigation and wrote down all that occurred. The missionaries signed the declarations. Later, they brought the soldier to the dispensary because he had blindness in his right eye. Dr. Bakoko examined him, and it appeared the soldier had a brain tumor. They transferred him to Kinshasa.

#

The Kiri territory administrator, one of those who arrested me, came to meet with the missionaries. The Bandundu Province governor wanted to know more about the problem between the soldiers, the national police, and the mission. Father Paul and Father Daniel refused to meet with him, but I talked to him. "We are fed up with the way the soldiers and police treat the people. They have stolen their animals, made arbitrary arrests, tortured the people, and came into the mission and hospital with their guns."

Afterward, the administrator met with the soldiers, police, and local officials and read them the riot act. We saw a positive change, as the soldiers remained in their camp most of the time, and most no longer carried their weapons.

#

While I taught at school one day, I began to have pain in my lower abdomen and groin, which steadily got worse. I went home and laid down. Upon examination, I discovered I had a hernia. I managed to reduce it by myself, and the pain went away. I decided to wait until after Easter to have surgery.

On Sunday night, I got called to the girl's home because a drunk man had appeared outside of the fence, causing trouble. I got the man to leave. When I returned to my room, the pain came back. This time the hernia had strangulated, and I did not think I could get it reduced. When the intestine popped back in, I felt better.

The following day, I told Dr. Bakoko he would have to operate on me. I told Luba, Bola, and the boarding home director that I needed to have surgery and not to tell anyone until I had gone into the operating room. First, I helped Sister Goretti stock the pharmacy to replace the depleted medicine inventory. Then, I taught nursing students for three hours and taught an English class. I got home and laid down for an hour.

At 3:00, I received spinal anesthesia, and by 4:15, the operation had ended. The director then told the students. The news created a near panic, so the students gathered outside the operating room. As they carried me out on a stretcher, I looked up, gave them the "hi" sign, and they were relieved. The hospital and the mission are about one block apart. I had an entourage of people gather in front of, alongside, and behind me. As news spread throughout the village, more people came. I stayed in the back bedroom to rest. Luba and Bola stayed with me for two nights.

#

You may have seen on the news that at the age of 29, Joseph Kabila took office ten days after his father's assassination, President Laurent-Desire Kabila. He is trying to mend relations with the international community. He also wants a peaceful solution to the war. He is very inexperienced, and it is not clear if he is in control.

#

Soon after I had recovered from my hernia surgery, two doctors from the World Health Organization arrived to talk about the Ebola virus and monkeypox. They gave a four-hour session. They were worried about the outbreaks of Ebola as there had been a recent outbreak on the Uganda-Congo border. Monkeypox is almost identical to smallpox, except it has a lower mortality rate. However, it is very contagious. There were 75 cases with five deaths in a village near Kiri last year.

The World Health Organization expressed concern that the Botoa would not get vaccinated. I assured them we had everything organized to do the vaccinations. After the two doctors left, the 70 Botoa barefoot doctors came for a training session to give the vaccine. The barefoot doctors would go door to door to ensure all children under age five got vaccinated.

#

In July, I left for the U.S. to spend time with family, returning to Kinshasa in October. I visited the Protestant rural health office. They contracted to implement the USAID rural health zone project. Dr. William Clemmer, the person in charge, had been the medical director of a Baptist hospital in Vanga. He told me that Kiri and Pendjua were on the list to receive help after the first of the year. We had a problem because Dr. Botuli, who finished his public health studies in Belgium on June 30, still had not returned.

Dr. Clemmer proposed that I become the regional medical director. Then he would send a qualified Congolese doctor to work at the hospital. I sent an email to find out if Dr. Botuli would return. I planned to see Dr. Clemmer the following day and ask him to wait until December 1 to decide who would be the zone medical director.

I spent the next four mornings running around Kinshasa, buying clothes for the Botoa students and merchandise for the Botoa stores. One section had dozens of small stores run by Chinese, Lebanese, Pakistani, and Senegalese. The clothes they sold were much cheaper than in the downtown stores. This section's roads were not paved and were either very dusty or very muddy, depending on if it rained or not. Crowds filled the shopping area, and I stood out, being the only white person there. Most shopkeepers were Muslim, and they were friendly.

#

I arrived home on November 4. A large crowd welcomed me, and my students were happy. They shouted, "Tator ateu bzakir esuki," which means, "Dad has come home! Hunger is over!" They often said this when their father came home from a hunt.

I learned there were many infants in the hospital with pneumonia. Since we did not have any oxygen tanks or respirators, a significant number died. We were in the middle of a long rainy season, and there were many mosquitoes, which meant there were many malaria cases. Malaria destroys the red blood cells, especially in children under the age of five. We had to give an average of four to five blood transfusions a week.

To add to my problems, Kiri's economic inspector arrested ten Botoa barefoot doctors claiming they did not have the qualifications. I sent a letter and explained that the medical director and the health ministry supported my project. I also wrote to the Kiri territory administrator, who then came to my office to talk about the program. I explained the training each barefoot doctor received, and I assumed there would be no further difficulties. An hour later, the administrator sent me a note. The inspector had a legal report and required a payment; otherwise, he would file the report. I refused to pay him, and then I told him they would see me in court.

I wrote to the Kiri hospital administrator. I informed him I would no longer help the hospital until the government stopped harassing my health workers.

In early December, I returned to Kiri. There were a few patients in the hospital, and there were no antibiotics or malaria medicine. The doctor had been absent since October, so the nurses had to do consultations and give treatments. If Dr. Botuli did not return, they would have to look for another doctor. USAID said they would not provide Kiri the health project unless they had a qualified and honest doctor.

## The New Commander
While in Kiri, the new military commander came to see me. He was young, educated, and spoke both English and French. He wanted to know how the soldiers in Pendjua behaved. "They are acting as they always have - stealing ducks, chickens, and goats from the people," I grumbled. "Things are going to be different," he said. "I want a good relationship with the missionaries." I remarked, "I've

heard the same promise from five or six other commanders." He insisted, "Brother, things will be different. You will see."

"Time will tell," I responded. Then, I went to the parish to prepare for my return to Pendjua. I left with a pickup truck full of smoked fish. We had room for three passengers in the back. When we arrived at a village ten miles from Kiri, four soldiers stopped us. Three were drunk. "We are going to Pendjua, and we need a ride," one of them demanded.

When I told them that we did not have room, the soldiers became angry and did not let us pass. I warned them, "We are going to Kiri, and I will advise your commander." When I informed him, he became both embarrassed and angry. He gave us a letter to advise the soldiers to let us pass, or they would risk arrest. We left Kiri again, heading for Pendjua. We came across the same soldiers, and I gave them the letter. One soldier brandished his bayonet and threatened the passengers. The soldier in charge asked if he could accompany us, as there were two other soldiers on the road ahead. I reluctantly agreed to let him get in the truck. He had a jug full of moonshine and became drunk by the time we had gone halfway. We dumped him off at the house where the other soldiers were.

#

That evening, the parish secretary came and told Father Paul that a soldier arrested his wife and held her at the soldier's house. Father Paul rushed to the house and asked them to release the secretary's wife. They refused. So, Father Paul sat on their porch and refused to leave because he thought they would rape her. Even after the soldiers threatened to beat him, he did not move one inch. Finally, they let the lady go, and Father Paul returned home. I prepared a report to send to the new commander.

The next day, my secretary, Marie, arrived at my office in tears. She encountered a soldier, who tipped over her wheelchair and dumped her onto the ground. Then, he cut the wheelchair and punctured one tire. When I saw that four of the soldiers were drunk, I decided to be prudent and not confront them. Again, I wrote a report to the commander. The soldiers were a bunch of misfits, and we would be better off without them. They always tell me that they are here to protect us. I always respond by saying, "We prefer to take our chances with the rebels if they come."

#

On Saturday, the new, young commander from Kiri arrived with a male nurse, and he wanted to buy some medicines for the army dispensary. The commander asked me how the latest group of soldiers behaved. I recalled how he had told me that things would be better.

I replied, "Well, the new group of soldiers are no better. They become drunk every night, steal ducks and chickens, and rape the young girls." I added, "Your soldiers do not deserve to be called CAF – Congolese Armed Forces, but should be called CAB – Congolese Armed Brigands." The commander did not laugh. "Why are your soldiers here?" I demanded. "To protect you," he said.

I laughed. "Those drunks could not protect me. Ten Botoa hunters could eliminate them with their poison arrows in a matter of minutes." He did not laugh at that remark, either. "May I buy some medicines?" he solemnly asked. "Sure, but only if you replace the six drunkards with five soldiers who do not drink." Then, he conceded, "I don't think I can find five such soldiers, but I will try."

# Life as a Bush Doctor
## *2002*

The day after New Year was quiet, though I had no idea how it would end. A lady from the Equator region arrived with three nasty machete wounds. I had never seen such horrific injuries. A fight took place in her village the day before between her brother and another man. They fought with machetes, and when she tried to separate them, she almost got hacked to death.

She had a large cut from her spine, halfway across her back. The wound went so deep that it cut the muscles and the surface of her kidney. The six-inch wound on her left shoulder practically cut off her upper arm. The lacerations were infected, and she lost a lot of blood. We gave her blood transfusions and cleaned and dressed the injuries. We had to wait three days to operate and close the wounds. I considered it a miracle that she did not die.

#

I received a letter that Dr. Iluku, who helped at the hospital, would not return to Pendjua. The news discouraged me. Dr. Iluku said he became ill, and some evil spirits in Pendjua caused the illness. Many may be astonished a doctor believed such a thing. Still, traditional African beliefs were more influential than modern medicine. Dr. Bakoko would not return until July, and now I am the only doctor at the hospital for the next four or five months.

#

The senior students returned from Kiri on March 5. They went to take the first part of the state exams, and they said a lot of corruption took place. The state examiner asked for bribes and, in return, handed out the questions in advance. I became disgusted because we did not have corruption in our school, and we told our students to study hard to pass the test on their merits. It discouraged the students that seniors from other schools passed the exam because of corruption.

#

When the next day started, I certainly had no idea how it would end. An 18-year-old patient arrived from Molele, a village 20 miles away. He had a tree fall on him while he cut a field for his Ekonda master. The tree almost took off his arm just below the shoulder. It looked like mush all torn to shreds, and it would need to be amputated. We were unable to start the operation until 11:30 p.m., and we did not finish until 5:00 a.m. We took skin from his forearm to cover the wound.

#

On Thursday, we held a community meeting with Father Andy. The same subject always came up: how long will the missionaries stay in Pendjua? No one ever gave a date. I want to remain as many years as possible. I hate the thought of what will happen to my Botoa students if I leave. I wondered what would happen to the hospital. The hospital in Kiri no longer functioned, and the doctor had not returned. I do not know if the USAID project is still on course for the Kiri hospital and health zone. I wrote to the American doctor in charge of the project. I told him that I would not be responsible for Kiri.

Several days later, I went to Kiri and met with a delegation from USAID. In February, I had sent a letter to USAID. I informed them that if Dr. Mponge did not resign as the medical director for Kiri and the health zone, I refused to be responsible for the project. The delegation said they came on behalf of Dr. Clemmer, the USAID project director, and agreed to replace Dr. Mponge. He had already embezzled significant funds.

COURAGE IN THE CONGO

They asked me to reconsider my resignation. The delegation wanted me to oversee the project and asked me to select a new doctor for Kiri. They said if I refused, then USAID would cancel the program for Kiri. I knew that would be a disaster. When the delegation left, I talked to Roger, the nurse supervisor in Kiri, until 11:30 p.m. He pleaded with me to withdraw my resignation and take charge of the project. I told him that I would reconsider, but they would have to find a good doctor for Kiri.

## The ANR

I did not expect that I would again become the subject of an ANR inquiry (National Agency of Investigation). This agency is the same group that arrested me in December of 2000. I received a summons to come to Kiri for an inquiry into the conflict with Dr. Mponge. He accused me of inciting the population against him. He accused me while at the ANR office in Kinshasa. This charge made me distraught.

I gathered documents concerning my different engagements in Kiri and made copies for the ANR. After evening prayer at the boy's home, they expressed their fear about my trip. They thought the ANR would take me away to Kinshasa again. They said, "If you do not return on Friday, we will walk to Kiri and attack the ANR." I assured them they did not have anything to worry about, and I would return on Friday.

I went to the ANR office, and the agents asked me many questions about the work I did in Kiri. They asked about my relations with the Congolese doctors who worked in Kiri and my opinion of Dr. Mponge. I did not hold back. I told them Dr. Mponge managed to bankrupt the hospital within one year, and he rarely treated patients. Each time he came to Kiri, a delegation then came to see me. They complained about Dr. Mponge and told me the doctor did not care about the patients, the personnel, or the hospital. I did not need to incite the population against the doctor, as everyone had already turned against him and asked him to leave.

After three hours of questioning, the agent said he would write a report and that I had no reason to worry. Afterward, the boarding home director and I went to a fishing village and bought 2,000 smoked fish to take back. When the boys saw the Toyota arrive, they jumped and yelled for joy. I hoped this would be the last episode with the ANR.

#

A few days after my return, the boarding home director accompanied me to Kiri. We also took six patients who were returning there. The group included the military camp commander and his wife, who came to Pendjua to deliver her baby. I have become friends with the commander. Whenever I make a complaint against a soldier, he punishes the soldier. He pulled all the soldiers out of Pendjua. I then learned that the commander received a transfer to Inongo. I will remember him as the only good soldier I have ever known in my time here.

When I arrived in Kiri, Dr. Otto, the vaccination program director, brought a new doctor to meet me. Dr. Mponge would not return to Kiri, which closed a sad period for the people. I arranged to meet Dr. Maurice. He was 42 years old and finished his studies in 1989. While he served as the medical director of a hospital in Bas-Congo in 1998, the war broke out. The rebels attacked his village, and Dr. Maurice and his family fled to Kinshasa. He had worked in a clinic there since 1999, but he did not like living in the city. Based on my first impression, I believed that Dr. Maurice had the experience to be the hospital and health zone director.

I informed both doctors I did not want to be associated with the Kiri hospital and health zone because of all the problems. I advised them of the recent accusation against me and the ANR inquiry. Dr. Otto stated that if I refused to be responsible, they would cancel the project, and Kiri would have nothing. The situation created a real dilemma for me.

When I had first arrived in Kiri, 15 patients were at my door. They pleaded to go to Pendjua. It seemed like a needless tragedy to see so many sick people who did not have a doctor, and the hospital did not have any medicines. In good conscience, I did not think I could abandon Kiri.

I again met with Dr. Maurice. I told him about the difficulties at the Kiri hospital and that the doctors in the interior did not make as much money because the people were poor. I asked him more questions about his work history and his family. Then, I told him I would try to find the money to pay a small supplement, but there would not be any contract or obligations.

#

Once I arrived home, I admitted a 14-year-old boy from Kiri to the hospital who suffered from osteomyelitis, an infection of the bone. He had received treatment in Kiri for the past three months. Now he had a pathological fracture of his femur. He needed radical surgery, which I cannot do here. I told the family that they must take their son to the University in Kinshasa, and I offered to pay for the boat ticket. Then, I made a splint with some plaster to use to stabilize the fracture.

#

Then, I had a female patient with a ruptured extra-uterine pregnancy. She had gone into shock and needed at least two units of blood before the emergency operation could start. No family members were available, so the pharmacist and I each gave a pint of our blood. With many prayers, she made it through the surgery.

That afternoon, I gave the boarding school students a lesson on AIDS. They asked many questions. They wanted to know why there had not yet been a case of AIDS among the Botoa. I believed it was because of the Ekonda taboo to have sex with a Botoa. However, the situation has been changing in the cities. In Kiri, the Botoa prostitutes had Ekonda clients, so it would only be a matter of time before AIDS affected the Botoa. The soldiers had raped many Botoa women the past five years, and they would spread AIDS among the Botoa.

#

Later in the week, two sixth-graders bought whiskey from the school director's wife and became very drunk. I became angry and went to talk to her, along with the other teachers and teacher's wives who sold moonshine. They all lived in the teacher's housing. I warned them, "If you continue to make moonshine, I will report you to the priest coordinator for the schools." They begged me not to write the report. "It is inconceivable that educators contribute to the delinquency of the youth," I continued. "I'm serious, and if you do not stop making and selling your homebrew, I will act."

#

The previous night, a mother gave birth to a little girl who had a defect in her abdominal wall, and her intestines were outside the abdomen in a sac. I had not seen anything like it, so I got my surgery book and read how to repair it. I was apprehensive about operating on a newborn baby. Though we were not too hopeful, we had no choice but to try. With great effort, we managed to get the intestines back into her abdomen and sew her up. Later, the baby girl had bowel movements and started to breastfeed. Indeed, I could feel the hand of the Lord upon this miracle baby and us.

### Senior Trip

Boboko Joseph recently finished his senior year in the biology and chemistry option, and Mobilia Andre is a senior in the teacher's program. These two young men accompanied me to Kinshasa. When we arrived, we took a taxi to the procure. They stayed in rooms on the third floor that faced the Congo River. I had a place across the hall. We went up on the roof. It had a railing around the edge, and we saw the Congo River, the port, and the railroad yard. Brazzaville, the capital of the Republic of the Congo, could be seen across the river. We saw the buildings at the city center, of which the tallest had forty stories. Mbolia Andre turned to me and asked, "Where did the white people get the intelligence to do all this?"

We took a car and visited the national teacher's college. This college is where Mbolia Andre wanted to attend when he finished high school in 2003. Next, we went to the university to visit the medical school. Boboko Joseph wanted to be a medical doctor. He has been first in his class every year for twelve years, so I believed that he could succeed.

#

The next day, I went to the USAID office with Dr. Maurice. He had already been to the office the previous day. They told him that unless Brother Jerry agreed to oversee the project, USAID would not help Kiri. I knew it would be difficult to refuse. If I did, Kiri would no longer have access to medicines. I told USAID that I would oversee the project if there were no financial obligations on my part. I advised Dr. Maurice that he must be honest and do a good job directing the hospital and health zone. I added that if he did not, I would inform USAID and have them stop the project. We made an appointment to return and sign the papers.

#

During our second week in Kinshasa, we went to the CICM printing plant and bookstore. The boys learned how they made books. They were wide-eyed and amazed at how the machines worked. We bought books for the schools.

In the afternoon, the chauffeur took us to another bookstore. There were three lanes of traffic stopped at a stop sign. We were in the middle with cars all around when a policeman stepped in front of us. He motioned for us to pull over to the side of the road once the traffic started moving. A very obese policewoman opened my door and squeezed in beside me. She asked the driver for his license and insurance card. "You went through a stoplight at the preceding corner," she accused us.

"That's a lie." I retorted. "If it were true, then the cars behind us went through as well, and you should arrest them." Both the policeman and policewoman said we had to go to the station. I knew they were looking for a bribe to avoid the inconvenience of going there. I told her that the boys and I would walk to our destination. Then I said, "The chauffeur can go to the station, but we are only passengers, and the car is not ours." She hesitated, and then I insisted she open the door and let us out since we had not violated the law.

She replied, "No, Father, we will drive you to your destination." I replied, "Fine." We went to the bookstore and exited the car. The chauffeur and the two police left. Five minutes later, the chauffeur arrived back at the bookstore. The police had asked him for 300 Francs to buy a beer. The chauffeur only had 30 Francs, which they refused, and sent him on his way. As he left, they said, "That Father doesn't want to share his money with us, poor police."

#

After returning from Kinshasa later in the month, Dr. Maurice came to see me about the medicines USAID had committed to sending. We had paid a Congolese man to transport the medication. The man had arrived in Nioki, near Kutu, but he had run out of fuel. The boat had a hole in the hull, and the motor did not work. We heard the man already sold the 800 liters of kerosene and began to sell the medicines. I contacted the procure in Kutu and asked if the mission's barge could pick up the remaining medications when it returned from Kinshasa. I felt sorry for Dr. Maurice as he struggled to manage the Kiri hospital and still did not have any medicines.

#

The diocesan school director informed me that eleven of the seniors who majored in teaching did not pass the state exam. Five were Botoa. I shook my head in disbelief. I doubted the state exams had ever arrived in Kinshasa, and I suspected they never got corrected. Corruption ran rampant at the Kiri exam center. Many were jealous of the Pendjua high school, so I imagined that anything could have happened. The students will study hard again all year and hope for better results next year.

#

After I returned from a meeting with Dr. Maurice in Kiri, I received a note from a school teacher in Mboyolo. He informed me the father of Nseka, an 8th-grade student, had died. A poisonous snake bit him while he fished. I waited until supper to tell Nseka. When I told him, he cried and cried, and everyone became deeply saddened. Nseka kept throwing himself down on the ground. I held him and did my best to console him. We had an evening prayer vigil. The choir sang songs they composed, as well as some traditional songs. On Saturday, I gave Nseka some money, and he and four other boys, headed for Mboyolo.

#

I arrived in Kinshasa on November 23 and met with Dr. Bakoko, who still planned to return to Pendjua. I also met with SANRU and USAID to discuss the health projects for Kiri and Pendjua. SANRU is the abbreviation for Sante Rurale (rural health) and is a division of the Church of Christ of the Congo. USAID gave SANRU the contract to supervise the health projects. The projects would be for five years, and they would provide medicines and materials for the hospitals and health centers.

Before meeting with Dr. Clemmer, I went to see the administrator. He wanted to talk about the financial report Dr. Maurice sent. Each month, SANRU sent $500 for the supervision of the health centers and office supplies. Dr. Maurice wrote that he used the money to transport the medicines from Inongo to Kiri. This claim proved to be false, as the mission's barge carried all medication. Dr. Maurice created fake invoices dated October 10 and 20. However, the medicines had already arrived on October 6. I felt sick at heart to discover Dr. Maurice had been dishonest. I asked the administrator if he wanted to cancel the Kiri project, and he replied he would not. However, going forward, he would place the $500 in an account in Kinshasa, and I would supervise its use.

The lady who did the purchasing for the procure accompanied me. We went to Kato, where the Chinese, Lebanese, and Senegalese operated hundreds of shops. All of a sudden, a gang of six thieves attacked us. After much pushing and shoving and shouting, the thieves fled empty-handed. Some storekeepers came to our aid. I held tight to my briefcase during the struggle. I felt relief that the thieves did not have knives or guns.

The chauffeur, the lady purchaser, and I returned to Kato to purchase the remaining items on my list. Thirty minutes later, a torrential downpour began and lasted for three hours. I bought an umbrella and managed to shop while wading through mid-calf high water. When we returned to the office, the roads were like rivers and filled with stalled vehicles. Our four-wheel-drive Toyota Land Cruiser did not have any problems navigating the flooded streets.

#

At week's end, the chauffer and I picked up Dr. Bakoko, his wife and son, to catch a flight to Inongo. When we arrived, some workers started to take the baggage off the plane. I told them they were mistaken, as we were to continue to Kiri.

The agent from Kiri said the plane had engine problems and must return to Kinshasa. Both Dr. Bakoko and I doubted the agent had told the truth. I asked the pilot if the aircraft had engine problems, and he replied, "Certainly not." The agent knew the plane would not go to Kiri, but he wanted the ticket sales commission. He promised to arrange transportation by boat to Kiri. I had my doubts; however, we were stranded in Inongo on our trip back to Pendjua.

We arrived back home on December 11. The travel agent could not arrange transportation to Kiri. However, I managed to get an outboard motor and a boat from a Congolese doctor. I bought 200 liters of gas and 7 liters of oil. We loaded the boat, paid the port authority, and were on our way. The trip usually took at least seven hours. We were an hour from Kiri when the sun went down. The chauffeur made a wrong turn, and we were lost. After we found the right channel to take, we arrived in Kiri at 8:00, tired but happy.

#

Upon arriving in Pendjua, I had an altercation with the local officials and the chief of police. The Kiri territory administrator ordered the police chief to collect a bicycle tax of 1,000 Francs per bicycle. They confiscated the bike of the nurse who came from Monbago to pick up medicines. The health center bikes were exempt from tax, so I went to see them. They refused to release the cycle, so we got into an argument. "Since you are against the missionaries, I am going to close the health center and file a report with the administrator," I warned them. They still refused to release the bike, so I sent a report to the Kiri administrator.

#

In late December, I made two trips to Kiri. I met with Dr. Maurice concerning his October finance report. He did not know I knew he gave a false statement and used the $500 for his personal needs. I began, "I know you have a lot of expenses since your wife and five children are still living in Kinshasa." Then, I added, "I know

209

you do not earn a lot of money yet." I then showed him the report and the false bills he made out. "You will have to do better because if you don't, then the project will be canceled by SANRU, and the people of Kiri will suffer again."

"Thank you, Brother Jerry. I made a mistake," he admitted. "I promise not to steal again."

#

The day after Christmas, I had another altercation with the chief of police. He came to see the deacon. I yelled at him for not obeying the administrator and not returning the bike. The police chief became angry. "The administrator cannot do anything against me!" he shouted.

I replied, "I will tell that to the administrator when I go to Kiri tomorrow." At 4:00 p.m., the deacon had come to see me, and he was upset. The police chief came to his house with a revolver and told him he would kill him if he continued to agree with the missionaries. I advised the deacon to accompany me to Kiri and report the incident to the administrator.

On the way to Kiri, the deacon relayed more details to me, "The police chief returned to my house last night with a revolver. He put the barrel to my head and said that even if he killed me, they would not arrest him. He said he would just get reassigned to another territory." We arrived in Kiri and went straight to the administrator's office and gave him a report.

# Kiri Hospital
## *2003*

In mid-January, I traveled to Kiri. In the afternoon, I met with the hospital accountant and learned the situation did not look favorable. Dr. Maurice left for Kinshasa, and he took all the money. I hoped he planned to buy medicine. We would have to wait for his return to find out how or if he spent the money. I stayed overnight at the parish. There were four diocesan priests there, and they had a difficult time making ends meet. They usually ate supper at 7:00, but no one had arrived when I walked into the dining room. That seemed unusual. At 8:00, Father Christian called me to come and eat. We each had one piece of bread and water. I felt embarrassed, as I knew they felt terrible that we had nothing else to eat.

#

In late January, I arrived in Kutu for the annual retreat. Before going, Father Daniel, the three confreres from Beronge, and I met. We discussed our continued presence in Pendjua and Beronge. Father Paul would likely not return, and therefore we would not have a priest to do pastoral work in the villages. Father Daniel considered leaving for good at the end of 2004. Father Mike Reyes would also possibly depart.

They decided to hand Beronge over to the diocese, and the remainder would stay in Pendjua. I could not bear the thought of leaving. I feared that the Botoa projects would disappear without our

211

presence, and the Ekonda would again oppress the Botoa. In the two days after the retreat, I participated in meetings. Everyone agreed the two missions were a priority because of the Pygmies. They were the poorest of the poor and the most marginalized. The problem would worsen as the number of confreres continued to diminish.

They confirmed that Father Paul would not return, and Father Yves would return after Easter. In June, Father Mike will return to the Philippines. Two young confreres would remain in Beronge, and the mission would come under the diocese's authority in 2004, and the two confreres would transfer to Pendjua. They also decided that the missionary presence in Pendjua would end in 2008. I found some relief in knowing that we would remain here for now.

\#

Upon my return, I met with Luba, Bola, and Jean Louis. Jean Louis has been trying to organize an association to help the Pygmies. I met him last year in Kinshasa and encouraged him to return to Pendjua. Jean Louis resided in Booke, a small village 50 kilometers away. He wrote an agricultural project I helped him edit before sending it to various foundations to request funding. Jean Louis had already begun to organize two teams consisting of men and women from Booke to cut and plant demonstration fields. I provided them with axes and machetes. Every household had to dig a latrine and cut the weeds before they received a machete.

\#

Next, I met with Dr. Kwata from SANRU-USAID regarding a letter accusing Dr. Maurice of irregular accounting practices. He said Dr. Maurice did not use the funds for their designated purposes. I told Dr. Kwata that some of the accusations were true, and we discussed them at the council meeting. I explained that we established financial guidelines, and I hoped Dr. Maurice would follow them. This situation put me in a tight spot because if SANRU canceled the project, Kiri would not have any medicines.

\#

In need of some recreational time, I went to a soccer match between the Pendjua team and a neighboring team. The game did not last thirty minutes. The other side placed a fetish on the goal post, and a Pendjua player knocked it off. The other team refused to play because their magic fetish got destroyed. Witchcraft is still actively used here. The people go to the witch doctor to buy a fetish to help them succeed in an exam or have a successful hunting or fishing trip. They also use them to have a good harvest, win at sports, find a girlfriend, be healed from an illness, or harm an enemy.

The Botoa students claimed that after they won all the soccer games last year, the Ekonda said that happened because Brother Jerry prayed. They said that I receive power from God, and that kept the opposing teams from winning. I told the boys they had won because they worked hard, trained a lot, and played as a team. They did not seem convinced.

#

Later, I went to Kiri to meet with Father Andy and two new Filipino confreres, Vincent and Ronnie. They had finished their theology studies and would now do a two-year internship. They were also in Kinshasa for one year to work in an urban setting. Now, they would come to Pendjua and Beronge for a rural experience.

The following day we left for Beronge. On Saturday, Father Mike gave a recollection of his six years of missionary life in Beronge, and we held a going-away party. Father Andy shared about missionaries. Missionaries are to proclaim the Good News and be witnesses of God's love to all, especially the poor.

Vincent, the new, 28-year-old confrere, had attended school at a CICM parish in the Philippines. Vincent worked very hard. He put in a plywood ceiling in the mission house and painted the walls and ceiling. While he repaired the chicken house, one of the brick walls fell over. So, Vincent fixed all the walls in the chicken yard. He wanted to raise chickens and ducks. I hoped we could keep the thieves away.

The good news came that Father Daniel arrived in Kinshasa. A few days later, he made it to Kutu, and he arrived at our mission on June 14. A large crowd came to welcome him back. We were now back to a community of four, with Father Yves, Father Daniel, Vincent, and I. I enjoyed the new spirit of our community.

*Monkeypox*

A terrible disease first appeared last week. It is a virus that causes a condition called monkeypox, and it is similar to smallpox. The rash and symptoms of the two diseases are almost identical. However, the mortality rate is lower. The virus spreads by contact with an infected animal, usually a monkey or a squirrel. The infected person is also contagious to other people. A 12-year-old Botoa boy became the first patient with the disease. The nurses first admitted him on Saturday, and they thought he had a severe chickenpox case.

We evacuated the hospital and quarantined the boy and his family. The other patients went to another ward under quarantine, and we took measures to protect the nursing personnel. Everyone panicked, so I took it upon myself to care for and treat the boy. Two more children came to the hospital with lesions, but they were not as sick as the first boy. We informed the World Health Organization office in Inongo, and they will advise Kinshasa. Now we waited for instructions on how to proceed. Times like these tested our faith and trust in God.

By Thursday, the boy with the monkeypox appeared to improve. He could sit up and stand. He asked for a T-shirt and a pair of shorts. But, by Friday morning, he had convulsions and then became unconscious. He died at noon on Friday. I surmised he developed encephalitis or possibly Reyes syndrome. The other two children were in good condition. I became upset when I learned that the nursing director did not visit the very sick patients during the three-day weekend. After a conversation, the family of the quarantined boy received excellent treatment.

*Jean Louis Ebengo*

I am also happy to report that the new Kiri territory administrator, though not an Ekonda, seems to be very pro-Botoa. I like having the highest government authority on our side. The Pygmies are victims of many cases of abuse from local Ekonda officials. The administrator asked Jean Louis to make a report every time a violation occurred, and he would punish the perpetrator.

Jean Louis was excellent at reporting on abuses the officials did to the Botoa. The sector's secretary went to a Botoa village with falsified documents. He claimed that 40 acres of their land belonged to him. Then, the chief of Liamba forced Botoa women to carry thirty sacks of corn on their backs for 15 miles. Another official forced the Botoa to build a mud home for his concubine.

Jean Louis and I prepared reports for the administrator and the new Pendjua sector chief. The new sector leader came from the Mosengili tribe. The administrator promised to put an end to the abuses. I warned Jean Louis that there would be many Ekonda who would now hate him. He always had bodyguards armed with machetes, bows, and arrows whenever he traveled.

Representatives from USAID, Innovative Research Management, and the government arrived in Kiri. They held a forum on the abuse by the military, national police, and local government officials. The people gave examples, and Jean Louis reported on injustices suffered by the Botoa. These reports made an impact on the American representatives.

\#

Upon returning to Pendjua, I had a conflict with the police chief and the village chief. The two men became angry and wrote a letter that accused me of stirring up a rebellion. They were also mad at Jean Louis since he filed many reports on the police and local officials' abuses against the Botoa. I believed we had the Kiri administrator's total support, so I did not have any fear.

\#

I traveled to Kiri to buy fish. While there, I met with Dr. Maurice. He did not look forward to the meeting since I had sent a report to the USAID office about his terrible management of the zone. Dr. Maurice acted his usual cheerful and friendly self, and he told me USAID accused him of mismanagement, which he denied. He said he had enough of Kiri and would leave in one month.

\#

Later that month, I drove Father Yves, Father Daniel, and Vincent to Kiri. My confreres were amazed at how I navigated the bridges without falling through. Our group left for Inongo on

Thursday morning. We thought we could make it in one day since we used the tugboat instead of the barge. A massive storm rolled in before we got to the lake, and we had to pull to the side of the road for two hours. When we got onto the lake, a strong wind forced us to pull over near a logging camp. The waves on the lake were rough all day, so we spent the night there.

Six people were on the boat, and we had a small six-foot by six-foot cabin with wood benches in it. One seat had cushions, so the three oldest passengers slept on it. No one slept well. We started again at 4:00 a.m. After we crossed the lake and followed the bank toward Inongo, another storm came up and forced us to shore. When the captain went to start the motor, the batteries were dead. The captain and two others paddled a canoe to Inongo. They came back four hours later, and the nightmare journey resumed.

On Saturday, Father Yves gave a recollection. He talked about his 50 years of professed life. Father Yves, known as the saint of Lake Mai Ndombe, had deep faith rooted in Christ. He admired Saint Paul, the great missionary. All the events made for a very memorable day.

#

In October, I traveled to Kinshasa. At first, we went by boat from Kesa to Nioki. A massive storm came up behind us and followed us to Nioki. We unloaded our luggage and rushed into a riverside hold before the torrential downpour hit. The rain stopped at 1:00 a.m., and the plane arrived at noon the following day.

I came to Kinshasa for medical care, rest, and a little work. I discovered another basal cell cancer on my left cheek that had been there for about eight months. I went to the Kinshasa Medical Center. Most of the doctors were Congolese, but they had received training in Belgium. I met with the dermatologist. He did not do a biopsy on me since the lesion appeared to be precancerous. Then, he gave me a fluorouracil cream to apply.

I went to USAID to talk to Dr. Minuki about the problems in Kiri. He read my July report about the disastrous situation, and the news about Dr. Maurice disappointed him. SANRU left 200 cartons of medicine at the procure. A person from Kiri delivered one hundred containers. According to Dr. Maurice, another person, Dolysi, would bring the other 100 cartons. Since Dolysi and I were friends, I contacted him. He claimed he did not know anything about transporting the remaining 100 packages. I suspected Dr. Maurice might have intended to pick them up and sell them when he came to Kinshasa in November.

As I waited to depart to Kiri, Dr. William Clemmer, the project manager, walked in. He had not expected to see me. His administrative team planned to talk about the problems in the Kiri health zone and Dr. Maurice. We decided to send a team to do an audit in Kiri. I arrived back at the mission on November 9 after a four-week absence.

#

A few days later, I returned to Kiri for the USAID-SANRU audit of the health zone and hospital. The evidence showed that Dr. Maurice stole a lot of money. He also sold equipment and material SANRU had sent. The administrator relentlessly questioned the doctor, the accountant, the doctor's girlfriend, and a lady responsible for the pharmacy. When I met with the team, the administrator got very angry. He said that someone planned the disorder to cover up the theft. He said he would suspend Dr. Maurice and pull the Kiri project unless I agreed to manage the pharmacy and the accounting.

"I already have enough work in Pendjua," I responded, "especially since Dr. Bakoko is working in Inongo. We don't know if he will return or not." Everyone expected me to agree to the plan to ensure health care for the 100,000 inhabitants in the Kiri health zone. I told them I would sleep on it and give them an answer in the morning. I did not sleep well. I got up at 3:00 a.m. and prayed to discern what to do. I decided I could not refuse their proposal.

The administrator and medical director of the Inongo district came to see me. I told them I agreed to manage the pharmacy and the accounting. We then met with the health zone staff. The administrator suspended Dr. Maurice and gave me the keys to the pharmacy and the safe. There were ten village elders, the Kiri territory administrator, and other officials present. They all began to applaud. Dr. Maurice walked out in anger.

#

After three days in Kiri, I left for home. When I arrived, I found a note slid under my door that read, "How can a father abandon his children? Don't you like us anymore? Why are you always absent?" I talked to the students and explained, "If I did not agree to manage the pharmacy in Kiri, then 100,000 people would be without health care. Is it right for me to refuse to help those people? What do you want me to do?" They agreed I should help the people in Kiri, and they would accept my absences.

I spent Saturday afternoon with my "abandoned" children. We had a "masolo ya bankoko," an event where someone who returns from a trip talks about their journey. They informed me about what happened to them while I had been absent. I gave the boys new shirts and the girls new dresses. The gifts made them very happy and were a sign I had not abandoned or neglected them. The boys and girls were the joy of my life. I thought about what the Lord had told His disciples. "No one has left his home, brothers, sisters, mother, father, children, or fields because of Me who will not receive a hundred times as much here in this world."[6]

### Bokoko

At the end of November, a Botoa student, who had many troubles and no longer stayed at the boarding home, died. Precisely what happened is not clear. I heard that on November 15, the boy drank a lot and stayed with a friend in Lakula. He did not go back to his village. During the night, he went looking for a girl. Someone threw a large stone that struck him in his left lower chest. The next day he went home and complained of pain. He came to the hospital on November 20, and Dr. Charles admitted him after diagnosing a chest wound.

Unknown to us, the family continued to treat him with enemas of toxic herbs. After five days, he had severe abdominal pain. He underwent surgery, and they found he had a perforated stomach and a ruptured spleen. He died on the operating table. The

---

[6] Mark 10:29-30 ISV

previous day, he told his family and nurse that Bokoko had thrown the stone. Bokoko, a senior, had recently passed the senior biology and chemistry state exam. He denied the accusation, and there were no witnesses. The deceased boy had a conflict with Bokoko, so I wondered if he named him out of spite.

The authorities jailed Bokoko in Kiri to wait until the investigator finished his work and sent his report to the court in Inongo. Everyone believed Bokoko would be found innocent and that he would be acquitted. I felt sorry that this happened because Bokoko planned to leave for Kinshasa this week to begin studying at the university. I prayed for both families.

### The Theft

In early December, the nurse supervisor came to work and noticed a hole in the veranda's ceiling, and someone opened the front window. When Richard, the accountant, arrived, he opened the door. He discovered that the safe was gone and he saw a hole in the ceiling above the door. Someone had broken into the office and robbed the safe that contained 235,900 Congolese Francs ($646.00). The Pendjua sector chief came to investigate. Everyone agreed that the holes in the ceiling were too small for a thief to enter through.

They believed Richard stole the safe with the help of an accomplice. Due to his disabilities and use of a wheelchair, he would have needed help. Richard denied taking the safe and claimed thieves entered through the holes in the ceiling. The chief talked to the judge in Inongo. The judge instructed him to bring Richard to Inongo unless he admitted to the robbery. Later, Richard signed a document and promised to reimburse the money. However, he continued to claim his innocence. The health zone director suspended Richard. This event made me sad because Richard worked for me for 14 years, and it would not be possible to find another job.

\#

Sometimes, it seems like another week, another tragedy. An Ekonda girl in junior high school collapsed and died. I believed she had a cardiac arrest as a result of congenital heart disease. I had treated her older brother for heart disease for the past five years. The students were upset and believed she died due to sorcery. Then, a third-grade student died of cerebral malaria. His parents were a nurse-midwife and a high school teacher. Everyone became upset because two students had passed away within ten days.

I found a letter the interns slid under my door. They wrote, "Brother, last week, we buried one of our students, and another this week. The Bantu, who know how to reason well, told us they had a dream that a storekeeper from Kiri buried a fetish on the school grounds. As a result, five male Botoa interns, five female Botoa interns, four male Bantu students, and four female Bantu students will die. Brother, do not think we are lying because it's true. The Bantu told us so. If you want to do good, go to Kiri and bring Father Ngongo here to remove the fetish. If not, we are going to die. If you doubt us and one intern dies, we will all quit school."

Usually, I laughed at this silliness, but, this time I could not. I did not take the student's beliefs and fears lightly. So, I went and talked to the principal. He and the teachers agreed that they also wanted Father Ngongo to come. I promised I would speak with Father Yves. After evening prayers, I gave the letter to Father Yves to read. We agreed we should celebrate a Mass on the school grounds and bless the classrooms to dispel the fear that existed in the two schools.

#

The police chief came and said he caught the thieves who robbed the money from the accountant's office. Last Monday, he and I both received an anonymous letter. It named four Botoa boys as thieves because they bought clothes and other items at local stores. When they arrested the four boys, they said a man named Bolunga gave them the money. Bolunga fled into the forest, and they had not captured him. I asked the chief how the robbers entered the office, and he said they came through the holes in the ceiling. He did not inspect the holes, so I had him go and look at them. When he came and looked, I asked him, "Do you think a person could fit through a hole in the ceiling that measures eight inches by 13.5 inches?"

"Inano, a seventh-year junior high school student, could," he responded. "Bring Inano here so we can measure him," I said. The distance between Inano's shoulders measured 15 inches. Even so, the chief's report noted that the accountant did not commit the crime and should be allowed to return to work. The health zone supervisor refused to let Richard return because no one believed a thief could enter through the ceiling's holes.

I felt sorry for Richard, even if he were guilty. Due to his severe handicap, he could never find another job here. I wrote two letters to Richard to counsel him. I told him it would be wise to admit he stole the money, return what remained, and then return to work. However, Richard continued to declare that he did not commit the theft. I believed that the increase in poverty and misery caused a significant rise in dishonesty and thefts.

#

On the same day, tragedy struck the same couple whose 12-year-old son died on December 15. This time, their three-year-old boy came to the hospital with fever and delirium. They treated him with quinine for cerebral malaria. However, he died that day. I now wondered if the two boys may have had meningitis. It could be possible even though they did not have the classic signs of meningitis, such as a stiff neck.

#

On Sunday, the choir wore the new robes Sister Henriette, and the tailor sewed. The choir sang their hearts out. I became sentimental and choked up by the performance. I could not imagine how 23 years ago there were only 20 Pygmy children in primary school. Today, there were over 2,000 Pygmy children in primary schools. We had 100 in junior and senior high, a choir of 45 Pygmy high school students, 20 school teachers, and eight nurses. I thanked Jesus for sending me to Pendjua to bring the Good News to the poor and oppressed.

# Civil Rights
*2004*

I have an update on the theft that occurred in the accountant's office on December 2 of last year. The person that many considered to be the principal thief, a Botoa man, turned himself in on December 25. He told the police that he and Richard went to the office. He said Richard opened the office with his key, and they left with the money box. Richard gave him 40,000 FC (about $80). The police chief proudly informed me that Richard was a thief. I replied, "What else is new?" I knew Richard had stolen the money all along.

Richard again denied stealing the money, and he added that the Botoa man lied about the theft. They transferred both men to Inongo, where they would go to the district court. I still could not understand why Richard did such a thing.

#

Later, Jean Louis came to visit me. He gave me a report on the eight villages that cut collective fields. All eight communities finished cutting, burning, and planting the fields. Jean Louis had become a defender of the Botoa's civil rights. He recently had a run-in with a Bantu chief who wanted to force the Botoa women in Wema to transport manioc roots for a Bantu farmer and not pay them. This practice continued to be a common occurrence here.

The farmers bribed the chief, and he forced the Botoa women to transport the manioc. However, Jean Louis told the women not to obey, and he informed the chief he would accuse him of abuse of power. He retracted his order, and the farmer had to pay the women.

He also ran into a case of abuse of power by another Bantu chief. The chief made all the Botoa work in his fields without pay, even though the constitution forbade this practice. Most village leaders used the Botoa as their "slaves," but Jean Louis planned to end this abuse. Jean Louis wrote a report and sent it to the territory administrator and the district attorney in Inongo. The Botoa referred to Jean Louis as their Moses.

## *Ikuku*

Ikuku, a seventh-grade boy, developed a high temperature, headache, and chills, so I thought he had malaria. I administered a perfusion with quinine, and on Sunday, he felt better, and he did not have a fever. I continued to give him quinine. Later, I went to the home to see him, and he cried out, "boboko" and "lokobo chukani!" (I cannot move my left arm and leg). I examined him, and sure enough, he had partial paralysis.

His temperature hit 104, and he had a severe headache. I thought, "Oh, my God, does he have brain abscess meningitis?" I did a spinal tap and found the tell-tale pus, and the gram stain showed pneumococcus bacteria. I gave him an IV with penicillin every two hours and an IV with chloramphenicol every six hours. It was all I could do since we did not have more potent antibiotics.

On Monday, the boy's condition worsened, and he fell into a coma. In the U.S., doctors would drain the brain abscess, but we had no way to do it here. I gave the boys an update and asked them to pray for Ikuku. On Tuesday, Ikuku woke up, and he recognized me. After several days he sat up, talked, and ate. I believed that his road to recovery had begun. His left arm and leg were still partially paralyzed. Everyone thanked the Lord for healing little Ikuku.

#

I prayed for Ikuku as I packed my suitcases and prepared to leave on my trip. I would go to Kiri, then travel by speedboat to Kutu, and then catch a plane in Nioki to Kinshasa. The schoolboys and girls were nervous about my departure. I was uneasy, but I knew the children would be in good hands with Father Yves and Father Vincent in charge.

On Tuesday, I awoke early, and we loaded the boat and departed at 5:30. I chose to go to Kutu and then Nioki. From Nioki, they had a regularly scheduled flight each Wednesday. We first left for Inongo. The lake turned rough, and the 14-foot aluminum boat bounced up and down on the waves. The worn seat cushions contributed to my sore and bruised back. The craft leaked in several places, but I felt better knowing that I had the life jacket my brother Bill gave me.

We ate lunch in Inongo and then went on to Kutu. Father Andy and I enjoyed seeing each other. Once in Nioki, the Brothers of Charity took me to their place while I waited for my plane. An Austrian man owned this small private passenger plane. He always arrived on time, and I met him in Nioki at 1:30 p.m. We arrived in Kinshasa, and a chauffeur took me to the procure.

I planned to spend a week in Kinshasa, then go to Belgium to visit the Sisters from Pendjua and some confreres. From there, I would go to Washington, D.C. I wanted to be present for the blessing ceremony for a container of material for the hospital that a Catholic organization called Crosslinks donated to me. Laura, the secretary at Missionhurst, and her husband agreed to pay for transportation from the U.S. to Kiri. I am grateful for their generosity.

#

April 25 was World Malaria Day. I heard on the radio that a child died every 30 seconds from malaria in Africa. Some countries were running out of anti-malaria drugs as companies did not produce enough. I left a six-month supply at the hospital and ordered more from Holland.

#

From May to August, I went home to the U.S. to visit my family and arrived back at Pendjua before school started in September. Upon my return, the president of the justice and peace committee came to see me. He became very excited as he shared his story. He told me the people of Imenge came to Pendjua and accused

Jean Louis of organizing a rebellion against the Bantu. He said Jean Louis and a group of Botoa armed with bows, arrows, and machetes chased the Bantu from the fields they cut in the Pygmy's forest. I sent a messenger to tell Jean Louis to come to Pendjua. He had already left for here and would arrive on Friday morning.

Jean Louis said the Bantu lied. He and his two brothers were inspecting the forest when they came across two Bantu cutting fields without permission. He told them to leave. In the meantime, the Pendjua chief, who hated Jean Louis, sent a message to the governor in Inongo. He asked him to send troops to quell a rebellion. We decided Jean Louis should go to Inongo and talk to the governor. We sent a message to tell him that a revolution had not taken place.

Jean Louis returned from Inongo. The district governor and judge had both supported him. They wrote to the Pendjua sector chief and told him to stop the Bantu from confiscating the Botoa's land. The local officials hated Jean Louis. They were afraid of him because he had the support of the district and provincial authorities. They had never seen such a fearless and determined Pygmy. He fought for the civil rights of the Pygmies, and they saw him as their Martin Luther King. I prayed that the Bantu would not kill him.

#

The barge arrived in Kiri in mid-November, and I went to supervise the unloading. The cargo contained hospital beds, equipment, a container Crosslinks sent, and 52 cartons of medicine. It also carried many books, African-print cloth, children's clothes, eight barrels of diesel fuel, and nine kerosene barrels.

We started unloading early in the morning. We had three tractors with wagons because the mission's large truck broke down. We finished loading the carts at noon, and the tractors left. The governor from Inongo came and asked me to take him to Pendjua. I hadn't planned on returning until we finished unloading the barge.

By now, though very tired, I had no choice but to drive the governor. We stopped at five villages so that the governor could talk to the people. I told him to order the men to cut the brush and weeds along the road. When I returned to Kiri, they had cleared most of the growth and weeds. The governor visited the hospital, health zone office, schools, and boarding homes. He congratulated us on the work we did, and he told the people they were fortunate to have missionaries here. I had planned to return to Kiri, but a massive rainstorm delayed my trip.

We were at the river port early to unload the barge and load the wagons. We worked in the scorching heat and finished six hours later. I went to the parish, ate lunch, took a bucket bath (they no longer had running water), and then followed the tractors. We ran into a rainstorm halfway to Pendjua. Two large trees had fallen across the road, and the flooding washed out one bridge. We always carried two axes and two machetes when we traveled to remove trees and repair bridges.

#

Jean Louis came and reported on his two-week trip to inspect the collective fields in 14 villages. Many Botoa harvested their first crop of corn and manioc. The money they received motivated them to cut more areas. A Botoa widow and her 18-year-old son from Liese came to see Jean Louis because their Ekonda "master" confiscated their land to cut fields. This type of activity had become more frequent, and it outraged me. Jean Louis left to investigate.

He returned in mid-December to give a session to six Botoa who were part of the rural development. Jean Louis followed up on the Botoa widow and her son, who had their land taken from them by their Ekonda "master." The local chief in Liese judged in favor of the Ekonda and fined the boy 2,000 FC, took his clothes off, and whipped him. Jean Louis took the case to the Pendjua sector chief, and he ruled in favor of the widow and her son. So, the Ekonda had to give back the land. They arrested the local leader, and he repaid the 2,000 FC. If it were not for Jean Louis, the widow and her son would have never recovered their land.

#

Near the end of the month, I received my balance sheets for my accounts and had an unpleasant surprise. The procure office charged me $4,700 for import tax for the container Crosslinks sent. They shipped the container under cover of a tax-exempt organization. I hoped to recover the money; otherwise, I would overdraw my account, which would be a disaster.

#

Later that night, we could not find Simba anywhere. My dog, Simba, usually slept in my room at night. I worried that someone stole her or that she went into the forest to chase antelope, and a snake possibly bit her. I turned off my light at 8:30 p.m. and was in bed by nine, but I woke up an hour later to the sound of pounding on my door. I called the night watchman, who was asleep, and asked if he heard someone knocking on the door. He said, "No," so I went back to bed, and ten minutes later, the same loud noise occurred, but I did not see anyone. The third time the sound occurred, I realized that it came from the room where we held the radio transmitter. The watchman came with his bow and arrow, and I grabbed a machete. We opened the door and out pranced Simba! She was happy to see me, and I was delighted to see her. The year ended on a good note.

# The "Prophet" Moses
*2005*

The high schools began their second semester though the school system faced much chaos. The bishop's conference informed the government that they no longer required the parents to pay a teacher's bonus. They want to force the government to pay teachers a living wage. Without the extra money, teachers only received between $5.00 and $10.00 a month. As a result, most teachers refused to work. The parents of students in public and Protestant schools also refused to pay the bonus, so their schools closed.

I feared that if the parents no longer paid the bonus, our teachers might quit. If the high school closed, I stood to lose a lot of money. I met with the principal and teachers, and they agreed to continue to teach. I paid my teachers between $20.00 and $50.00 a month. I decided to provide funds to cover the parent's bonus to the grade school teachers. This school, the best one in the Pendjua sector, is where I supported 180 Botoa students. This decision cost me $140 a month.

I would not pay the teachers until March, as the commercial people did not have enough money. A plane arrived in Kiri with the cash, mail, boxes of t-shirts, belts, soccer shirts, soccer nets, and more.

#

I received a letter from William A. Schultz, Executive Director of the Medical College of Wisconsin. He informed me that they selected me to receive the Humanitarian Award to recognize my charitable work. They offered to pay for my airfare if I got permission to come home. I felt this might be problematic since I just returned recently, and I only had permission to go back every three years.

I talked to the Father Provincial in Kinshasa on the radio, and he permitted me to go to the U.S. to attend the alumni dinner. We did not have any email service in Pendjua. So, I transmitted a message to Lonkesa-Kutu by radio to advise Mr. Schultz that I could come home. The staff there sent an email on my behalf.

#

A few days later, I read about the United Nations' goals from a Missionhurst communication. That same week, Tony Blair, prime minister of Great Britain, announced the African Commission's report. Here are statistics that struck me: 40,000,000 children did not receive primary education, and 28,000,000 were HIV positive. There were 11,000,000 AIDS orphans, and a child under age five died every 30 seconds from malaria. He said that Africa had become the scar on the consciences of the developed world, and wealthy countries could not allow Africa to slide further behind.

*Moses*

I have previously written that the Bantu believe the fetishes of their enemies cause all illnesses and deaths. They go to local witch doctors to obtain fetishes (charms). These charms are supposed to help them get money, a job, have a good harvest or a successful hunt, find a spouse, have children, protect them from their enemies, harm others, and more. They often become afraid of their fetishes and want to get rid of them, but they fear to do so. In recent years, many sects have sprung up and claim to have special powers. They do this to make money and take advantage of the fact people live in misery.

A young man set up shop in a village near Kiri and claimed to receive God's miraculous powers. People flocked to him by the hundreds and called him a prophet. He called himself Moses. I heard that he operated on hernias, hydroceles, and goiters without cutting the skin. The prophet rubbed "special water" on them, and their hernias disappeared. They said he cured sterility, the blind, deaf, mutes, deformed arms, and more. However, he specialized in removing fetishes and identifying a person's enemies. The people said all these claims were valid. I told the director I want to send some of our blind, deaf, and mute patients to prove he was a hoax. I found it unusual that this guy did not ask for money.

Last Thursday, a freshmen boy started to cry because someone stole his dictionary. On Friday, I asked the students to return the dictionary. I said, "If the thief does not return it, I will write to the "prophet" and have him identify the thief." That night the dictionary showed up on the boy's bed. I had a good laugh.

In another incident, Father Daniel's store clerk went to Kiri to see the "prophet" to get rid of some fetishes. The prophet asked him to give him all the fetishes, which he did. Then the prophet said, "You haven't given me all the fetishes." The man said, "Yes, I have." So, the prophet made him drink some of his "special water." They believed that if the person did not give up all his fetishes, then he would die. When the man had walked ten miles away from Kiri, he dropped dead. Everyone believed that the man lied to the prophet.

An elderly blind man from Pendjua went to see the "prophet." The story going around claimed that when the blind man returned, he could see. I asked the cook if he saw the man. The cook said the man walked by himself and did not need anyone to lead him around. Later, Mama Antoinette saw the man and reported that he walked with a stick and bumped into everything, so he remained blind. Two couples were leaving next week to take their deaf-mute children to see the "prophet." We would find out if he cured them. I remained skeptical.

#

At the end of the week, I gave an open book test to the eighth graders. One boarding school student started to cry as I passed out the books. I gave him a book, told him to stop crying, and answer the questions. The boy continued to cry, and I leaned down and asked him what made him cry.

"My cousin came from my village and told me my 20-year-old brother has died in Kiri," he wept. I sent the boy back to the home and told him to wait for me, and I would give him some money for funeral expenses. When I arrived at the house, I asked the boy what caused his brother's death. "My father took him to see the prophet to get rid of his fetishes, but my brother did not give them all up, so he died." Upon further questioning, I discovered I had treated the brother for congenital heart disease and heart failure. I figured that the 40-mile walk to Kiri became too much for him.

#

The "prophet" Moses' mother lived in Pendjua, and he came to visit her before I left for Kiri. The villagers and students rushed to see him. I did not get to see him, but I told my head nurse to send three patients to him – one with gangrene of the leg who needed an amputation, one with a hernia, and a deaf-mute. Moses left early, so the patients did not get to see the "miracle worker."

## Humanitarian of the Year

In late April, I traveled back to the U.S. and went to Milwaukee, Wisconsin. I spoke to the medical students where I had attended school and told them about the Pygmies and how the barefoot doctor program started. I talked about the importance of education to help get the Botoa out of poverty. Then, I told them about all we did to improve the health situation in the Congo. In the end, I said, "I think we have the greatest profession in the world. The only reason for us to be is to serve. And I hope some of you will serve the world when you finish your studies."

I received the Humanitarian of the Year Award. After I received the award and gave a speech, I received a standing ovation. I stayed in Milwaukee to attend my 40th class reunion dinner, and then I left Illinois on May 15 for my journey back to Pendjua.

#

I flew to Kinshasa and arrived at the procure. I went to see the provincial treasurer and inquired if the donations from

September 2004 to April 2005 got credited to my account. Father Joe wondered why I had not received the listings. I found out why. I asked Father Andy and the three Sisters in charge of the procure if they knew why. They looked at one another, and then Father Andy said that they were embarrassed to tell me. In January, a CICM confrere in Kinshasa got caught taking letters from Europe and the U.S. out of the mailroom. It turned out that he opened all the envelopes to look for money and then destroyed the letters.

On Sunday, I planned to leave early. Sister Rosaria, the principal of the Catholic high school in Kiri, accompanied me. We took a larger craft since we had at least 400 pounds of baggage. Within a short time, we discovered the boat had several leaks. When we got to the lake, a strong wind whipped up that worsened as we went along. After two hours of tossing about, we decided to stop at a village until the wind died.

Our lives were in danger every time we traveled in rickety old aluminum boats. We asked the villagers for some vines to tie the baggage to the seats to keep them off the leaky floor. I always had my life jacket with me in case the boat sank. The wind died down, and we continued to Inongo, where we stopped for lunch. Father Mongo told me that everyone expressed amazement to see me alive. A rumor went around that the "prophet" Moses caused me to have an accident in the U.S. and claimed I died. Father Mongo told the people at Sunday Mass that they would be the first to know if anything happened to me. He assured them that Brother Jerry would arrive in Inongo at noon. I find it funny how rumors got started.

With the lake now calm, we decided to continue to Kiri. We arrived in the evening, and Father Yves waited for us. I left early the next day and arrived in Pendjua at noon. Many people were amazed to see me alive and well. They also heard the stories going around about my death. One claimed I had seen Moses before leaving Kiri. Since I refused to give him the cross I wore, Moses put a hex on me, and I died in an accident. The people believed the story.

#

I visited the students, and they were excited to see me. Hundreds of people continued to visit the "prophet" Moses with the hope of a cure for various diseases or to remove fetishes and curses. I did not know anyone who he cured. I knew of deaf-mutes who remained so, blind people who were still blind, and cancer and AIDS patients who did not get cured. I thought the people would realize the hoax that Moses perpetrated, but they did not.

The people who went to see Moses also bathed in his pond. Supposedly, it contained "holy water" to protect them from evils and every kind of illness. Men, women, children, Bantu, and Pygmies all bathed in this water naked. People believed there would be a killer epidemic. Therefore, all children had to wash in this water to be protected. Most parents in Pendjua took their children there. During the last three weeks, two planes came from Kinshasa, each with 20 passengers who sought out Moses.

#

Some people brought a young man to the hospital who had a severe asthma attack and went into a coma. It took a day and a half for him to arrive at the hospital. I was at a disadvantage since we did not have oxygen or respirators. So, I treated him with IV fluids, cortisone, bronchial dilators, antibiotics, and a prayer. He began to respond the next day.

The hospital would run out of IV fluids soon, so I ordered 100 liters since planes began to arrive in Kiri again. Flights resumed because the Ekonda, who lived in Kinshasa, wanted to go and see Moses. They desired to get rid of fetishes and bathe in the pond, to protect themselves from evildoers. At least 20 passengers arrived each Friday for the past four weeks. I still waited for the 70 cartons of medicine held at the procure in Kinshasa since May. There were no commercial boats between Kinshasa and Kiri during this time. I feared that we would become more isolated.

#

In August, I celebrated the 25th anniversary of my religious vows. I thanked the Lord for these joy-filled years. They were the most satisfying of my life, and I wouldn't trade them with anyone.

#

I went to Kiri to supervise the unloading of 2,300 pounds of medicine and 2,000 pounds of school supplies and items for the homes. Luba and Bola went with me. The roads worsened as there were five torrential downpours each week. Knee-deep water flowed over the dikes, and the bridges were underwater. Whenever we came to a bridge, Luba and Bola stood on the logs, so I knew where to place the wheels. We arrived in Kiri and went to the port where the boat docked. While we were there, the "prophet" Moses came and attracted a huge crowd. I did not get a chance to greet him but hoped to talk to him someday.

A group of ten village notables came to see me. They asked me who would maintain the road and bridges when Father Daniel left. "You will have to maintain the road, but we will help you," I told them. "You must cut the brush to open the road and gather rocks to fill the holes, but the mission will provide the back loader, diesel fuel, and chauffeur."

When I started the health center in 1983, the people maintained the roads to allow me to come to their villages in my Toyota jeep. When Father Daniel came in 1995, he paid the men to keep the roadways in good order, so they now expect to be paid. The people needed to understand that development did not mean they had to depend on the mission for everything.

#

Twenty-two Botoa barefoot doctors came for a one-week session on tuberculosis, diarrhea, treatment of first and second-degree burns, and learning about the elections. The independent electoral commission registered voters in the interior, and they used portable computers and a camera. Each voter will receive a plastic identification card. A training team in Kiri taught 100 people how to register voters in the Kiri territory.

The registration would not be easy as the equipment had to be transported either on foot, by bicycle, or in dugout canoes. The mission tried to educate the Botoa about the importance of registering and voting. The Catholic Church sent out voter education material to all the parishes in the country. The people were excited to have an opportunity to vote, and they placed their hope in having an elected government.

#

234

Dr. Bakoko arrived to meet with the health care personnel and the population. He had worked at the Pendjua hospital from 1995-2001 and then went to Europe to study public health. He returned in late 2002 as the health director for the new Pendjua health zone. He left in late 2003 to become the leprosy program coordinator for the Mai Ndombe district.

He met with 60 representatives from the population. Afterward, he told me the people were satisfied with the hospital care but not with the health zone. They insisted that if the World Bank project happened, I must oversee the finances and medicines since corruption ran rampant in the Congo. On the radio, I heard that the military withdrew money to pay 250,000 soldiers each month; however, there were only 150,000 soldiers in the military.

### Moses' Apostles

A troubling episode concerning the "Moses" phenomenon occurred. A group of his "apostles" who lived in Pendjua went to the village blacksmith's home. They accused him of having fetishes to harm the people. They beat him, stripped his clothes off, stole his money, a machete, two large pots, and other items. Then they paraded him through the village. A small group of Christians came to his aid and took him to the hospital. They called me to the emergency room. He did not have any severe injuries, though the incident made me furious.

I went to the police chief and asked him why he did not arrest these criminals. There were 13 men involved, and four were sons of businessmen. The police chief replied that he was all alone, as the other five policemen were in Kiri at a seminar. Later, the police chief, the village chief, and the sector chief came to see me. They asked me to send a message to the Kiri territory administrator to request ten police officers to arrest the criminals. I sent it, and the administrator sent me a reply and asked me to send the Toyota pickup to Kiri. The chauffeur left at noon. He returned the next day, and by noon all 13 were in jail.

The "apostles" carried "magic staffs" to protect themselves, and they told the people the police would not be able to touch them.

Well, their magic staffs must have lost their magic. The officer asked me to provide transportation to take the five ringleaders to Kiri. It will be interesting to see what will happen with them. Everyone said that Moses would set them free.

#

In advance of the elections, Luba, Bola, Jean Louis, and I held a brainstorming session. We tried to find ways to motivate the Botoa to register for voting and how to help them register. If they did not have an ID card or a worker's card, then they would need five designated witnesses to swear the person was a resident of that village. Ninety percent of the Botoa did not have ID cards, so that prevented them from registering. It reminded me of the 1960s in the southern U.S. when Afro-Americans had difficulty registering to vote. All Botoa barefoot doctors, teachers, and nurses had cards, so they organized groups consisting of five witnesses each. I believed we would register everyone.

#

A new NGO began to operate in the area, and the coordinator visited me. They hoped to organize farmer's cooperatives. However, they set the demonstration co-op up as a plantation and paid the Botoa ten cents a day to cut, burn, and plant the fields. I told them they were not a co-op, but instead, they exploited the Botoa, and if they continued to do so, I would oppose them. The coordinator left without a word. I feared they would try to buy the Botoa's land. "I have to convince the Botoa not to sell their land," I told Jean Louis.

#

On October 30, we held a going-away party for Father Daniel. He talked about his forty years in the Congo and how sad it made him that he must leave. After Mass, the school children and youth groups marched, sang, danced, and put on skits to thank him for all he did for them. Father Daniel left on Tuesday amidst many tearful farewells. Father Yves and I would try to keep the agriculture and road projects going. However, it would depend on our ability to finance them.

#

In November, Dr. Charles became the temporary medical director for the Pendjua health zone. The Bandundu province medical inspector sent Dr. Bakoko to Pendjua to install Dr. Charles as the health director. When they took an inventory, they discovered there were only 10 liters of kerosene for the three vaccine refrigerators. On March 1, USAID had sent enough kerosene for 13 months. The office staff figured Dr. Mpeti had been selling the kerosene since September. This incident made the health zone administrator very unhappy.

This matter discouraged me, and one may wonder why I choose to stay. I hold the firm conviction that Jesus called me here to be God's channel of love, compassion, and healing to the poor, especially the Botoa Pygmies. A few setbacks or failures will not cause me to give up.

#

Later that month, the primary school director came to the hospital in critical condition. Last Friday, he had what I diagnosed as strep throat, so I treated him with penicillin and aspirin. Then he developed muscle contractions and lockjaw. These symptoms were typical of tetanus. He did not recall any wound; however, he could not swallow anything, even water, as that provoked spasms in his throat. We did not have caloric perfusions to give him, so he lost a lot of weight. We also did not have oxygen tanks or respirators to treat him. I gave him muscle relaxers every four hours and IV fluids. Fortunately, I had four vials of tetanus antitoxin.

#

Two voter registration centers had problems. Hundreds of Botoa men and women from Ikongo came to Pendjua to register because the Ikongo center demanded money. Jean Louis reported that hundreds of Botoa had not registered in Itendo because the police required the Botoa to give them a chicken before registering.

#

One day, I noticed a crack in the sun-dried brick wall at the end of the dormitory. The next day, I saw dirt piled up on the outside, and water had soaked into the clay bricks. Concerned about safety, we dug all the dirt out and noticed the bottom two layers of bricks were wet and soft. However, I thought they were still strong enough so that the wall would not collapse.

The next day, I stopped to check it out, and as I stood there, the entire wall collapsed. It fell to the outside, so it did not damage the wardrobes and beds. I am thankful that it did not fall at night, as the students would have panicked. We placed two-by-fours to hold up the roof, and I hired three bricklayers to repair the wall. The students wanted to stay in the dorm though it did not have an end wall, so I put up plastic sheeting.

#

I waited for a flight to Kinshasa, as I had business to attend to there. After six days, the plane arrived. There were 18 passengers and only 16 seats. I entered with the first few people. Then the shouting and pushing began. All 18 passengers got on board, and they asked the two left standing to leave. They refused. At least ten of the passengers had been in Kiri to see Moses. The two without seats kept saying they did not have any money and could not stay. The pilot refused to take off until the two standing passengers left. We were delayed for forty minutes until the police came and forced the two unhappy passengers to disembark.

The primary school director, who had tetanus, and his wife managed to get on the plane. The director had four children in Kinshasa, and they wanted him to come there. When we arrived, I went to the hospital to explain the signs, symptoms, and treatments I had done with him.

#

The following day, I set off for SANRU to determine why they did not send the $4,800 worth of medicine they had promised to ship in May. Dr. Minuku, the coordinator, said they never received the order. I placed a new order, and the pharmacist said he could only fill one-third of it. It frustrated me that I could not get the entire order.

A week later, I remained in Kinshasa. I went to Vice President Z'ahidi Ngoma's office to ask him to obtain five or six scholarships for Pygmy college students. He could help me get accreditation for the last five Botoa primary schools. Also, he could get the teachers at all ten schools onto the state payroll.

There were four vice-presidents, and Z'ahidi acted as the vice president representing the non-armed opposition. The other three were warlords of the three rebel groups fighting the Congolese army of President Joseph Kabila. If the new constitution passed, there would be elections to end the four transitional governments.

I ran into Dr. Clemmer at SANRU and asked him why I could not receive the entire $4,800 worth of medicines. He typed a letter on his computer and told the pharmacist to give me the whole order. The next day, a truck hauled the medications to the boat scheduled to leave for Kiri tomorrow. I thanked heaven that Dr. Clemmer helped me.

#

I caught a flight to Kiri on December 19. I met a Congolese lady from Paris on the plane. She had taken her two boys to see Moses, and they stayed at the parish house where I stayed. I believed the two boys had autism. I continued to be amazed they came from so far away to see Moses. His local popularity had faded as people realized he did not cure any real illnesses.

The barge arrived in Kiri, loaded with all the items I ordered. The chauffeurs were there with two tractors and wagons. We were up early the following day to start unloading. We cut the boards that UNESCO had donated to make 450 desks for the Botoa schools.

We planned to leave for home the next day, but we had a delay. A torrential downpour woke us. When the rain stopped, the caravan of two tractors, wagons, and the Toyota left for the mission. My children were thrilled when we pulled into the boarding school to unload 2,000 smoked fish. They also wanted their Christmas gifts of shirts for the boys and blouses for the girls.

# The Diagnosis
## *2006*

In early January, four patients had meningitis, and I thought an epidemic would start. One evening, they carried a sophomore boy, Bankoto Bruno, to the mission because he had a severe headache and a 104-degree temperature. He had cerebral malaria, so I started him on quinine and kept him at the mission house in a spare bedroom. Bruno had improved some the next day, but I decided to keep him there another 24 hours.

By the next night, his temperature rose to 104 degrees. He became delirious and shook severely and had convulsions. I gave him quinine again and a sponge bath to bring his temperature down. I did not get much sleep as I worried that he might die; however, he felt better on Monday. Then, on Thursday, he felt well enough to go to school. It always took a lot to keep him from going to his classes.

#

On Friday night, I had some free time for reading. The English medical journal "Lancet" published an article about the Congo's health situation. They reported that 38,000 people died each month from diseases and malnutrition because the war caused a total collapse of the health system. Prime Minister Tony Blair once said, "In a world where prosperity grows, the fact that 4 million infants in Africa will die before their fifth birthday is an obscenity which must haunt our daily thoughts."

*A Mother's Love*

January 16 will be a day I will never forget. Father Yves asked me to sit with him in the dining room. He told me he received a message saying my Mom had passed away. On January 14, my mother, Rita Galloway, died peacefully in her sleep at 93.

Afterward, I went to my room and closed the drape to signal that I did not want to be disturbed. Then, I journaled:

"I know everyone thinks their Mom is the best, but Mom WAS the best and most fantastic mother one could have. She was indeed a gentle mother, a gentlewoman, generous, and always caring for others, inspiring us to have concern for the poor. Mom was a woman of faith and helped us to grow in the faith and love of Jesus. She always encouraged us to do our best.

I know I would not have gone to college if it hadn't been for her encouragement. She always supported our decisions. When I changed from dentistry to medicine, Dad wasn't happy, but she said, 'Do it.' When I decided not to become a cardiologist but to dedicate my life to the service of the poor, Dad was very unhappy. Still, she said, 'Do it.' And when I answered Jesus' call to become a religious missionary, Dad wasn't happy once again. Still, she said, 'Do it.'

I know I caused Mom some pain and suffering, but she always prayed for me and forgave me. During the '60s and '70s, when I was a left-wing radical leaving the church and denying God's existence, she prayed and patiently waited for me to come to my senses. And when I became a born-again Catholic, she celebrated."

#

By the end of January, many children had cerebral malaria and severe hemolytic anemia caused by meningitis. I admitted two more cases. A six-year-old Botoa boy came into the hospital with a high temperature and convulsions. The nurses treated him with an IV of quinine as they thought he had cerebral malaria. When I saw the boy, I thought the same thing. The following day, he gained consciousness but still had a high temperature and a stiff neck, so I did a test that revealed meningitis.

I ordered the test given to everyone with a fever and convulsions. We used to do this test in the past, but somehow the policy had been neglected. The second case involved an 18-year-old Botoa girl. Her situation had become very critical, and she died ten hours after being admitted. I learned that she had been sick for three days at home and that Moses' "apostles" had treated her with their "magic water." Maybe someday, the people would see this guy as a fraud and would no longer go to him.

#

My best ninth-grade student, Mbongi John, did not show up to school. When I asked John's older brother why John did not come to school, he told me John had fallen sick and would be absent. John's father showed up and said his son had become very ill with a high temperature, headaches, and neck pain. I realized that if he had meningitis, he might die. I bawled out the father for not bringing his son to the hospital.

John stood only four-foot-tall and weighed just 65 pounds. The village men could have carried him here in one of their homemade portable chairs. I ordered the father to go home and bring John to the hospital. They arrived with him the next day. It turned out he had malaria.

I asked John why he did not come to the hospital sooner. He said his family thought a sorcerer caused the illness. They took him to a village where one of Moses' "apostles" had a pond with "blessed" water. They bathed him in the water for four days, and when he did not get any better, John told his father to go and see Dr. Jerry. It made me mad that they didn't bring John to me first.

## The Pronouncement

In March, I was back in Kinshasa, not by choice but a necessity. I had to have the recurrent squamous cell carcinoma removed from my left eyebrow. Due to many delays, I was still in Kinshasa in April, much to my chagrin. I woke up at 11:00 p.m. one night and did some reading. When I got up to get water, everything went black. The next thing I knew, I woke up lying on the floor. An ambulance took me to the CMK hospital. While in intensive care, they gave me two transfusions. I received two more on Monday. An echograph showed a "mass" in my upper abdomen. They told me I must go to Belgium for an endoscopy and biopsy.

I thought about the banner in our den at home. It has a curved road running from top to bottom, and Dr. Tom Dooley's saying, 'I have promises to keep and miles to walk before I sleep.' I prayed, "You completed the mission the Father gave You. Give me at least two years to finish the task You gave me. You cannot abruptly abandon the least of your brothers and sisters."

I told Father Andy if the tumor is benign, I will have the operation in Belgium and return to Pendjua. If it is cancer, I will go to the U.S. for surgery to remove it. Then I will visit family and friends, Missionhurst, and return to Pendjua until my time is up.

I left for Belgium, and at the hospital in Namur, the doctor ordered many exams and scans. Then, I had a frank talk with the doctor. He told me the tumor in the stomach wall would almost certainly be cancerous. The doctor scheduled an operation for May 3. However, I told him I would go to the U.S. for the surgery.

I had an incredible inner peace. I prayed I would be able to return for at least two years to arrange the transition. I want the hospital, health centers, barefoot doctor program, the Botoa education program, and the boarding homes to continue long after I am gone. I am confident I will have two years to continue to live and work in Pendjua.

#

I arrived at Missionhurst in Arlington, Virginia, and I received the preliminary report. The tumor was malignant lymphoma. Dr. Christie explained that the non-Hodgkin lymphoma type B with large cells had the highest cure rate. I told the doctor I needed two years, and he looked a bit taken aback. I explained that I needed to go back to prepare the people for the transition.

He said they would administer chemotherapy every 21 days for six to eight treatments. "I have to go back to Pendjua no later than mid-September," I told him. "If I need eight treatments, I will give myself the last two in Pendjua." Dr. Christie replied, "We will talk about it later."

I am worried about my children. The students already have much anxiety and wonder what will happen to their boarding homes. I think about and pray for my children each day. I pray I can be with them for a few years to prepare them for the day when I will not be there. The Botoa want me to stay until the Lord comes for me. My Pygmy friends and students always say that my bones belong to them. They want me buried in the ground of their ancestors so their children and grandchildren can visit me.

The pathologist received the biopsy tissue and said I had a MALT lymphoma that they would not treat with chemotherapy but with an antibody called Rituxan. This drug did not have significant side effects. I would receive treatments of one infusion every week for four weeks every six months for two years. The doctor told me that the cancer was 100 percent curable.

#

On my way back to Kinshasa, I heard that when news of my illness spread, Cardinal Etsou in Kinshasa asked all the parishes to pray for "the apostle of the Pygmies."

I finally made it back. Much to my surprise, I found Father Yves staying at the procure. He had a bicycle accident in July and suffered severe back pain. Father Yves could not get out of bed by himself. I looked at his X-rays, and he had compressed vertebrae and decalcification of the bones. He had a low blood count, and his feet and legs swelled. I told Sister La Clerck that I thought Father Yves had multiple myeloma, and the doctors in Belgium should check for it.

#

I flew to Kiri, and my friends were happy to see me. When we crossed into the Pendjua sector, people yelled and cheered as we passed through each village. We arrived after dark, but a large group gathered to greet me. They were also eager to hear news about Father Yves.

I discovered the Rituxan had a delayed side effect – it wiped out my taste buds. My sweet and sour taste buds only functioned a little. I could not tell the difference between the taste of different meats, bread, manioc, rice, and vegetables. It seemed strange to eat just to survive. I looked at it as a small price to pay for a few more years of life.

#

I rode along the path behind the school to the boarding homes. Next to the trail, there were large holes from where students dug clay to make bricks. On my way, I lost my balance and fell into a four-foot hole, landing on my right shoulder. My bike landed on top of me, and I could not climb out of the pit. Two students came by and helped me out. I had dirt in my ears, nose, and mouth. My right shoulder experienced a lot of pain, and I could barely move it. I cleaned myself up and returned to school to give my two English classes an exam. I could not lift my arm to write on the board, so the principal wrote out the questions.

#

I've had painful sores in my mouth for three weeks. I tried three different antibiotics and anti-fungal medicines. These sores were common in immune-compromised patients. I hoped and prayed the lesions would not get worse and would go away. The painful sores in my mouth got worse. I have not been able to eat any solid foods. My meals are soup, oatmeal, and pudding. I decided to fly to Kinshasa to get some medicine to help clear up the sores.

Everyone panicked, and many friends came to see me in the afternoon. The school interns were in a panic because the Bantu students told them I would return to the U.S. for good. Many threatened to quit school. They asked me to talk to the students. I promised them I would only go to Kinshasa and not on to America.

"The oncologist is optimistic. However, if I do not recover, I will die right here with you at my bedside," I assured them. "I'll be buried on the boarding school grounds. The boarding schools will not close. All the inheritances from my parents, aunts, and uncles will form a foundation to support the homes and the Botoa barefoot doctor project." Some had tears running down their faces, but they were relieved to hear I would not abandon them.

#

I left Kiri on Tuesday, and the flight provided a scenic view, as the scattered, fluffy white clouds beneath us. We passed over the massive rainforest, covered with floodwater. Then we flew over the savannah and saw scattered farms of ten to twenty acres. We followed the river to Kinshasa. The trip started on the Lutoy River at Kiri and then on to Lake Mai Ndombe. From there, we took the Fimi River, which became the Kwa River, where the great Kasai River joins at Mushie. Then the Kwa flows into the great Congo River to Kinshasa. When I arrived, Father Andy picked me up.

I need medical care for the sores in my mouth. The medicine did not help and made them worse. I tried antibiotics, but they had no effect, so I decided it could be a fungal infection that cancer patients may get. I tried two medicines, again with no change, and I could not eat solid foods. My friend, Doctor La Clerck, came to see me, and she thought the condition could be thrush (candidiasis). She gave me fluconazole to try.

I remained in Kinshasa, not by choice but a necessity. I should have left yesterday; however, Father Andy and the other confreres and Sisters insisted I stay. Earlier this week, my symptoms became worse. On Monday, I woke up with more painful sores in my mouth. The inside of my lip burned, inflamed by a swollen sore, and I could hardly talk or swallow. I decided that the problem could not be from thrush (fungus) as I took medication for three weeks.

I made an appointment with the dermatologist who treated me two years ago for cancer on my face. After the exam, he said I have an allergic reaction to the Celebrex that I took for my arthritis. I should have thought of this since in the 1980's I had read about a tuberculosis medicine that caused severe rashes and mouth sores.

#

I talked to Bishop Philippe and shared my desire to stay in Pendjua until the end of my life. I told him I wanted my burial on the boarding school grounds. Philippe replied, "Jerry, that is wonderful. God must be influencing you to do this. Your permanent presence in Pendjua will be the witness of God's love for the poor."

#

All Kinshasa workers went home early because they expected the Supreme Court to announce the presidential elections' winner. It seemed inevitable that Kabila would be the victor, and many feared that Bemba's militia might cause trouble. I saw it as a real feat that everyone had a chance to vote, considering the issues and the country's vastness.

#

I left for Pendjua in early December. By then, I experienced a drastic amount of weight loss. I am uncertain if the loss is due to being unable to eat or due to lymphoma. I ate three full meals in the previous two days, and I felt strong but continued to need more rest. If the weight loss were due to lymphoma, then the second series of cancer treatments I will take will help.

When I arrived, the boys from the homes came streaming out to shake my hand and hug me. I came to tears. Many villagers came. "I returned even though I'm not completely cured," I told them. "I promised you I would not go to America, and I'd return even if the treatments did not cure me. My village is here. My parents, brothers, sisters, children, and friends are here. When the time comes, my burial will be here." The people went wild and clapped and sang.

#

The following week was the saddest and most emotionally draining week of my life. Brother John came and told me Father Yves died. I was overcome with sadness and went back to my home. It was unbelievable for me to think my intimate friend and spiritual director was dead.

Father Yves and I were two of the happiest missionaries in the Kinshasa CICM province. We were of one heart and one soul. We looked forward to working together and preparing two Congolese diocesan priests to take over in July of 2008. His thoughts and his heart were in Pendjua. He hoped and prayed to join us again. Now I knew we would not see one another until I joined him in heaven.

### Bekasi John

I went to the boarding school that evening to see Bekasi John, one of my seventh-graders. He had been sick for two days. They brought him to my room at 6:00 a.m. with a fever of 103 degrees and shaking chills. I started him on quinine. At noon, I told

Bola, who held sick calls at the boarding home, to give Bekasi John enough quinine for five days.

A week later, Bola reported that Bekasi John felt better. The next night, the older boys carried him on their backs and brought him to my room. They said he had colic and had been vomiting. He had a headache but did not have a fever. I looked at his treatment chart and noticed Bola gave him Fansidar. Fansidar is a less effective malaria medicine but is usually good enough. Bekasi John suffered from dehydration, and I hospitalized him to provide him with IV fluids and monitor him.

The next day, I checked on Bekasi John on my way to the office. He had pulled his IV out, and I could not believe that I found no one with him. He talked about some ancestor who bewitched him and caused his sickness.

As I rested that afternoon, an intern knocked on my door and told me I should go quickly to the hospital because Bekasi John fell critically ill. I rushed over and found him in a frantic state as three boys tried to hold him down. When I touched him, I knew he had a temperature of 104. I instructed someone to go and get an IV of quinine and glucose.

John had cerebral malaria. We had a hard time holding him down to get the IV needle in. I gave him 10 milligrams of valium in an IV, and it did not affect him. One boy laid on John's chest, one on his legs, and another held his left arm. I secured his right arm that had the IV needle in it. I told someone to go and get three more boys. I did not have the strength to sit there, holding the boy's arm. He fell asleep. I let out a sigh and said, "Thank you, Lord."

When I went home, I pleaded with God not to let my boy die. Then, I got called to the radio transmitter to talk to two students in Kinshasa. I stopped at the hospital to find John still asleep. When I returned, two boys came running and told me John did not seem to be breathing right. I rushed again to the hospital, and the nurse had already pulled the IV out. "How did he die?" I asked the nurse. "He had respiratory arrest and then cardiac arrest," she responded.

I fell on the bed and cried, "Oh, God, no!" We all broke down and cried. I gathered myself, went home, and sent for the carpenter to make a casket. The boys and girls ran to the hospital and screamed and cried. George followed me to the mission, and I said to him, "John is dead. I cannot believe he is dead. His poor parents will be so distraught. Oh, God, my boy is dead."

I gave the boys a bar of soap to wash the body. Then, I got out some African cloth. One had pretty blue images of the virgin Mary. The other a pretty red with pictures of Jesus and prayers in Lingala on it. I told George to arrange everything, and I would come for the mourning period. I went to my room and collapsed into my chair. I had nothing left but my faith to bring me through this crisis.

The boys took the desks from the classrooms and made a large semi-circle in the front yard. They moved the lights outside, put a bed on the veranda, and laid Bekasi John on the bed. They covered him to the neck with the red African-print cloth with the images of Jesus.

My chair sat on one side of the bed. On the other, two men were seated. The hospital secretary sat in one chair, and in the other, to my surprise, sat Nsambi, a barefoot doctor. Nsambi was Bekasi's father. He brought a basket of manioc roots for the parent's contribution. When he arrived, he found out that his son had been the one who died. This realization deepened my sadness as I tried to console him.

#

At 9:00 p.m., some boys brought a sick intern to my house, who had a temperature of 103 degrees, chills, and a headache. I treated him for malaria and told the boys to bring him back to my house in the morning. The boys brought him and left him on my bed before heading to school. I finished at the hospital and went and found the boy in a near coma. We took him to the hospital on a stretcher. I performed a spinal tap that showed he had meningitis. He went into a comatose state. I sat at his bedside from 11:00 a.m. until 10:00 p.m. without eating or drinking. I could do nothing but pray. I vowed that I would not allow another boy or girl to die without me being present.

The boys organized teams, so there were always six at his bedside. At 5:00 p.m., the boy's breathing became irregular.

Everyone became frightened. I said, "Jesus, it is better that I die, and he lives." Three hours later, the boy opened his eyes, and I asked, "Do you know me?" He nodded, yes. Praise the Lord! I went home five hours later and collapsed into bed.

#

On December 23, I took my third Rituxan treatment. My blood count dropped to 0.8, though I had taken 800 milligrams of iron in an IV, ten shots of vitamin B12, and folic acid tablets during the last three weeks. A few days later, I realized I needed a blood transfusion. My heart rate measured 130 beats per minute, and I had shortness of breath. John gave me a unit of blood, and I felt better.

Later that night, they brought one of my little fellows, who weighed a mere 28 pounds, to my house. He had chills and a fever of 103. I treated him with quinine, and the following day, his temperature lowered to 99 degrees. Though he felt a little better, I gave him more quinine.

Later, he became dizzy and had a headache. The older boys brought him to my room. He had a bad stomachache, so I gave him some worm medicine and decided to keep him in my place. He slept on my bed. Later, I gave him some milk, and he immediately vomited. The boy began to cry and said his head and neck hurt. His temperature shot up to 104, so I picked him up and crossed the road to the hospital to do a spinal tap. He also had meningitis. We started him on an IV. He never lost consciousness, though he did become delirious.

#

I received the bad news two more interns in the hospital had meningitis. I went over there as fast as I could. Little Bruno was one of them. Since he remained conscious and had received treatments for the second day, I held out hope for him. The other one, a little sixth-grade girl and the smartest one in her class, had fallen into a deep coma.

The girl became ill on December 26 and went into a coma two days later. They brought her to the hospital on the 30th. The girl had been unconscious for two days without antibiotics, so I did not have much hope for her. The mother did not bring her sooner because she believed evil spirits caused the illness. So, she used fetishes to try to cure the girl. The girl died at midnight. We took her to the girl's home. There were 18 students there, and I gave them soap and African-print cloth. They made a casket for her.

# The Final Wish
*2007*

I took my fourth and final Rituxan treatment. During the week, I developed shaking chills and a temperature of 102 degrees, so I took some malaria medicine and went to bed. The next day, I still had a fever, so I switched to quinine, the oldest and most effective anti-malaria drug. However, I did not like its side effects – ringing in the ears, decreased hearing, and dizziness.

The following week came with challenges. I thought I developed a "rare" complication from the Rituxan therapy. I had a total body rash called Steven-Johnson syndrome, which could be dangerous. They usually treat this rash with high prednisone doses, which I feared to take because of my second complication.

My daily high temperatures of 102 to 103 became worse. It dawned on me my white blood count must be too low, and I had no defense for bacterial infections. I scheduled a white blood count for Friday. My previous one showed a count of 2,200, though normal would be between 5,000 and 7,000. I need neutrophil infusions as I have too much work to do. On Wednesday, at Mass, I became weak and thought I would pass out. I made it back to my room. If I passed out in church, it would have created a panic. Mama Antoinette donated blood, and I received another transfusion.

#

In late January, I had to stay in bed almost all day. I had high temperatures two to three times a day. Early one morning, I had shaking chills and covered up with two blankets. Dr. Charles and the head nurse wanted to treat me once more for malaria, so they gave me quinine by IV. But I did not think it could be malaria. I planned to go to Kinshasa to get infusions of white blood cells and have blood and skin tests done. I needed to find the cause of the fevers.

When we arrived in Kinshasa, I went to the CMK hospital for tests to find the fevers' cause. I told my primary doctor, "I do not want to go to the U.S." Then, I said, "I am going back home to Pendjua in three weeks. I'm an old missionary and have lived and worked with the Pygmies for 26 years. I belong to them. That is my final wish."

On February 4, I remained in Kinshasa. I met with the dermatologist, and he confirmed that I had severe Stevens-Johnson syndrome. After high doses of prednisone, my fever went away. The new Father Provincial came to see me and told me the Kinshasa confreres were very concerned about my health. The Congolese doctors did not know anything about my type of illness. The confreres wanted me to go to the U.S., and the Father Provincial invoked my vow of obedience to accept his decision to send me to the U.S., and I agreed.

#

First, I flew to Brussels, and I remained there to rest before going on to Missionhurst in Arlington, Virginia. The doctor said the medical problems were likely a severe reaction to the Rituxan and not related to the lymphoma. He got me an appointment with a dermatologist.

The dermatologist said, "You are very fortunate to be alive." I had toxic epidermal necrolysis, one of the most life-threatening skin disorders, and I had all the symptoms and signs. My top layer of skin blistered and peeled, and I had a painful red rash that spread quickly. I had scalded-looking rawness of the flesh, fever and chills, lesions in my mouth and lungs, and cracked bleeding lips that formed a crust.

The complications are the inability to eat, severe weight loss, malnutrition, bacterial skin infections, septicemia (blood poisoning), and shock. My weight had fallen to 120 pounds. The doctor told me I had done everything right. However, I should have gone to Kinshasa sooner for blood cultures and to start the prednisone treatment. She kept saying over and over, "You are lucky that you did not die." I said, "I have great faith in God. He protects those who love and serve Him."

I sent a note to my sister, Sister Mary Blaise Galloway, and thanked her for her work to get my letters out to everyone. I wrote the letters all these years not just to look for contributions, but in some sense, more importantly, to talk about my spiritual journey. I hope to inspire others in their spiritual journey and their relationship with Jesus.

#

A PET scan showed a residual indolent tumor near my stomach, with no evidence of malignancy. Other fibrous tissues would take time to disappear. My cancer had gone into remission, and my health problems were due to a severe allergic reaction to Rituxan. After visiting family and friends in Illinois, I left for Belgium on April 19 and continued to the Congo.

#

While home in the U.S., my siblings begged me to remain. I replied that I wanted to be with my family in Pendjua, and I would stay there until I died. I told them that my Botoa brothers and sisters always said, 'Your bones belong to us, and they are going to stay with us so that our children and we can visit you.'

I spoke to Bishop Philippe about my desire. He was thrilled and agreed to allow me to stay in Pendjua. He said, "It is a grace that the Lord wishes you remain with the Pygmies for eternity."

#

When I arrived at the villages in the Pendjua sector, people lined the streets. They screamed and beat drums and informed the other villagers of my arrival. Almost everyone packed the roadways, and there were over 300 people at the mission. I had never experienced such a welcome since I came here in 1981.

The sound of singing filled the air as my students gathered outside my room early Sunday morning. When I stepped out of my room, the crowd practically crushed me. "What a joyful return!" I exclaimed. Joy overwhelmed me, and I thanked God for bringing me back home.

#

I met with 40 village elders. They thought I would not return, and the hospital would close. They wanted to know what would happen to the vehicles (four tractors, one truck, four backhoes, and the Toyota) and the machine that cleaned the rice. I told them, "Everything will belong to the diocese, except for one tractor, which will go to the hospital and the boarding homes." They were not happy because the bishop came from the Basakata group. They thought he would give everything to the Basakata people, who dominated the diocese's southern part. The Basakata and the Ekonda were enemies. Tribalism remained extreme among the people.

# Epilogue

Dr. Jerry Galloway soon became unable to write letters due to his health.

Father Maurice Nsambo, the Provincial Superior, continues the story. On July 15, Jerry flew to Pendjua, and on July 18, he went into convulsions and had a very high fever. He asked us to transfer him to Kinshasa. On Monday, July 23, a plane rushed to get him.

Once at the Medical Center, he expressed the desire to go to the U.S. to get the appropriate care and then return to Pendjua. The doctors said he could not travel in his condition. On Monday, the 30th, he entered eternal life.

Sister Mary Blaise wrote a final letter on July 30, 2007:

"One of Brother Jerry's favorite quotes was from Tom Dooley. A banner hung on the wall in our den in our Aurora home for many years. It said, 'I have miles to go before I sleep.' Yes, Jerry was our little brother and our second Tom Dooley. We will miss you, Jerry. I will end with an Irish poem."

'Fill the World with Love'

In the evening of my life, I shall look to the sunset,
At the moment in my life when the night is due.
And the question I shall ask only I can answer,
Was I brave and strong and true?
Did I fill the world with love my whole life through?

Your brother Bill and I will answer this poem for Jerry with a definite YES."

The End

# After Word

Sister Mary Blaise (Bonnie Galloway) was committed to seeing her brother's story written.

Dear Readers,

As a young girl growing up in Mendota, Illinois, little did I know that my younger brother, Jerry Joseph Galloway, would spend much of his life as a doctor, helping the poor in Pendjua, Democratic Republic of the Congo, Africa. He was a normal American boy growing up, attending schools, and becoming a medical doctor.

Jerry served in the Peace Corps in the Congo. After working in a health care program for the poor in Beaufort, South Carolina, Jerry joined the religious order called Congregation of the Immaculate Heart of Mary (CICM) in Arlington, Virginia. He dedicated his life to serving the poorest of the poor in Pendjua.

I am very grateful to my cousin, Kent Galloway, for sharing the story of Jerry's wonderful work with the people of Pendjua.

Sister Mary Blaise

# Post Script

Many of the buildings and programs that Jerry maintained have collapsed due to a lack of funding. A group of young Pygmies is working to establish the Jerry Galloway Foundation to raise money for schools and books to continue education for the Pygmies.

#

I hope this book has brought an increased awareness of the plight of the Pygmies. Medical aid to fight Ebola, malaria, measles, and other diseases is needed. Books and schools for the Pygmies are in great need. I hope to inspire others to support humanitarian efforts to help the Pygmies.

Printed in Great Britain
by Amazon

64374281R00161